ElderPark

Violated

Violated

A SHOCKING and HARROWING
SURVIVAL STORY from the notorious
ROTHERHAM ABUSE SCANDAL

Sarah Wilson

WITH GERALDINE McKELVIE

HARPER
element

To protect the identities of individuals involved in Sarah's story some details,
including names, places and dates, have been changed.

HarperElement
An imprint of HarperCollins*Publishers*
1 London Bridge Street
London SE1 9GF

www.harpercollins.co.uk

First published by HarperElement 2015

1 3 5 7 9 10 8 6 4 2

A catalogue record of this book is
available from the British Library

ISBN 978-0-00-814126-4

Printed and bound in Great Britain by
Clays Ltd, St Ives plc

PROLOGUE

My eyes fixed on a cobweb in the corner of the room as I heard footsteps on the stairs. The door creaked open and I shifted on the lumpy mattress on the floor. They'd left me there a few hours earlier and now it was dark, so dark. If I strained really hard, though, I could still see the outline of the cobweb. It gave me something to focus on, to distract me from what was going on in the cold darkness of that room.

A figure appeared in the doorway, but he was just a silhouette, the latest in the line of faceless men who'd come to me that night. Was he the sixth or the seventh? I'd lost count. I didn't meet his gaze; I couldn't bear it. I kept looking at the cobweb as I felt him place his weight on top of me. The smell of his sweat and cheap soap filled my nostrils.

He didn't have to tug at my trousers because they were already round my ankles, but I could feel him wrestling with his own, undoing his belt, impatient and erect as he tore open a condom wrapper. The vodka they'd given me had numbed me a little, but not enough, and anyway, by now I was beginning to sober up. As he entered me, pain tore through me and I bit my lip so hard I tasted blood.

No one seemed to care about the state of this godforsaken house, just as no one seemed to care about me. When I had been brought there it had been light, and I had been taken straight to this room, where mould streaked the blue walls. I wondered how long the cobweb had been there. Had it been days, weeks, months? I wanted to cry but no tears would come. I wondered how long I'd be left in this filthy room, in a strange town miles from home.

The man said nothing as he writhed around on top of me, only grunting a little. I was too scared to tell him he was being too rough. How could I say that to him? After all, they kept telling me it was all my fault. I was a little slag, they said, I was white trash. I'd brought it all upon myself so this was what I deserved: to lie on a dirty, lumpy mattress, awaiting a never-ending queue of men, all old enough to be my dad.

Gradually, his breathing got quicker and he muttered something in a language I didn't understand. His hands wandered towards my chest and, as he gripped the breasts just beginning to develop, I asked myself: what does he find attractive about me? I'm only thirteen – and he can't even see my face.

Eventually, it was over. He put his trousers back on and walked out without a word. Once again, I was alone in the dark room, lying on the filthy, horrible mattress, staring at the cobweb and wondering just how many more men would come before I'd be allowed to go home.

This story probably sounds shocking to many people, but for me, what happened that night was nothing unusual. I was only a child, but even by the age of thirteen, to me it was normal to be bundled into a car and driven around England to be abused by men – paedophiles. Some of these men showered me with gifts and told me they loved me; others didn't say a single word to me as they lay on top of me, violating me in the most disgusting way imaginable.

All of the men who abused me were of Asian origin, almost all British Pakistanis, but as I lay there night after night, I didn't care where they came from or what colour their skin was. In years to come, what happened to me, and many other girls, as victims of the Rotherham sex ring would become a national scandal. Professors would write reports, politicians would resign and people on the news would talk about girls like me and how we'd been failed by the very people who were supposed to protect us.

My nightmare began a long, long time before Rotherham was on the front page of the newspapers, and the memory of that time will stay with me long after our town has disappeared from the headlines. Over the years that followed the abuse, I slowly came to realise that I wasn't a little slag like they'd told me so many times, but a victim. But I refuse to be a victim forever, so I'm sharing this with you now because I don't want what happened to me to happen again, ever, to any other child. This is my story. It's the story of a victim but, more importantly, it's also the story of a survivor.

CHAPTER ONE

EARLY DAYS

I suppose it's fair to say I've never had an easy life.

I was born in Rotherham, a big industrial town just a few miles from Sheffield, in September 1991, blissfully unaware that my parents' relationship was already starting to unravel. My mum, Maggie, and my dad, Mark, had got together in the late eighties. They'd met when Mum's sister, my auntie Annette, started going out with Dad's cousin. Dad had come to Rotherham to visit them and he got talking to Mum when she popped round one night. Mum had just come out of an unhappy marriage and was bringing up my older brothers, Mark and Robert, on her own when Dad asked her out for a drink. Mum was petite, with sandy curly hair, and he had obviously taken a shine to her. He said all the right things when she needed a shoulder to cry on, and soon they were an item.

But Mum and Dad were very different people. Mum had lived in Rotherham all her life and was from a traditional, hardworking Yorkshire family, the second of seven siblings. Granddad worked in the local steelworks, while Nan had a job at the KP Nuts factory. Mum followed her there after she left school, although she could never get a permanent contract because there was never enough work.

Dad, on the other hand, was a bit of a tearaway. He was short, with dark hair and tattoos all over his arms and legs. He'd been born in Rotherham too, but his family had moved to Horncastle, a little market town in Lincolnshire, when he was a small child. He'd been expelled from school when he was really young and sent to what they used to call a borstal – a sort of mini-prison for kids that the schools couldn't control. He never really told us why and we never asked. Growing up, there were lots of things about Dad's life that seemed to be a big secret. Sure, he could sweet-talk Mum and say all the right things, but the truth was that he hardly ever had a proper job and Mum never really knew what he was getting up to when he went out in his van for hours on end.

Mum says I was a delicate little thing, with a small covering of fair hair, and she fell in love with me straight away. Two days after I was born, she was allowed to take me home to our red terraced house on a street called Psalters Lane, which was a sort of unofficial border between two of the big council estates in Rotherham: Kimberworth and Ferham. Even now, I can remember our house as clear as day, especially the living room. It was decorated with two different types of green-and-white wallpaper separated by a border, as was the fashion back then, but it wasn't exactly a happy place.

Mum tried her best to make ends meet, working lots of jobs in shops and pubs when there were no hours to be had at the factory. It was real struggle, but it wasn't like Dad was the only person we knew who was out of work. Rotherham had once been a booming, vibrant town, but by the time I came along a sense of foreboding was spreading across South Yorkshire. The old industries, like coal mining and steel, were in decline, but there were no new ones to replace them, and soon Rotherham would become one of the most deprived parts of Western Europe.

By the early nineties, lots of immigrants had settled in Rotherham, which got some people's backs up. They were nearly all Asian, mostly Pakistani. They were much stricter with their families than us locals, perhaps because they were such devout Muslims. Most of them would go mad if they caught their kids smoking or drinking. Loads of the kids weren't allowed boyfriends or girlfriends because their families wanted them to have arranged marriages with other people from their community.

That's not to say the Muslim kids didn't try to bend the rules; they just had to be a bit more secretive about what they were up to than their friends.

Lots of the Asian families who came to Rotherham were given houses in Kimberworth and Ferham, and gradually they began to open corner shops and takeaways on the otherwise abandoned streets. Some people resented them and ranted that it wasn't fair on local businesses and they'd come over here to steal our jobs. My family didn't really think that, though. To be honest, it seemed a bit racist. Most of these people just wanted a better life for their families, and who could blame them for that?

Still, depression and desperation were everywhere in the town, and our house was no different. Mum was frazzled trying to look after Mark, who was eight, and Robert, who was three, as well as tending to a new baby, and Dad wasn't much help. To make matters worse, I kept developing nasty chest infections and I was always projectile vomiting everywhere. Mum knew something wasn't quite right and she was never far from the doctors' surgery. I was given lots of antibiotics but nothing helped, and no one really knew what was wrong with me.

Then, in February 1992, our local surgery got a new GP. She was the first female doctor we'd ever had. Believe it or not, that was a big deal. She clearly knew her stuff, though, because within minutes of examining me she'd looked up some textbooks and called the hospital for a second opinion. She didn't tell Mum, but she feared I had heart problems. Soon, I was taken to Rotherham District General Hospital, where I'd been born just five months before.

Mum and Dad didn't know why I had to have lots of tests, and at one point social services were called in. One of the doctors thought my parents just weren't feeding me because I was so skinny and my legs were a weird shape. Mum was horrified. Of course she'd been feeding me – I just couldn't keep anything down!

Eventually, doctors found two holes and a leaking valve in my heart. Mum was beside herself when they told her I'd have to have heart surgery. She came with me in the ambulance to Leeds Killingbeck Hospital, where I ended up staying for a month. Not only was Mum worried sick about me, she had the boys to think of. Leeds was at least a 45-minute drive away from Rotherham, and that was only when you didn't hit traffic. Thankfully, family mucked in to help, but Granddad was really ill at this point. He was in hospital with heart problems too, so Mum was really having a terrible time. She stayed at the hospital with me while Dad went back to Rotherham to fetch me some of my toys. Just when things seemed like they couldn't get any worse, our car was broken into in the hospital car park and lots of my toys were stolen. Mum was gutted, as she'd really scrimped and saved to buy me them.

I had my operation in the middle of March, and thankfully it all went fine. Mum and Dad were both there when I was taken from theatre to intensive care, but Dad disappeared shortly afterwards. He told Mum he was popping back to Rotherham to sort some fresh clothes and get some money, but he didn't reappear. No one had a mobile phone back then, so Mum couldn't even ring him to check up on him. We didn't see him for days, and Mum was absolutely raging, but eventually he turned up again and charmed her out of her bad mood, without really explaining what he'd been up to. That was just how it was with Dad.

A week after my surgery, I was transferred back to the hospital in Rotherham. This suited Mum, as Granddad was being treated there too. She'd often wheel him down the corridor to see me, and by all accounts I was the apple of his eye. But as I started to get stronger, Granddad got weaker. Not only did he have heart problems, but he also had diabetes and asthma. Barely a month after my operation, he passed away. He was only fifty-seven and Mum was heartbroken, but to this day we believe he wanted to give all of the life he had left in him to me.

A few weeks after Granddad's funeral, Dad was arrested. Mum discovered he'd broken into an insurance brokers' and stolen a safe. He'd only been caught because some police officers stopped him when they noticed one of the lights on the back of the van wasn't working. He was sent to jail for six months. Mum was at breaking point. But still he somehow managed to worm his way back into our lives when he got out. Mark and Robert never had much contact with their dad, and Mum didn't want the same thing to happen to me, so she let him move back in. A few months later, my sister Laura was conceived.

If Dad had been flaky and unreliable before, he was even worse when he got out of jail. I don't know what happened to him in there, and I probably never will, but Mum knew he'd changed the second he walked through the door, back into our council house with its green-and-white walls.

My earliest memory of him is a little sketchy, but it has stayed with me my whole life. I mustn't have been two yet, as Mum was heavily pregnant with Laura, but I can vaguely remember her tumbling down the stairs with her huge baby bump, tears streaking her face, and Dad standing on the landing above with a face like thunder. I think I was sitting in my pushchair at the time, watching it all happen in slow motion in front of me, frightened and confused. I'm not sure if that was the first time Dad hit Mum, but it certainly wasn't the last, and I vividly remember the other occasions as I got older and more aware of what was happening.

Laura was born in August 1993 and we were close from the start, playing little games and doing all of the things that sisters like to do. Of course, we had our squabbles, too. One of my aunties had a video camera and there is some really funny footage from when we were little of me going in a massive huff when I catch Laura riding my bike!

Laura and I never spoke about what was going on with Mum and Dad – we were too young – but we were both scared by all the fights and the shouting. I wanted to protect her, but I didn't know how. We'd hear them rowing loads, at all different times of the day and night. When we were really little, we loved watching the cartoon *Pingu*, which was all about the life of a little penguin. I remember sitting in front of the television, hearing crashing sounds coming from upstairs. We'd just keep watching the TV, so it could drown out the noise and we could pretend that everything was okay.

At night, we'd huddle together in our room and play with our dolls, trying to block out the shouting and screaming downstairs, but sometimes, when we heard Mum begging Dad to calm down as he threw things around the room, it was all too much.

One time, I heard Mum cry out in pain and I just knew that Dad had hit her. I was so frightened I crept downstairs – my knuckles white with fear as I clutched my favourite Barbie doll – and called 999. I only knew that was how to get hold of the police because I'd seen it on TV. I didn't really think about what I was doing, and I could barely speak when the operator answered. I just whispered that my daddy had hit my mummy and told them what I thought was our address before hanging up and darting back up to my room, terrified that Dad would catch me and know what I'd done. I know the coppers turned up, but I can't remember what happened when they arrived. All I can recall is that horrible, sick feeling I would get in the pit of my stomach when I heard Dad raise his voice. I wasn't sure if he knew it was me who'd called them, or what he might do if he did find out. I was terrified he'd do something to really hurt Mum, or maybe start on one of us as a punishment. I worried about what I would be able to do to stop him. What could I do? A five-year-old child against a fully grown man?

Mum chucked Dad out a few times, but he always came back. I think she was scared to say no when he wanted to give their relationship another try. Who wouldn't be? Who would want to be left on their own with four kids? Still, every time Dad left I prayed we'd finally seen the back of him. Living with him was like being in a war zone, and Mum was on eggshells all the time. We never knew when Dad was going to explode in a fit of fury. The smallest thing would set him off and he'd tear round the house like a tornado.

For some kids in my position, school might have seemed like a refuge from everything that was going on at home, but not for me. From the moment I walked through the doors of Ferham Primary School for the first time, I knew I wouldn't fit in. My home life had made me feel vulnerable and lost, and the bullies picked up on that, which made me an easy target. The school was a real mix of Asian and white kids, and almost everyone taunted me in their own way. There were a few ringleaders, though, mainly girls who pulled my hair and called me names – normal kid stuff, you'd think, but it just never seemed to stop. The three really mean girls were Jenny, Anna and Carolyn. They picked on me for all sorts of things, for anything they could think of – from the gap in my teeth to the fact that Mum couldn't afford to buy me the latest trainers. As they played their little games in the playground, giggling with the other girls in my class, I'd stand at the side and watch, trying to swallow the lump in my throat and wondering why they didn't want me to join in with them.

They made me feel bad and ugly. Like most five-year-olds, I hadn't really thought about how I looked before I started school, but Jenny, Carolyn and Anna noticed everything. They constantly told me I looked horrible and that my clothes were stupid.

'Look at Sarah's jumper,' Carolyn sniggered one afternoon. 'Where did you buy that, Wilko?'

I might have been among the poorer kids in the class, but back in the nineties no one in Ferham really had much money and none of us was in a position to turn our noses up at anything. But this hardly mattered to these girls.

'Wilko for Wilson!' Anna giggled. 'No wonder you look so shit. Your mum can't afford to shop anywhere else.'

I'd sometimes see the other girls in my class playing in the street after school or in town with their parents in pretty tops or girlie little dresses. I stuck out like a sore thumb in my black, shapeless shellsuits, hand-me-downs from my big brothers. The more the bullies taunted me, the less I thought about what I wore or how I looked because I simply couldn't win. Even when Mum had enough money to treat Laura and me to some new clothes, I always begged her to buy me another pair of trackie bottoms. At least that way no one could accuse me of trying to look pretty.

I never felt like I fitted in there, and so I didn't listen much in class. I was far from stupid but I was never top of the class or the teacher's pet. That would have just given the bullies another reason to single me out, and all I wanted was to fade into the background. I desperately hoped that I could be invisible, that the other kids would just not notice me and wouldn't give me grief.

It was a shame the way that school worked out, because ever since I was really young I'd wanted to do something with my life. I had dreams of what I could do when I was older. While lots of children would flinch at the sight of blood, I'd never been squeamish and I was always first on the scene when one of my brothers or sister got a cut or a bruise. When I was really little, before I started school, I told everyone that I wanted to be a nurse when I grew up, but after the first few years of primary school I stopped dreaming about stuff like that. Just getting through each day was an effort. Things got even worse later, when I lost my baby teeth and my big teeth started to come in.

'Sarah, what's wrong with your face?' Jenny said one morning, as we copied down some sums from the blackboard.

I turned scarlet and looked at the ground, saying nothing.

'Look at the gap in your teeth,' Carolyn said. 'I'm glad my teeth don't look like yours.'

It wasn't just about my appearance, though. Any time a classmate spoke to me, or invited me to join in one of their games, the girls would tell them they'd catch some horrible disease if they came anywhere near me.

'Don't play with Sarah,' Jenny would say. 'She's got the lurgy!'

'You'll catch her germs,' Anna would add, hand on her hip. 'Play with us instead.'

Each time this happened, my new friend would scuttle off, leaving me standing alone in the playground. Some would give me an apologetic backwards glance, and I got the sense that they didn't really want to play with the class bullies, but they were too scared to say no or to stick up for me because that would have made them a target too. Others didn't give me a second thought as they ran off, delighted at having been asked to spend their lunch hour with the most popular girls in the class.

I never confided in Mum about what was going on at school because I didn't want any more hassle and I knew she'd just get really angry at the bullies. If I'd told her any of the names they called me, she'd have been down at the headteacher's office like a shot, and I didn't want anyone to think I was telling on them – that would have just meant more trouble, and that was all I needed! Sometimes, when I felt really miserable and lonely, I ached to tell her, but there was always something going on with

Dad and the time never seemed right. Still, a mum's instinct is a powerful thing and she always had an inkling I was being picked on. Although I know she begged my teachers to keep an eye on me, the girls who bullied me never seemed to get in any kind of trouble.

Then, when I was six, there was finally a glimmer of hope. Mum sat us down and explained that Dad wouldn't be coming home. Don't ask me why, but I knew this time was different to all the rest. She'd been at the end of her tether for a while and I think she had finally realised she couldn't go on like this – for our sake as much as her own. She had summoned up the courage to go to the police about Dad at last. She never told us what had happened, but from that day things were different. Dad wasn't sent back to jail, but Mum was granted an injunction, which meant he was banned from contacting us for a bit.

Mum really wanted a fresh start, and our house in Psalters Lane held too many bad memories. It took her a little while to get a new house, but a few months later we moved a few miles away, to another part of Rotherham called East Dene. Gradually, I started to come out of my shell. My new school was a bit better and I liked most of the teachers. I made a little group of friends and I even started to pay more attention in class.

We also had some nice neighbours, who had a pond in their garden with lots of frogs. They also had a son my age, called John. I took a bit of a shine to him and we used to tell people we were boyfriend and girlfriend, although we were always falling out! Those were good, fun times.

Things even started to pick up with Dad. He'd tried to get custody of us shortly after he and Mum split up, but of course he didn't get very far. Mum was having none of it, plus he had a criminal record. But he had a new girlfriend called Ellen who seemed really nice, and Mum eventually let us see him on weekends and school holidays. We had some nice times at Rother Valley Country Park, just down the road, and we even tried canoeing and rafting. Don't get me wrong, I always got the impression that Ellen was far more interested in us than Dad was, but it was nice that we could all be civil at least.

Then, just before my ninth birthday, Mum announced that we were moving back to Psalters Lane. She had lots of friends in Ferham and Kimberworth and I think she missed being so close to them. Another family had moved into our old house, with all its bad memories, but Mum had found us a new place on one of the little side streets, just off the main road. It was semi-detached, with a bit of a garden and three bedrooms. I'd share with Laura and Mark would share with Robert, just across the hall.

I wasn't sure how to feel as we packed our things and the removal van set off back towards Ferham. Of course,

I didn't really want to go back to my old school and face the girls who'd made my life a misery, but as the familiar red brick houses of Psalters Lane slid into view, I tried to convince myself I'd find a way of coping.

Sadly, when we got back to Psalters Lane my old school bullies became the least of my problems.

CHAPTER TWO

FITTING IN

As I'd imagined, going back to Ferham Primary School wasn't exactly a barrel of laughs. I'd barely walked back through the door when I caught sight of Jenny, one of the bullies from my old class. She smirked as her eyes travelled towards my feet. I was wearing a pair of Hi-Tec trainers Mum had worked really hard to buy me, but I suspected they'd attract a nasty comment as they weren't Nike or Adidas.

'Hey, Sarah!' she hollered across the playground. 'Still can't afford decent trainers, then?'

I felt my face flush scarlet as I told her to shut up. Over the next few days, the misery continued. I felt so lonely. One day, Carolyn spat in my food at lunch, and they were constantly pulling my hair. I'd feel someone yank on my ponytail then I'd turn round to see the three of them sniggering. Sometimes the rest of the class would join in, too.

The teachers just pretended not to notice.

A little while later, a new show came on ITV and everyone in the class was watching it. It was called *Pop Idol* and it featured lots of up-and-coming singers who competed against each other to win a record deal. One of the favourites to win was a teenager called Gareth Gates. Loads of the girls in my class really fancied him, but like me he had a slight gap between his two front teeth.

'Jenny,' Anna said loudly enough for most of the class to hear. 'Don't you think Sarah looks like Gareth Gates?'

The familiar sound of sniggering filled the air as I silently burned with rage and humiliation. For the next few weeks most people refused to call me Sarah. Instead, Jenny, Carolyn, Anna and lots of their friends simply called me Gareth.

I was convinced my teacher, Mrs Cunningham, must have heard them taunting me, but she never told them off and it seemed so unfair. One day, Anna called me Gareth again and I'd had enough. I turned round in my chair to see lots of my classmates laughing into their jotters.

'Shut the fuck up!' I hissed.

'What did you just say, Sarah?' Mrs Cunningham asked, eyes wide with fury.

'It's not my fault!' I replied, voice shaking with rage. 'They keep calling me Gareth Gates.'

'I will not tolerate swearing in my class,' she said coldly. 'Go to the headteacher's office now.'

These girls – and some of the boys – had been picking on me for years, but now I was the one in trouble. It didn't make any sense and it just seemed so unfair. I'd had enough. I didn't know how the bullying was going to stop if no one was protecting me – how could it ever get any better? I lost it. Something inside me just snapped.

'You're a fucking slag,' I spat back. The words had barely formed in my brain and even I was surprised I'd said them out loud. Mrs Cunningham's mouth fell open in shock and I could hear my classmates both gasping and tittering in amusement. But I didn't want to apologise. I just stood there staring at my teacher while she tried to figure out what to do with me. If she'd done her job properly and told the other kids off in the first place, none of this would have happened. Eventually, she marched me round to the headteacher's office herself and I was excluded for two days.

Perhaps I should have been disappointed in myself. I hated school and it was a good way to have a couple of days off. None of the kids I knew saw an exclusion as a punishment – quite the opposite.

Of course, Mum wasn't too happy when she picked me up, but she wasn't as mad as I thought she'd be. I'd always been a nice girl and this was pretty out of character, so I think she knew something was up.

'Sarah, are you being picked on at school?' she asked me that evening.

'No,' I snapped back. 'Just leave it, Mum.'

And that was that. I just didn't want to talk about it. Luckily, I had made one new friend since I'd come back to Psalters Lane. Her name was Lynsey and she lived on our road. She went to another primary school a few streets away and she didn't know anyone who bullied me. She was around the same age as me and she was a laugh. We'd muck about together on the street and it was so lovely to have a friend. One day she asked me to come and help her babysit for a family friend.

'Her name is Elaine,' she explained. 'She's nice.'

Elaine lived around fifteen minutes away from Ferham and, as we walked there, Lynsey told me that she had two children, aged three and one.

'They're dead cute,' she went on. 'I help watch them most nights, though. Elaine's always out.'

I thought that was a bit strange: why did Elaine go out every night and leave her kids with a girl who was still at primary school? I figured that maybe she worked in a pub like Mum, but it still seemed a weird thing to do when her children were so young.

But the second I walked into Elaine's house I could tell

she was nothing like Mum. It was absolutely filthy and no place for kids. It wasn't just the fact that the floors were littered with junk and the pots were piled high in the kitchen sink – after all, everyone leaves things lying around from time to time – it just looked like it hadn't had a proper clean in years. There was mould growing on the walls and all of the surfaces were grimy and dirty. It smelt damp and horrible.

Elaine must have been in her late teens, early twenties at most, but to me she looked ancient. She was standing in the living room smoking when we walked in, wearing a creased vest top and faded blue jeans. Her face was lined with tiredness, as if she hadn't slept in days. Her limp brown hair was scraped back into a harsh ponytail and there were huge dark circles under her eyes.

'All right, Lynsey,' she said casually. The youngest child – Josh, I discovered – was screaming in the background, while his older sister Kylie was stamping her feet loudly. Elaine didn't take much notice. 'You still okay to babysit tonight?'

'Yeah, sure,' said Lynsey, over the noise of the kids. 'This is Sarah.'

'All right?' Elaine said, but I could tell she wasn't really in the mood to make conversation.

Kylie and Josh were still shouting in the background, crying out for attention, but it was like Elaine couldn't hear them. Eventually, Lynsey picked Josh up and tried to comfort him, but I wasn't paying attention to them any more. Instead, I watched transfixed as Elaine took a crumpled tenner and a bag of white powder from her pocket. She emptied the white powder onto her grubby coffee table, which was already littered with fag ends that no one had bothered to clean up. Then she rolled up the tenner and started to snort the powder through it. I genuinely had no idea what was going on, but it looked a bit ridiculous so I had to stifle a giggle.

I left Elaine's early that night, but the next evening Lynsey invited me back and I asked Mum if I could stay out a bit later. Elaine's house was horrible and dirty, but something made me want to go back. At last I had a friend, and it was really nice to be able to hang out with someone my own age who seemed to like me. As we walked back up the hill the next night, I asked Lynsey what the white powder was.

She looked uncomfortable. 'I think it's a drug,' she replied.

'A drug?' I echoed.

'Yeah, cocaine,' Lynsey said. 'But she only takes it sometimes.'

When we got to the house Elaine was getting ready to go out, and she looked a lot different from the dishevelled woman I'd met the day before. Gone were the creased vest top and faded jeans; now she was wearing a tight black dress and high-heeled boots which came all the way up to her knee. Her hair was down and it looked like she'd washed it. She'd also put on some bright-red lipstick.

'I'm off,' she said. 'See you later.'

I soon discovered that Lynsey often wasn't alone when Elaine was out. Elaine had a little cousin called David, who was fourteen. He used to come round too, and he'd bring all his mates. I quickly realised that Elaine's was a bit of a dosshouse. Now, as a mother myself, I'm horrified that young children – babies, even – were allowed anywhere near a place like that, but at the time I wasn't thinking about it; I was just fascinated at how totally different it was from my own home, my own way of life.

There were around six teenage boys sitting cross-legged on the floor when I walked into the living room – Elaine only had one couch and it was totally falling apart, with holes where the stuffing oozed out – and there were lots of strange-looking green leaves on the table. One of David's mates was sucking on a big, gold thing that looked like a pipe.

'Ever tried a bong?' he asked me, without introducing himself. 'Have a shot. You'll love it.'

'A what?' I said.

'It's weed,' Lynsey whispered.

I'd heard people talking about weed before, but I had no idea what it would do to my body if I took it. But David's friend handed the bong to Lynsey and she inhaled deeply, giggling a little nervously. Then, she passed it to me. I could feel my heart hammering in my chest. What would Mum do if she found out I'd taken drugs – me, a nine-year-old girl? She'd go absolutely spare, of course. But as I'd always been an outcast at school, the idea of having cool, older friends appealed to me. I wanted to fit in so, although I was too young to even know what I was doing, I took the bong from Lynsey and, palms sweaty, I breathed in.

I spluttered as the fumes entered my lungs, and the older boys started to laugh, but I kept going as I didn't want to lose face. After I'd taken a few puffs, I passed the bong back but my brain was already starting to feel a bit fuzzy. A few minutes later, the room was spinning and I started to retch. Bile was rising in my throat, as if I was going to be sick, but nothing else would come.

'Lynsey,' I said, tugging on the sleeve of her hoodie. 'Lynsey, I feel really weird.'

'Relax,' she replied. 'It's just 'cause it's your first time.'

'No,' I said, making no attempt to hide the desperation in my voice. 'No, you don't get it. I think there's something wrong with me.'

Overhearing us, David asked what was wrong.

24

'What have you just given me?' I asked. By now, I was almost in tears. 'I feel really sick.'

I couldn't understand why David and his mates were laughing, and it only made me more scared. The tears which had been threatening to fall now began to spill down my face, but still the boys didn't take any notice.

'What's going on?' I sobbed. 'What are you going to do to me?'

'Now you've tried weed, you'll not be allowed to go home,' David said.

My throat tightened with panic. 'What?' I stammered.

'You won't even get to say bye to your mum,' said the boy who had given me the bong. He still hadn't told me his name.

'The doctors are on their way to get you now,' David went on. 'They're coming to pick you up.'

Of course, none of this made sense, and my brain felt so cloudy that I convinced myself the boys were telling the truth. And anyway, I was only nine. The thought of never seeing my mum again was really frightening, and in my mind at that moment it could easily have been true. I could feel the terror rising in my chest but I was powerless to stop it. My weak heart was racing and tears were streaming down my face. I no longer knew who was saying what; all I knew was that I needed to get out of Elaine's, and fast, and get home to Mum before all of these horrible people took me away to God knows where.

I let out a shrill scream, but it was like the noise had come from someone else's body, not mine. Lynsey was looking at the ground – I think she felt a bit bad for me – but the boys were hooting and howling with laughter. I sprang to my feet, really terrified now, and raced to the front door, but David got there before me, blocking it with his body.

'You can't leave, Sarah,' he said. 'The doctors are coming, remember? They're going to lock you up with all the crazy people.'

Fear and paranoia flooded my body as I tried to wrestle with him, but it was no use: I was a little nine-year-old girl, barely reaching his chest, and he was a fourteen-year-old boy, with the body of a man.

'Please, let me out!' I begged him. 'Please let me go home to my mum!'

The corners of David's mouth were turning up, as if he was trying not to giggle, but I didn't see – I was still dizzy. I ran back into the living room where Lynsey was still sitting on the floor. She had the bong in her hands. Suddenly, I felt like I was going to be sick, as if it was really happening this time. My stomach was churning violently and I ran to the corner of the room, retching loudly.

'Look!' David shouted. 'She's going to whitey!'

He and his mates started whooping with laughter again. As my stomach settled, I turned back round to face David.

'Please, can I go?' I whispered.

'What did I tell you?' he replied. 'Doctors are on their way.'

Helpless, I turned to Lynsey. 'Lynsey, they won't let me out!' I cried. 'Lynsey, you need to help me! Call the police!'

The boys thought this was hilarious, but Lynsey shot David an uneasy glance and I could tell he was starting to feel a bit mean.

'Calm down,' he said. 'We're only messing.'

I still felt shaky when I got home, but luckily Mum wasn't there. She'd started working shifts at a local pub and Mark had been left in charge of us. I got myself a glass of water and climbed into bed. Laura was already fast asleep at the other side of the room. But a few minutes later, I knew I was going to be sick – or 'whitey', as the boys had called it – for real. I ran into the bathroom and threw up, praying Mark hadn't heard.

The next morning, I still felt edgy and paranoid, and I was convinced Mum would guess straight away what I'd been up to, but she'd come in late from work and she was tired and busy, chattering away to me about school and whether or not I needed my PE kit that day.

I'd hated the weed. It was horrible, plus the boys that hung around at Elaine's didn't seem very nice. But despite that, when Lynsey asked me back a few nights later, for some reason I said yes. I guess it was something to do, and being with Lynsey made me feel like I belonged somewhere. I needed that, now I was back to having no friends at school.

'God, you were so stoned the other night,' Lynsey said as we walked to Elaine's. 'I thought you were going to whitey everywhere.'

'I did when I got in,' I admitted. 'It was horrible.'

'You'll get used to it,' Lynsey said. 'I was dead paranoid the first time, too, but now it's just a laugh.'

Gradually, the boys stopped taking the piss out of me, but they kept giving me weed. I suppose they were only really kids themselves and they didn't see it as a big deal. For the next year and a half, Lynsey and I spent lots of our free time at Elaine's. She was my only real friend and I felt safe with her, safe even in that house, despite all the crazy stuff that went on there. It was an escape from being so lonely at school and at home. At last I had somewhere to go with someone who actually wanted to spend time with me.

It wasn't long before I started smoking fags, too. It was just the done thing at Elaine's, plus she would sometimes give us some for free as a 'treat' for watching the kids when she was out. I suppose it should have been obvious to me that she was working as a prostitute. After all, not many single, teenage mums can afford to buy cocaine like it's going out of fashion. But I'd just turned ten at that point and I didn't even really know what a prostitute was. I just thought Elaine was always busy with her mates or working the odd shift in a pub here and there. It was only years later, when I got talking to a girl who knew her, that I found out what was really going on when she disappeared in her short dresses and high-heeled boots.

In the summer of 2002, just before I started Year 6, Lynsey and I also started drinking. Sometimes the boys we knew from Elaine's would take us down to Ferham Park and buy a couple of bottles of cheap cider. For all that my first experience with weed had been horrible, I loved getting drunk from the start. As soon as the cider hit my bloodstream it gave me a bit of a buzz. For the first time in my life I was loud and confident, and even David and his mates thought I was a laugh. At least I think they did – I'm still not quite sure if they were still laughing *at* me. Of course, I always drank a bit too much and I'd often end up throwing up in the bushes, but I didn't really care. It was all in the name of good fun, right?

Sometimes Elaine would buy us cider too, if we agreed to the odd chore or to stay an hour or so longer with the kids. She knew what age we were but she needed something to bribe us with, and it seemed the easiest way of getting us to do her a favour here and there. Mostly, she was all right, but sometimes she could have a right temper on her. I suppose it was because of all the drugs she took, but back then I just thought she was really moody. One day, she asked me to wash some pots for her. It seemed a bit pointless, because the house was a total tip and I never saw her cook much, but I agreed anyway as I wanted her to buy me some booze when she went to the shop. I was scrubbing them for ages and I thought they looked much better, as they'd really been minging before, but when Elaine came in to inspect them she began hurling them against the wall.

'You stupid bitch!' she thundered. 'You can't even wash fucking pots right!'

'What's wrong with them?' I asked, bewildered.

'Look at this one!' she said, her voice still raised as she held the pot in the air. For a second, I wondered if she was going to hit me with it, but instead she pointed to the tiniest speck of dirt on the handle. It didn't look like food; it was probably just muck from her dirty kitchen.

'Sorry,' I replied, shrugging my shoulders.

'Yeah, well, so you should be!' she snapped. 'This is a fucking disgrace. After all I do for you, you can't even wash a pot right.'

Half an hour later, though, she was back to being okay again, and she still bought me some cider when she went to the shop. That was the thing with Elaine. She could be a right cow, but her mood swings never lasted long.

I quickly became an expert at hiding my smoking and drinking from Mum. Most nights she was on a late shift, so I'd make sure I got home before closing time and go straight upstairs to bed, back to the room I shared with Laura and all of our dolls, before anyone could ask me who I'd been with or what I'd been doing. Sometimes I even told Mum I'd been at Elaine's, but obviously I made out that I'd just been helping with the kids. For all that Rotherham has its downsides, there is a real sense of community among some people, and lots of them will often go above and beyond to help others out. I think Mum just thought it was nice that Lynsey and I wanted to give Elaine a hand, because that's what people did.

Ferham is a small place, and by the time I reached Year 6 word had spread that I was hanging around with a group of older, cool mates. Slowly, people stopped giving me a hard time, and some of the people who used to bully me wanted to be my mate. Even Jenny, Carolyn and Anna stopped being really mean to me. I was glad they didn't want to tease me any more, but I couldn't be bothered being mates with them. Even at the age of eleven, I knew it was all a bit fake. Ever since the row with Mrs Cunningham that led to me being excluded, I was determined that I wasn't taking any more shit from them.

For a girl who was once so desperate to blend into the background, I was now the talk of the school. It didn't help that I was almost always hungover or on some sort of comedown from all the weed I'd been smoking. I wouldn't let anyone cross me – teachers or pupils – and I was soon getting excluded every other week for fighting or disrupting the class. If someone so much as breathed a wrong word to me, I'd batter them.

Mum was really angry and she soon began to suspect I'd been up to no good. She started quizzing me about who I'd been hanging around with and what I'd been doing, but it didn't make me stop. She later told me that she feared I was still being bullied and begged the school to investigate, but they weren't really interested. I think by that point I'd just become a bit of a nuisance to them and they couldn't wait for me to leave to go to secondary school.

For Mum, alarm bells really started ringing when Laura began to pick up on my bad behaviour. By this point, Laura was starting to show the signs of having mild learning difficulties. She wasn't as much trouble as I was, far from it, but she was always a little bit behind the others in her class when it came to reading and numbers, and she could never concentrate on her work because she was constantly hyper. Looking back, Mum thinks she had some form of ADHD, but those things weren't talked about so much back then and she was never diagnosed.

One lunchbreak, I got into a fight with a girl in my class and, spying me across the playground, Laura ran over and tried to join in. She didn't get very far – I would never let my little sister fight my battles – but the damage had been done, as one of the dinner ladies had come out of the canteen to see what all the commotion was. She told the headteacher and all three of us were excluded for a few days.

Poor Mum was at the end of her tether and made us stay in our room for ages. She was so mad she wouldn't even let us watch *The Powerpuff Girls*, our favourite cartoon, never mind go out and play with our mates.

'You used to be a lovely little girl,' she told me, over and over, despair in her eyes. 'What's happening to you?'

I think Mum hoped my bad behaviour was just a phase, but I was careering off the rails by now and no one could stop me. I don't know if I was really happy, but I know that I was glad I wasn't being bullied and I felt relieved that I had a group of mates who could look out for me and I could have a laugh with. In my young eyes, Mum wasn't protecting me – she was just trying to stop my fun.

CHAPTER THREE

NADINE

It was in early 2003, a few months before I left the primary school I hated so much, that I first met Nadine.

With four of us to support on her own, Mum was taking all the hours she could get at the pub and was soon doing double shifts. This meant she often worked from the early afternoon right through until closing time, and sometimes she couldn't find anyone to babysit us. By this point, the boys were old enough to fend for themselves, but Laura and I would have to go and sit in the pub after school while we waited for Mark or one of my aunties to pick us up and take us home for dinner. No one seemed to mind; it was a pretty relaxed place and most of the staff brought their kids along. I can't deny that we were bored out of our minds. We were desperate to be out with our mates, but Mum insisted on keeping an eye on us as we were so young. Given my recent behaviour, I suspected it was also because she didn't want to let me out of her sight.

The pub was around half an hour's walk from our primary school. It was owned by a woman called Carole, who had a right mouth on her. It had been there for as long as I could remember, but Carole and her husband had only owned it for a few years. They gave it the odd lick of paint but it still looked a bit shabby. Back then, everyone smoked in pubs and the white walls quickly became yellow and stained. Not that anyone minded – it was hardly like there were loads of better places to go round our way.

Some of the customers were okay, but others were a bit dodgy. It was always dead quiet during the day because most of them only came in at night. It wasn't like some pubs, where you could go for dinner or a nice bar snack. It didn't even have a kitchen. The best you could hope for was a packet of crisps.

There were two rooms: the main bar area and a lounge we called the 'tap room'. In the tap room, people of all ages would sit and smoke weed openly. It was a funny sight: scruffy teenagers and wayward old men passing joints around for hours on end. There were always tons of underage people in there, some of them barely older than Laura and me. Carole turned a bit of a blind eye to it. I don't think she was really that bothered, and in all the time Mum worked there I never saw the coppers come in.

Laura and I usually hung around in the tap room while we waited for Mum. Its saving grace was that it had a pool table and we were allowed to have a few games, provided none of the regulars wanted to use it. But that day, some had come in early, so we'd been told to sit in the bar instead.

'This is shit,' I moaned to Laura, and she rolled her eyes in agreement.

It was then that I saw Nadine for the first time, standing at the back door. Nadine was a big girl, much bigger than Laura or me, but it wasn't just her size that drew my eyes to her. She had frizzy, mousy brown hair with cheap blonde highlights that needed topping up. She was still wearing her school uniform, and her stomach spilled out of her white shirt over her short black skirt, which barely covered her bum. She'd only fastened a few of her shirt buttons and I tried not to stare at her huge breasts – I realised I could see her bra. I could tell from her school tie, which she'd carelessly fastened in a loose knot round her neck, that she was at one of the local high schools, or the comp, as we called it. She looked much older than me and I soon discovered she was fifteen and in Year 10. She intimidated me, but not just because of how big she was. There was just something about her. Even before we'd spoken a single word, I knew she was the kind of person you had to respect, or there would be trouble.

'Who are you?' she asked, eyeballing Laura and me. It sounded like an accusation. Laura looked to me helplessly.

'I'm Sarah and this is my sister Laura,' I replied, trying not to sound nervous. 'Our mum works here.'

'Yeah, I've seen you around,' Nadine said to me, ignoring Laura.

'So who do you chill with, then?'

Around Rotherham, 'chilling' was code for drinking and taking drugs. It sounds silly, but I instantly felt proud that Nadine was speaking to me, almost like I was her equal. Knowing they were around her age, I rhymed off the names of some of the boys from Elaine's, desperate to seem cool and grown up.

'Oh, yeah?' she said. I hoped that she was impressed, but I wasn't sure. 'Anyway, I'm off. It's shit in here tonight.'

There was no one serving at the bar so Nadine barged behind the counter and grabbed a litre bottle of vodka. She obviously did it all the time, because she didn't even look round to see if anyone was watching her, and Carole wasn't exactly the kind of person who'd pay to get CCTV installed. Then she swung her handbag over her arm and disappeared out of the back door.

The next evening, I saw Nadine again. Laura and I were waiting for Mum in the tap room when she swept in and planted herself down next to me. She smelled of fags and cheap perfume.

'So, how old are you, Sarah?' she asked. She lit up a fag and took a puff, before passing it to me. I took it from her as Laura shifted uncomfortably. I knew she felt weird about me smoking, but I didn't feel bad. Instead, it gave me a bit of a buzz. There were just two years between us but I suddenly felt much older and cooler.

'I'm in Year 6,' I said. Nadine raised her eyebrows.

'Year 6,' she snorted. 'God.'

'Yeah, but I fucking hate it,' I replied, before proudly adding: 'I'm always getting excluded.'

'Right,' Nadine said. 'You at Ferham Primary?'

'Yeah,' I replied, stubbing out the fag she'd given me as I blew out the last of its smoke. 'What a shithole.'

'I sometimes go chilling there at night with my mates,' Nadine said. 'It's a laugh.' She lit up another fag, blowing smoke in my face. I tried not to flinch. 'Actually, I'm going there in a bit. Want to come?'

'Okay,' I said, as casually as I could. 'Cool.'

To this day, I can't explain why I was so hypnotised by Nadine. Perhaps it was because she was so loud and confident. She was hardly a good role model. As I replay this scene in my head almost thirteen years later, I desperately want to give myself a shake and tell myself not to go; to stay at the pub with Laura and Mum and forget all about her.

But that's not what happened. Of course, I did go with Nadine. For as long as I could remember, my classmates had made me feel like a freak, but now this cool older girl wanted to be my mate. Sure, I had some older mates from Elaine's, but Nadine seemed different. I was already under her spell.

I had no way of knowing that my new friend would soon open the door to another world, a world I really didn't want to enter. For all my bravado, my eleven-year-old self had no idea what horrors lay in store. Nadine and I weren't going to swap CDs and talk about nail varnish like other young girls.

Nadine was someone to hang around with, someone who might even give me some of her stolen booze.

I went into the back of the pub, where Mum was cleaning some glasses.

'Can I go to the park for a bit?' I asked.

I explained that I'd made a new friend called Nadine, but I didn't let on how old she was, so Mum said yes. Her shift didn't finish until late that night, and I knew Mark was babysitting because he was due to pick Laura and me up soon to take us home for dinner.

'Don't stay out too late – you've got school tomorrow,' she told me, but I didn't pay much attention. I knew

Mark wouldn't be bothered if I came in a bit later than I was meant to.

Half an hour later, Nadine summoned me to the back door of the pub. She'd obviously been home because she'd changed out of her school uniform and was wearing jeans and a hoodie. I grabbed my school bag, feeling a mix of nerves and anticipation. I expected her to nick another bottle of booze from behind the bar, and I was a little disappointed when she didn't.

'Let's go,' she said.

But as we walked along the road towards my school, Nadine fished a crumpled £20 note out of the pocket of her jeans.

'I took this from my mum's purse,' she boasted. 'Daft cow. What do you drink?'

'Cider, usually,' I replied.

'We'll get vodka,' she said. 'It's well better.'

I'd never tried vodka before but I got the impression I didn't have much say in the matter. We stopped at a local corner shop and there was a scruffy looking man stood outside, asking people if they had any spare change.

'I just pay the smackheads to go in and get my booze,' Nadine said.

I watched as she handed the man a handful of change – it couldn't have been more than a pound in total, but he seemed happy.

'What you after?' he asked.

'A litre bottle of vodka and two bottles of Coke,' Nadine replied.

A few minutes later, the man reappeared with a blue carrier bag and we walked to the playground. The sun was beginning to set and it looked a bit different at night, without all the kids buzzing around.

'Looks like it's just us,' Nadine said. I felt a surge of satisfaction as I realised she'd chosen to hang around with me, on my own.

Some people might find it shocking that all I wanted to do at eleven was mess about with older people and get drunk out of my head. Some girls my age were still playing with dolls. But back then I was so desperate to fit in, I'd have done anything to feel accepted. Plus, it wasn't like we had much else to do. We could rarely afford cinema trips or fancy toys like some kids could, so we had to make our own entertainment somehow or go mad with boredom. In a town with lots of poverty and not much hope, drinking and taking drugs often seemed like the only option.

Nadine took a Coke bottle from the carrier bag and poured half of it onto the ground. It fizzed as it made a puddle at my feet. She then topped it up with vodka and handed it to me, before making one up for herself. I took a huge swig and it took everything in my power not to gag. The vodka was much stronger than the cheap cider I was used to. Even mixed with Coke, it tasted foul and burned my mouth. Nadine laughed so much she snorted.

'You all right there?' she said.

'Yeah,' I said, screwing up my face as I took another sip. 'I just always drink cider, that's all.'

'It tastes minging at first,' she admitted, gulping from her own bottle. 'But you get used to it. And it gets you pissed faster.'

I figured that the more drunk I got, the less I'd be able to taste the vodka, so I necked my bottle as fast as I could and soon Nadine was topping me up again. But this time there was no Coke left so I had to drink the vodka on its own. It tasted even worse, but it didn't stop me.

I quickly realised that Nadine was absolutely obsessed with boys. She was way more experienced than I'd imagined. Back then, it didn't occur to me that she was still underage and that the men she spoke about were probably taking advantage of her. To me, it just seemed like she loved sex, and loved talking about it even more. At first, I thought the lads she said she'd slept with were in her class at school.

'Who do you think the fittest lad round here is?' she asked me. The vodka had made her pasty face flush red. I'd always been a bit of a tomboy and I'd never done anything more than hold hands with a boy – when I'd pretended to be going out with John back in East Dene when I was just six. I was still a kid and boyfriends were the last thing on my mind, so I just shrugged.

'Come on, Sarah,' she said, prodding me in the ribs. 'You must fancy someone.' She ran through the names of some boys we both knew, telling me who she thought was fit, who would be good in bed. I hoped the darkness hid the shock in my eyes. Of course, I knew the basic facts of life, but I didn't need details. I was only eleven, for God's sake.

'I shouldn't even be saying this,' Nadine went on. 'Not now I've got a boyfriend.'

'Is he in your year at school?' I asked.

'Ha!' Nadine replied. 'No, he's way older. He's a great shag. Older guys are much better in bed.'

'Oh, right,' I said.

'Just wait till you lose your virginity, Sarah,' Nadine said. 'You don't know what you're missing.'

When we'd finished the vodka it was time to go home. I stumbled when I tried to get up and Nadine snorted with laughter again.

'You're fucking smashed!' she said.

Mum wasn't home yet when I got in and Mark was watching telly in the living room.

'You all right?' he called after me.

43

'Yeah,' I said, trying to say as little as possible as I made my way upstairs. As usual, Laura was already asleep, and I passed out as soon as I climbed into bed. But a few hours later I woke up, my stomach churning violently. My head was pounding too. I could feel the vodka rising in my throat and I ran to the bathroom. I'd just opened the door when I vomited everywhere, not quite making it to the toilet bowl. Mum was home and in bed by this point, but she woke up as soon as she heard the commotion.

'Sorry, Mum,' I said. 'I feel terrible.'

I thought she would catch on straight away – that she'd realise I'd been drinking with Nadine – but she seemed none the wiser.

'Oh, you poor thing,' she clucked sympathetically. 'You must have a stomach bug. I'll get this mess cleaned up and you go back to bed.'

The next morning, I could barely lift my head off the pillow. My mouth was dry and sticky and my head was still throbbing. Mum opened the curtains and sunlight poured through the window. It hurt my eyes so much I pulled the covers over my head. The vodka had given me a much worse hangover than I was used to with cider.

'How are you feeling?' she asked.

'Terrible,' I groaned. 'I'm not going to school today.'

'Probably a good idea,' Mum said. 'Best not to spread your germs.'

From then on, I chilled with Nadine most nights. I still saw Lynsey occasionally, but a few months after I met Nadine the council moved Elaine to another house. Lynsey and the boys went there sometimes, but by this point someone had told Mum that Elaine took cocaine all the time. She went mad, telling me I wasn't allowed to help with her kids any more. Before, I'd have put up a fight, but now that I had Nadine to hang around with, I didn't need my old mates so much. It sounds bad, but I was just a kid and all caught up in this new, exciting friendship.

Nadine would meet me at the pub or the park after school. Sometimes she'd invite some of her mates from school, but mainly it was just the two of us. Nadine would usually steal a bottle of spirits from behind a bar or help herself to some money from her mum's purse so we could get someone to buy us cider, vodka or MD 20/20 – cheap fortified wine better known in these parts as 'Mad Dog'. We'd drink anything, as long as it didn't cost much and it got us pissed quickly.

I didn't think it was a big deal that Nadine stole from people. I just thought it was cool that she had the guts and she never seemed to get caught. Her parents must have noticed money going missing, but she never mentioned it. As for the bottles of booze from the pub, the place was full of dodgy characters so Nadine was

never the prime suspect any time Carole noticed something had disappeared.

Nadine and I didn't do much apart from smoke and
drink, either in the school playground or at the local
park. It was all we had in common, really, but that didn't
seem to matter. There was nothing else to do anyway.
The police would often drive past us and I'm sure they
knew what we were up to, but they didn't seem bothered.
They probably thought we were just a nuisance and that
stopping to tell us off was more hassle than it was worth.
Most of the time Mum would still be working when I got
home and Mark and Robert never said anything about
my drinking. If Mum was in, I went straight to bed,
hoping she wouldn't notice I was slurring my words and
unsteady on my feet.

The only nights I didn't see Nadine were when she
was with her boyfriend. She talked about him lots and
said his name was Amir. I didn't ask too many questions
as I was scared of saying something silly. I knew nothing
about having a proper, grown-up boyfriend. To me, it
seemed years away. I wondered if I'd ever get to meet
Amir, but I assumed Nadine was too embarrassed to
introduce us. After all, he was even older than Nadine.
She said he'd left school ages ago, so I guessed he must be
seventeen, maybe even eighteen. She was probably scared
I'd make her look babyish.

But one night, we were walking to the playground, clutching our bottles of cider, when Nadine's mobile phone started buzzing in her pocket. Her face lit up when she glanced at the screen. Over her shoulder, I saw that Amir's name had flashed up. The conversation was short.

'Okay,' she said. 'See you soon.' She hung up and a smile spread across her face.

'What is it?' I asked.

'Oh, Amir's going to come and chill with us,' she replied. 'He's bringing some mates. You'll like them.'

CHAPTER FOUR

THE NIGHTMARE BEGINS

When I first saw Amir and his friends standing in the playground, I was a bit confused. I recognised them straight away. There was a big group of Asian men who hung around outside my school, and I'd often seen them there at the end of the day. I'd never felt threatened by them, but I knew they were much older than I was. They must have been at least thirty.

'Hey,' Amir said casually, as Nadine and I pushed through the front gate. 'Who's this, then?'

I shot Nadine a bewildered look, but she pretended not to notice. Surely this couldn't be her boyfriend? He almost looked old enough to be her dad. Plus, Nadine had told me he was really fit, and this guy just looked a bit scruffy. He was really short, with messy black hair and stubble that looked days old.

'This is Sarah,' Nadine said. I wasn't sure why I felt uneasy as my eyes met Amir's, but my stomach twisted uncomfortably.

'Sarah,' Amir echoed, taking a drag of the joint in his left hand. 'I'm Amir. This is Rahim and Saif.'

I didn't pay much attention to Saif, but Rahim wouldn't stop looking at me. He was a bit scruffy too, but he was slightly better looking than Amir. If he hadn't had a massive beard, he might even have been fit. Still, he made me feel weird. I wondered why he wouldn't take his eyes off me and I wanted to tell him to stop, but I kept my mouth shut because I knew Nadine would tell me off if I showed her up.

'How old are you, Sarah?' Amir asked.

'I'm fifteen,' I replied, without thinking. 'I'm the same age as Nadine.'

I expected Nadine and the men to burst out laughing. There was no way I looked fifteen. Baby-faced and flat-chested in my kids' tracksuit, I was still very much a child. To my surprise, Nadine stayed silent as Rahim flashed Amir a smile.

Amir whispered something in Nadine's ear and she giggled. Then he led her away to another part of the playground. I could feel the panic welling up inside me as I realised I was alone with Rahim and Saif. I wanted to plead with Nadine to stay, but I already sensed that doing what Amir wanted was way more important to her than looking out for me.

I took a big gulp of the cider Nadine had just bought me as I realised Rahim's eyes were still boring into me.

'You're pretty, Sarah,' he said. 'I've noticed you around.'

The cider was beginning to make my brain feel cloudy, but even in my tipsy state I knew something didn't add up.

'Where have you seen me?' I asked nervously.

'Just around town,' Rahim replied. I fixed my eyes on the ground so I didn't have to make eye contact with him. It didn't take a genius to work out where Rahim had seen me: coming out of school, while he was standing outside.

I'd never paid much attention to him or any of his friends before. In light of everything that has been reported by the media, it sounds silly – but back then it didn't seem strange that there were always groups of Asian men gathered by the school gates. Lots of the kids in my class came from big Asian families and many of the men looked old enough to be their dads, while the younger men could easily have been uncles or older siblings. How was I to know what they were planning? Or why they were being so nice to me and what they wanted from me?

'Are you a virgin, Sarah?' Saif said. 'I bet you're not.'

I'd just taken another swig of cider and I almost spat it

out in shock. Of course I was a virgin, I was still at primary school, but the question felt like a test and I wasn't sure what the right answer was. Now I felt really uncomfortable. I looked over at where Nadine had gone but I couldn't see her. I could feel the panic rising; why would they ask that?

'Why do you want to know?' I asked, bewildered.

'We just do,' said Rahim. He waited for my answer, but I stayed silent. 'Well, are you?'

'Yeah,' I replied, my face burning scarlet with humiliation. I knew my answer might make me sound uncool, but I knew next to nothing about sex and I didn't want to trip myself up by lying.

Rahim and Saif laughed. I wasn't sure what to do, so I joined in.

'You must be joking,' Rahim said. 'There's no way you're a virgin. You're way too pretty to be a virgin.'

'I am,' I replied quietly. No one was laughing any more. Certainly not me.

'You're fifteen and you're still a virgin?' Saif said. I suddenly remembered I'd lied about my age. There was absolutely no chance Rahim and Saif believed me – they'd seen me coming out of my primary school, after all – but I felt I had to keep up the pretence so I didn't look like an idiot. To most people, fifteen still seems too young to have sex, and rightly so, but Nadine certainly wasn't a virgin and neither were any of her other friends. On our estate, with little else to do to occupy their time, most girls had sex for the first time long before their sixteenth birthdays.

'Yeah, so what?' I said, hoping they'd change the subject. I could feel my cheeks flushing with embarrassment. I thought about Nadine and her huge, womanly breasts and how different our bodies looked. I didn't even own a bra. How could anyone possibly believe we were the same age?

'Yeah, right,' Rahim said. 'No chance.'

'Tell her about the test,' Saif chipped in.

'Oh, yeah,' Rahim replied. 'The test.'

I gripped my cider bottle tightly as my insides tensed violently. 'Test?' I echoed. I was suddenly conscious of how squeaky and high-pitched my voice was, of how much I sounded like a child. Rahim grabbed my legs and pushed them together. I squirmed as he touched me.

'Relax, Sarah,' he told me. 'Why are you so uptight?'

'I'm fine,' I lied. Rahim didn't let go of my legs, each of his hands pressing against my thighs.

'What do you think?' he asked Saif.

'There's a gap,' Saif said, grinning. 'Definitely.'

I had no idea what they were talking about and Rahim was starting to hurt me. I wanted to ask him to let go, but I couldn't find my voice.

'That's what I thought,' Rahim said. He turned to me. 'We know you're not a virgin. You're lying.'

'What?' I replied, the panic clear in my voice. I had no idea how they could tell whether or not I'd had sex just by looking at my legs, but I didn't know enough to question them. Rahim's hands had now wandered around my legs, resting on the insides of my thighs, close to the crotch of my tracksuit bottoms. He kept them there for a moment before prising my legs open.

'Okay, close your legs again,' he told me. I did as he said. I didn't know what else to do – I was too young to know what was going on. He rested his hands near my crotch once more.

'I told you to relax,' he said. I sensed a hint of aggression in his voice and it scared me. 'Now, you see this little gap between your thighs?' I nodded meekly, not wanting to make him angry. 'That means you're not a virgin.'

'If you close your legs and your thighs are touching, you're a virgin,' Saif said. 'If they're not, you've had sex before.'

As an adult, I can see how completely ridiculous this 'test' was, but back then I was so naive that I began to doubt myself. I was sure I was a virgin, but what if I wasn't? If I'd never had sex before, why didn't my thighs touch like they should? A hundred different questions were swirling around in my brain. I was confused, full of self-doubt and beginning to believe these men who were much older and more experienced than me. Maybe I'd had sex when I'd been drunk and I'd blacked out and forgotten. Had I lost my virginity without realising?

'We can always tell,' Rahim added. 'So there's no point in lying to us. How many men have you had sex with?'

'I bet it's loads,' Saif said. I felt a lump forming in my throat and I had to swallow hard.

'Where's Nadine?' I asked desperately.

'Where do you think she is?' Rahim laughed. 'She's round the corner giving Amir a blow job.'

Even though Nadine was so outspoken about her sex life, I was still shocked. I didn't think she'd be brave enough to give someone a blow job in my school play-ground, where anyone could catch them – especially as Amir was so much older than she was. I thought they'd maybe be kissing, nothing more than that. I prayed she'd come back soon. I really didn't like standing in my school playground in the daylight with a group of much older men who were talking about stuff that made me feel nervous. For the first time since I'd started hanging around with Nadine, I really wanted to go home.

'Bet you know all about blow jobs too,' Saif said. 'I bet you give blow jobs all the time.'

'Would you like to give me a blow job?' Rahim asked.

I felt blood rushing to my head. I didn't know the first thing about blow jobs. To me, Rahim was creepy and disgusting. I didn't want to touch him, let alone do that with him.

'No,' I replied. 'I don't want to.'

'Oh, come on, Sarah,' he said. 'I really like you. I think you're lovely, I really do. I've wanted to talk to you for ages.' He slid his hand along my thigh again. 'You're special.'

'No,' I said again. 'What if we get caught?'

'We won't,' Rahim replied. 'No one comes round here at night – it's just us.'

'They might,' I said.

'They won't. No one will ever know,' he said. 'It can be our little secret.'

Those words reverberated round my head. *Our little secret*. At that moment, Nadine and Amir came back round the corner and I felt dizzy with relief.

Walking home, I confided in Nadine about Rahim.

'He asked me to give him a blow job,' I said, thinking she'd be shocked.

'Well, did you?' she asked.

'No, of course not.'

'Why not? He's well fit.'

'Because it's disgusting.'

Nadine looked at me like I was mad. 'It's not disgusting. Everybody does it. You should just get it over with.'

A few nights later, I met Nadine at the pub after school. As usual, she'd helped herself to some money from her mum's purse. We stopped at the shop and got another of the local down-and-outs to pick us up two bottles of Mad Dog before we headed for the school playground.

'Amir and Rahim are going to chill with us again,' she said casually. I could feel my face falling. I wanted it to go back to how it was before, just Nadine and me, having a laugh and getting drunk together. But now that I'd met Amir and his friends, I sensed things were different.

'Oh, right,' I replied, trying to sound enthusiastic. 'Cool.'

'Rahim really fancies you,' Nadine said. 'He thinks you're really pretty.'

I blushed and said nothing. In fact, I hardly opened my mouth for the rest of the walk to the school. I didn't like Rahim but, as much as it pains me to say it, I was still a tiny bit flattered by the compliment. No one had ever called me pretty before, and it was kind of nice to hear.

But as soon as I saw Rahim in the playground I had a sinking feeling in the pit of my stomach. His eyes fixed on me straight away and I felt awkward. Dressed in my tracksuit and trainers, without a scrap of make-up, I didn't feel glamorous, or pretty like he'd said I was. I felt like a little girl. I *was* a little girl. How could he, a man who had to be almost thirty, possibly fancy me?

'Hey, Sarah,' he said.

'Hi,' I mumbled in response. This time, Nadine and Amir didn't disappear straight away. The four of us sat together on the edge of the flower beds, chatting and drinking for a while. I say the four of us – I didn't say much. Nadine, Amir and Rahim talked about sex non-stop while I gulped back my bottle of Mad Dog, barely tasting it. I was now drinking heavily at least three times a week, but because I was so young I still got drunk pretty quickly.

'It must be shit being a virgin,' Nadine said, looking straight at me. 'Virgins don't know what they're missing.'

'You're right,' Rahim chimed in. 'They don't.'

For the next half an hour, they traded sex stories: where they'd done it, who they'd done it with, who they wanted to do it with. Nadine said Amir was her boyfriend but he didn't seem to mind her talking about all the lads she'd shagged before she met him. In fact, Amir and Rahim seemed more like teenage boys than grown men, their eyes widening every time Nadine spoke about all the things she'd done with boys.

'We should have a party at mine sometime,' Amir said. 'Have you got any other girls, Nadine?'

'Yeah, I could find you loads,' she replied.

I thought this was a bit odd: if Amir was going out with Nadine, why was he bothered about other girls?

'Yeah, bring some girls,' Rahim said. 'And we'll bring all our mates. There will be loads of lads too.'

As the sugary alcohol hit me, I loosened up a little. I became less aware of the creepy way Rahim was looking at me. Maybe if Nadine brought along some other friends he'd forget about me altogether and go for someone older. Before long, I even started to have a laugh. I'm just being uptight, I told myself. Nadine's older friends aren't so bad after all.

But I'd just lit a fag when I felt a cold hand settle on my knee. I tried to move away from Rahim, but he gripped my leg more tightly than before.

'When are you going to give me that blow job, then?' he asked, grinning at me. I inhaled sharply as I took a drag of my fag.

'I told you before,' I said quietly. 'No.'

'Oh, go on, Sarah,' Nadine piped up. 'He likes you. It won't kill you.'

I shot her a look. For the first time I was really angry with her, not that I would ever have dared tell her that. She knew fine well I didn't want to give Rahim a blow job. But she stayed silent, as did Amir. I realised all eyes were on me.

'I told you before,' Rahim said. 'It can be our little secret. We won't get caught.'

'Rahim, give us a minute,' Nadine said. 'Come with me, Sarah.'

Nadine took me just out of earshot of Amir and Rahim. I stupidly hoped she'd had a change of heart. Maybe she'd tell me I didn't need to do anything with Rahim if I didn't want to. I hoped she might even say I didn't need to see him ever again, because he gave me the creeps.

'What's up with you?' she asked. Her face was red and blotchy, the way it always went when she'd been drinking.

'I don't want to do anything with Rahim,' I replied. 'He's creepy.'

'Oh, come on, Sarah,' she said. 'He's not creepy, he's Amir's mate. Get a grip. He likes you.'

'But he's really old!' I protested.

'I told you before, older guys are better,' Nadine said. 'You might as well just get it over with. Once you've done it once, you'll know what to do.'

'I don't want to,' I repeated, my voice wavering.

Nadine was losing her patience now, and I could sense her irritation. 'If you don't give him a blow job now, he'll get one elsewhere.'

'But –' I began.

She cut me off sharply. 'Do you really want him to get head from someone else?' she asked. 'Is that what you want, Sarah?'

Sometimes Nadine asked me questions and I sensed there was only one answer I was allowed to give. This was one of those times. I was so scared of losing her that I'd have done anything to stop her from falling out with me.

'I suppose not,' I replied.

'Good,' she said.

There was nothing else I could say. Nadine was not someone you said no to; I had known that from the first time I'd met her in the pub. She'd intimidated me then and she was intimidating me now. I knew there was no way out of it.

We walked back over to Amir and Rahim. Nadine gave Rahim a little wink and he brushed his fingers against my leg.

'Come with me,' he ordered. I silently followed him to the other side of the playground, behind the school building. It was hard to believe that, just a few hours before, I'd been in one of the classrooms doing things a normal eleven-year-old should be doing, and now here I was with a man almost three times my age doing something I shouldn't even know about.

From then on, everything seemed to happen in slow motion. First, Rahim dropped his black tracksuit bottoms, then his white boxer shorts. Bile was rising in my throat as his clothes fell to the floor. I wanted to run away, to scream, but I was rooted to the spot, and when I opened my mouth no sound would come out.

'Remember, this is our little secret,' he whispered.

Without saying another word, he grabbed my head and pushed it into his crotch.

When I got home that night, Mum was in as it was her night off. I pushed past her and ran straight to my room. She was calling after me, asking if I was okay, but I didn't want to speak to her. I didn't want to speak to anyone.

The only thing I remember is that I wasn't crying. What I'd just done was horrible, so horrible it made me sick to my stomach, but as hard as I tried, the tears wouldn't come. I was completely numb.

I pushed my bedroom door open and Laura's bed was empty. After Dad left, she'd taken to sleeping in Mum's bed from time to time. I was glad she wasn't there. I needed to be alone more than I ever had before.

As I undressed, I felt dirty and ashamed. I wanted to get into the shower and scrub myself until my skin was red raw, but I didn't because Mum might suspect something was up if she heard the water running. I hadn't even known what to do; I'd just sort of guessed. But somehow, I felt like it was my fault. I wasn't sure why, but I felt like I was to blame for it happening.

I climbed into bed and pulled my covers over my head. I was still drunk and the room was spinning, but the thoughts inside my head seemed clearer than ever. I was home now, tucked up in my own bed with Mum downstairs, so why didn't I feel safe?

I closed my eyes and tried to sleep, but all I could see was Rahim, half-naked in the playground, trousers round his ankles, with his horrible, creepy grin.

Why did I feel like my life would never be the same again?

CHAPTER FIVE

GROOMED

After the night in the school playground, I sensed I'd be seeing a lot more of Amir and Rahim – and I was right. When I finally left primary school in the summer of 2003, you'd have thought I'd have been glad to see the back of it. But ironically, I ended up spending more time there than ever before.

I'd hated every minute of what Rahim had made me do to him that night in the playground, and as the long summer holidays stretched out in front of me, I thought hanging around with him and Amir every day would be torture.

But then, something strange happened. It started to be okay and I kind of enjoyed myself.

I didn't have a phone, so I'd usually arrange to meet Nadine at the playground in the afternoon and the men would join us shortly afterwards. We'd sit in the deserted playground and drink and smoke for hours on end. When we were with Amir and Rahim, they often paid for the alcohol and cigarettes, meaning Nadine didn't even have to steal from anyone.

Gradually, Amir and Rahim started to introduce us to their friends. Lots of them drove taxis, so they'd park up near the playground and we'd all pile into the cars. It sounds silly now, of course, but I was only eleven and I thought it was really cool to be out late and in a car, as Mum didn't have one at the time. There was always plenty of booze and fags to go around, and sometimes even some weed too.

With every free cigarette and bottle of cider they gave me, the sense of foreboding I'd had that night in the playground began to ebb away. Some guys drank and smoked with us, but even the ones who didn't were happy to treat us to whatever we wanted. It all seemed a bit too good to be true. They bought Nadine and me all this stuff and they never asked for anything in return. Rahim had made me give him another blow job one night, which was horrible, but even he wasn't hassling me to do anything any more. I just thought he and his mates were a bit daft, really, wasting their money on kids like us. If anything, we were taking advantage of them. I said this to Nadine once and she just shrugged.

'It's their choice,' she replied. If they were up for buying us loads of stuff, I wasn't going to complain.

I just wanted to be friends with the men. They might have been cool, but they were still dead old. Nadine was different, of course. Most nights, she'd disappear into a taxi with one of the guys and I'd watch the windows get all steamed up while I sat drinking and smoking in another car. Sometimes it was Amir, but she'd go off with his mates too. No one seemed to mind too much, and she loved telling me all about what she'd been up to as we walked home.

Everyone was just really chilled out, having a good time.

'This is right good,' I said to Nadine.

'I know, right?' she replied. 'Told you Amir and his mates were sound.'

As well as our trips to the school playground, we'd also meet the guys in Ferham Park, and soon they were taking us to house parties. The houses were really basic – some didn't even have proper furniture, but we barely noticed. We were too busy having fun – hanging out, drinking, smoking weed and listening to music. The people there were mainly men their age, almost all from Asian families, but there were other girls too, some even as young as me, and soon we were all the best of friends. One girl, Hayley, was always chilling with the gang, and she never seemed to have a curfew.

'My dad doesn't give a shit what time I come home,' she said. 'You should stay at mine sometime and we can stay out all night. It'll be a laugh.'

I was definitely tempted. Two of the other girls, Jade and Leah, were always round at Hayley's. It sounded fun, if a little chaotic – a bit like Elaine's old house had been like. I was coming in later every night, usually drunk or high on weed, sometimes both. Mum was getting more and more anxious, but I thought she was just being uptight and trying to stop my fun. She always wanted to know where I was and who I was with. One night, Nadine and I were chilling in a taxi outside the school with Amir and two of his mates, when the clock in the car told me it was gone midnight.

'It's five past twelve,' I whispered to Nadine. 'My mum is *so* going to kick off.'

'Let's stay out,' she said. 'It'll be a laugh.'

I didn't need to be asked twice. Half an hour later, Amir's taxi-driver mate had to go on a hire and we all split up, but instead of walking home, Nadine and I decided to camp out in a hut at the bottom of the playground.

'I wonder what everyone will say when they realise we've run away from home?' she said. I just giggled, thinking it was all a big adventure. I didn't realise that

Mum was beside herself and had already called the police to report me missing.

The police didn't track us down, but when we went home the next afternoon Mum was chalk-white and looked like she hadn't slept in days. She threw her arms around me and started crying, but before long she was giving me a massive lecture and ranting about how worried she'd been. I just zoned out.

A few weeks later, I started at Kimberworth Comprehensive School. I don't remember much about the first day because I was really hungover, but I think the teachers had already decided I was a bit of a nuisance before the bell sounded for hometime. I couldn't be bothered in any of my classes and I was really cheeky to most of the teachers. On the plus side, it was nothing like primary school. No one dared bully me. I thought I was really hard, and I wasn't scared of anyone.

It was around this time that I first tried cocaine. Nadine and I had gone to a house party with Amir and some of his mates. One guy, Omar, had me in the kitchen alone when he produced a bag of white powder from his pocket. I knew what it was straight away because I'd seen Elaine with it so many times. I thought he was going to take it himself, so I was surprised when he pressed it into my hand.

'Take this,' he said. 'You'll love it.'

Smoking weed was one thing, but cocaine was a whole different story and, for all my rebelliousness, the idea of trying it scared me a bit.

'I'm not sure –' I began.

'Honestly, Sarah,' Omar said, cutting me off. 'It's amazing. The best buzz ever.'

I held the packet in my hands for a few seconds, studying it closely.

'I'll try it later,' I told him. I thought he might insist I take it there and then, but he didn't. He just rested his hand on the small of my back for what seemed like a fraction of a second too long and flashed me a smile that made me feel a bit strange.

I hid the cocaine in the pocket of my tracksuit bottoms and told myself I'd get rid of it. But the next night, just before I'd arranged to meet Nadine, I found it in my pocket. I'd been watching TV with Laura – by this point we'd swapped the *The Powerpuff Girls* for *Tracy Beaker* or *My Parents Are Aliens* – when she announced that she was going out with her friends. Mum was in another room and I was in our bedroom. I could hear my heart thudding as I emptied the white powder onto my chest of drawers, not quite knowing exactly what would happen if Mum walked in. It gave me a strange sort of thrill, imagining her reaction.

I didn't have any banknotes so I snorted it straight off

the wooden surface. I had a whole gram and it took me four attempts to finish it. Within seconds, I felt a strange rush of energy and euphoria, like nothing I'd ever experienced before. I didn't feel paranoid like when I'd tried the bong at Elaine's. Instead, I was on top of the world.

Omar was right. Cocaine was amazing. From that moment I was hooked.

The feeling lasted for around an hour. As soon as it started to wear off I wanted more, but I had no idea how much drugs cost or where to get them. Luckily, Omar and some of the other guys always had something on them. I only had to ask, and sometimes I didn't even need to do that. Soon, I'd tried ecstasy and amphetamines too. I'd take anything I could get my hands on, anything that they offered to me.

If I'd been a nightmare for my teachers before, I was even worse now. Most mornings I'd either still be on an untouchable high or bang in the middle of a crushing comedown. If I'd taken cocaine, I'd be wiped out and just want to sleep, but the withdrawal from amphetamines – or 'phet', as we called it – made me so aggressive I'd want to fight anyone who so much as looked at me the wrong way. It didn't take me long to get excluded, when I battered a girl in my class. Now, I can't even remember who she was or why she'd annoyed me. I was in trouble so much that incidents like these just all merged into one.

I should have been ashamed of myself, but I was just delighted to get a few days off school, especially when Nadine agreed to wag some classes so we could hang out together. She didn't go to the same school as me, but we'd meet in Ferham Park as soon as our parents left for work.

Mum didn't know I was taking drugs, but by now she was aware that I was drinking and smoking all the time and she could see me spiralling out of control. It must have been like watching a car crash in slow motion, but I honestly felt like I was having the time of my life. I was completely and utterly oblivious to the fact that a gang of predatory paedophiles was slowly tightening its grip on my life, getting me hooked on the booze and drugs I couldn't buy for myself. The booze and drugs that I would soon rely on them for.

In Ferham, nothing stays secret for long, and Mum heard on the grapevine that Nadine and I were hanging around with guys twice our age. One night, not long after my twelfth birthday, we were standing with Amir and Rahim at the bottom of Psalters Lane when I saw her tearing down the hill like a woman possessed. She went straight for Amir, and I wanted the ground to swallow me up when she pushed him up against a wall by his throat.

'What do you think you're doing, hanging around with my daughter?' she spat. 'Do you know she's only twelve years old?'

I thought I might die on the spot, and I could feel the blood rush to my cheeks as I waited for Amir's reaction.

'Who, Sarah?' he smirked. 'What are you talking about? She's fifteen.'

'You're sick, you are!' Mum said, shaking her head. 'Anyone can see she's just a kid.'

Mum screamed abuse at Amir and Rahim for a few minutes, but they both laughed in her face. Dejected, she finally let Amir go. She ordered me to come home with her but I stayed rooted to the spot, refusing to move. I could see the tears in her eyes as she shook her head at me and began to walk off. I think she assumed I would follow her. I didn't.

'That's not my mum,' I told Amir. 'What a fucking psycho. I've never seen her before in my life.'

'She's mental,' Amir said. He was still laughing. 'I thought she was going to fucking strangle me.'

'I can't believe she's going about telling people I'm twelve,' I went on. 'What a weirdo.'

Amir and Rahim knew I was lying but it suited everyone to keep pretending I was fifteen, so that's what we did.

Nadine and I had already run away from home a few times when Amir and Rahim suggested they come with us. I was pissed off at Mum because she'd given me another lecture about my drinking. We decided to camp out behind the Aldi supermarket, less than a mile from Ferham. We were having a great laugh, taking drugs and drinking cider, when Nadine and the guys had an idea.

'I bet my mum has called the police,' Nadine said. 'We should pretend we've been kidnapped and ask them for ransom money.'

At first I thought she was joking, but Amir and Rahim were getting onboard with the plan and suddenly it was all happening. Now, I'm deeply ashamed that we put our parents through such trauma, but at the time it seemed like the best idea ever. We were swept up in the moment, high on drugs and drunk on cider. What could go wrong? It was just a laugh, wasn't it? So Amir phoned both our families and demanded they pay £12,000 if they wanted to see us alive again. Nadine and I got so caught up in the drama that we were screaming in the background for effect. I'd even started spending the ransom money in my head, forgetting that Mum would never have that kind of cash going spare. Except, while other girls my age might have fantasised about buying lots of clothes and make-up, I was thinking of splashing out on loads of expensive drugs and having a huge party with dozens of taxi drivers in their thirties.

At twelve.

Poor Mum genuinely thought my life was in danger. Amir told her he'd kill us on the spot if she called the police, so she organised a huge search party of her own. Loads of her friends were trawling South Yorkshire in their cars, desperate for some clues as to where we might be. We eventually walked home a few nights later because we'd got fed up of sleeping rough. Mum looked even worse than she had done all the other times I'd run away. She hadn't slept in days and her eyes were red and blotchy from crying. Now, I feel terrible, but back then I was just glad she had no energy left to give me a massive telling off.

By this point, we were well known to all of Amir and Rahim's friends, and a few nights later this really old guy pulled up in a car beside Nadine and me when we were walking near Ferham Park. I'd had loads of weed and I was really quite stoned. There were three younger guys in the car already but the old man told us to get in. He must have been about seventy, maybe even older. I'd seen one of the guys in the car before, but the old man was a total stranger. He had such a strong Pakistani accent that I could hardly make out what he was saying, but he mentioned Amir's name and I think he was telling Nadine he'd buy us booze. For the first time in months, I felt uneasy. It was one thing chilling with Amir's mates in their taxis outside the school, but I didn't recognise this man and he didn't say where he was taking us. I opened my mouth to protest, but Nadine literally shoved me into the back seat.

We were driving around for what felt like ages when the old guy dropped two of the younger men off at a house in an estate I didn't recognise. I hoped he'd take us back to Ferham, but he kept driving, chatting away to the man in the passenger seat in what I later realised was Punjabi, one of the main languages spoken in Pakistan.

'This is weird,' I said to Nadine. 'Who is this guy? He's ancient.'

'Calm down. He knows Amir,' she replied. 'He says he'll give us some vodka and then he'll pay for our taxi home.'

'Can't we just ask him to take us home now?' I said. The weed had gone to my head and I could feel the familiar fear and paranoia clouding my brain.

'Oh, Sarah, shut up,' she snapped. 'We're just going to chill with them – no big deal.'

In the end, the men took us to a grubby-looking Indian-style takeaway at the other end of Rotherham. The walls were yellow and dirty, and a stale cooking smell filled my nostrils. I later discovered it was coming from the ghee, a type of butter used to cook curries. I thought I might throw up because I was so stoned. I was probably drunk too. There weren't any customers in the front of the shop but the old man led us downstairs into the basement, his younger mate following silently behind us. It was dark and horrible and smelled even worse than the main part of the shop because it was so damp and cold.

A wave of nausea washed over me as my eyes began to focus. In the centre of the poorly lit room was a really old telly, the kind that comes with a video instead of a DVD player. On the screen there were three or four naked bodies writhing around, making all sorts of weird noises. Suddenly, it dawned on me: this sick old man, old enough to be my granddad, wanted us to watch a porn film with him. Even thinking of it now makes me shudder.

I tried to turn away from the screen but this time I knew I was going to be sick for real. The horrible video had tipped me over the edge. I bolted back upstairs as fast as I could. The old man and Nadine were shouting behind me, but I couldn't make out what they were saying. I burst out of the front door and I'd just made it onto the street when I threw up everywhere.

There was another Asian takeaway just across the road, and I could see one of the workers staring at me as I vomited on the street, but I was too out of it to be embarrassed. All I could think was: how can Amir hang around with these weirdos? And why would he tell them to pick us up when we didn't even know them?

The man in the takeaway across the road was trying to make eye contact with me but I couldn't hold his gaze because I felt so dizzy. I started to wonder if he often saw young girls like me out on the street, fleeing from the horrible basement.

'What the fuck was that all about?'

I became aware of Nadine's voice behind me, and I turned round to see her huge frame towering over me, her red face contorted with anger. But before I could answer her, the young man in the other takeaway was making his way over to us.

'You all right there, girls?' he asked. He was smiling and looked friendly. He was way older than us, of course, but at least he wasn't a pensioner.

'Just not feeling too good,' I replied.

'Why don't you come over to our shop and we'll give you some food?' he suggested. 'That might make you feel better.'

I looked to Nadine and she nodded. 'Yeah, okay then,' she said.

'Cool,' our new friend said. 'We'll get you something to eat then we'll give you some money for a taxi home.'

The man didn't tell us his name but I didn't really care. I just wanted an excuse to get away from the old guy and his basement, so I didn't ask any questions. The shop was quite cramped but he took us through to the back and gave us a chicken kebab and some chips. It was only when I started eating that I realised how hungry I was. I must have been really shovelling the food into my mouth because I was getting through it even faster than Nadine.

'Someone's got the munchies,' she said, raising an eyebrow.

Once we'd finished eating, Nadine asked the man for some taxi money like he'd promised.

'It's in my flat,' he told us. 'Come with me. I won't be long.'

The flat was only a couple of streets away. It had a little red door, and before he'd turned the key to let us in I could hear voices, male voices, speaking in a language we didn't understand. It wasn't Punjabi but the accents sounded Asian. The door to the living room was slightly ajar, and there were four men sitting on the floor, laughing and talking. I was still wasted, so I'm not sure how old they were, but they were all at least twenty-five.

I was sure the man from the new takeaway could hear my heart hammering in my chest as he locked us in. I'd thought he was a kind stranger, a sort of Good Samaritan who'd decided to rescue us from the creepy old man and his porn video, but now he seemed just as scary and weird as they had.

'So, what are you girls going to do for us, then?' he asked. He wasn't smiling any more.

We didn't have to ask what he meant. He started going on and on about the free food, how he'd given it to us for nothing and now he and his friends wanted us to pay them back, but the words wouldn't register because my mind was racing so fast, wondering how on earth this was happening because it was never part of the deal that these men would get anything in return.

'No,' I said, as firmly as I could, but my voice had started to tremble.

'No?' the man echoed. 'But how will you get home if we don't give you the money for a taxi?'

Suddenly, I was screaming. Nadine was shaking me, trying to get me to shut up, but even if I'd wanted to be quiet I wouldn't have been able to close my mouth. My screams were getting louder and louder, and the man was beginning to look worried, telling me to stop, but nothing would work. Eventually, he unlocked the door, shoving us out into the cold night. I think he was scared the neighbours might hear.

Nadine and I didn't know what to do – we were at the other side of town and I was in no state to walk all the way home. Nadine had no credit left on her mobile, so we legged it down the street away from the flat and kept running onto the main road. I sped up as we passed the first takeaway, just in case the old guy was still lurking around. We reached a payphone halfway down the street and Nadine stopped in her tracks, panting furiously.

'This is what happens when you act like that,' she said, fishing a few 10p pieces from the pocket of her jeans. 'They leave you in the middle of nowhere.'

I tried to ignore the anger in her voice. 'Who are you phoning?' I asked.

'Just this sex chat-up line. I always phone it when I'm stranded.'

'How does that work?'

'Oh, I just tell some idiot I'll give him a blow job and then he comes out in his car to get me.' Nadine said this as if it was the most natural thing in the world, the obvious solution to the problem. 'Always works, sad fuckers.'

There were two payphones, back to back, so I picked up the receiver on the second one and began to dial. Catching sight of me, Nadine put her hand over the mouthpiece and shot me one of her looks that always chilled me to the bone.

'You'd better not be ringing the coppers, Sarah,' she said. 'Seriously. I'll fucking kill you.'

But it was too late.

CHAPTER SIX

STOLEN INNOCENCE

Within seconds of my 999 call, a police car was tearing up the street, sirens blazing. I hadn't told them anything about the men, just that we were runaways and we needed to get home. Nadine was still on the phone, but she hung up as soon as she heard the commotion.

'You fucking idiot,' she said. 'Piggy bastards.'

Nadine hated the police and nearly always called them 'pigs' or 'piggy bastards'. She glowered as a female copper climbed out of the car and started asking us some questions about where we'd been. Neither of us gave anything away. The copper was all right, I guess, but she insisted on taking us down to the station before we could go home.

There was another officer driving the car but he didn't say much. When we pulled into the car park, the first copper took Nadine inside but told me to stay in the car. I'm still not sure why.

'Can't we just go home?' I asked him.

'We just need to make some routine inquiries,' he said. 'Has anything happened to you tonight? You know you can tell us if it has.'

I just folded my arms and said nothing. It seemed like ages before the other copper came back to the car, but Nadine wasn't with her. She got into the back with me and she had a serious expression on her face.

'Sarah,' she began slowly. 'Your friend has just made a very serious allegation against the group of men you were with tonight. Is there anything you want to tell me?'

She explained that Nadine had told her we'd gone back to the flat with the men from the second takeaway and I'd been gang-raped. I could barely believe what I was hearing, and I genuinely thought the police were playing mind games to try to trick me into telling them the truth. Nadine had been raging at me for phoning them. I thought she'd never grass those men up, far less make up a story that was ten times worse than what had actually happened. She was always sticking up for Amir and all the men that tagged along with him, so why was she trying to get them into trouble?

I told them it was a load of rubbish. They took us home separately and they never contacted me again about what Nadine had said. The next day, though, she thought it was a hoot.

'I told the pigs that those Pakis gang-raped you,' she said, laughing at the thought of me being violated by a group of strangers as if it was the funniest joke in the world.

At the time I was so confused but, looking back, I think Nadine was smarter than she made out. She was teaching me a lesson and it worked. I never phoned the police again as it all seemed far more trouble than it was worth.

As for the coppers, I think they already had me down as a bit of a time waster because I'd run away so much, and this was probably the final nail in the coffin. Whenever Mum reported me missing after that, they just didn't seem bothered about finding me. To them, it was like I'd decided to hang about with older men and get off my face on drugs and alcohol, and I'd have to live with the consequences. I wasn't yet a teenager, but years later I would discover that they'd described what was happening to me as a 'lifestyle choice'.

The more I saw of Nadine and this ever-expanding gang of Asian men, the worse things got at home. I'd always had a fiery relationship with my brother Robert, but the drugs made my temper even worse and we were always scrapping. This meant Mum was more stressed out than ever before, and even Laura and I weren't as close as we'd once been. She was ten, but she was still playing with prams and dolls in the back garden while I was being sucked into something that I couldn't seem to get myself out of, something that was being controlled by a group of men I didn't know – something that was so far away from the world of playing with dolls.

A few days after Nadine made up the gang-rape story, I was in my maths class when I caught sight of Robert outside the window. I couldn't hear what he was saying, but I knew he was trying to wind me up, making faces and pointing and laughing, as siblings often do. I'd been given loads of phet the night before, so I could feel an uncontrollable rage sweeping over me as I kicked over my seat and made for the classroom door.

'Where are you going, Sarah?' the teacher, Miss Jones, asked. She'd sprung up from her seat and she was now standing in front of me, blocking my way.

'My brother's out there,' I said. 'He's slagging me off. He's a dick. Let me at him.'

'Sarah,' Miss Jones said, as calmly as she could. She was used to me kicking off in class. 'Go down to the headmaster's office and give yourself five minutes to cool off, then we can discuss this properly.'

Miss Jones was quite petite – she couldn't have been more than about 5 foot, 3 inches – but I found myself wondering what would happen if I tried to knock her over. Robert was still outside the window, laughing with his mates.

'You have two options, love,' I said. 'You either move and let me go and smash his face in, or I'll put you on your arse and smash his face in anyway.'

Miss Jones just stood there, defiantly holding my gaze. I'd been in loads of fights with girls in my year, but I could see she thought I'd never have the guts to hit a teacher.

She was wrong.

Rage coursed through me as I swung a punch at her. Everything seemed to happen really slowly. I could see shock spreading across my teacher's face, and at the last minute she ducked out of my way. My hand went straight through the window, hitting it with such force that glass shattered everywhere. It seemed to take forever before the blood started gushing from my hand and down my arm. It was really sore, obviously, but I was still so angry I couldn't properly concentrate on the pain.

I'd hurt myself so badly that I had to have an operation and loads of stitches. I've still got the scars now. What was worse, though, was that I was permanently excluded from school. The headmaster told Mum I'd have to go to a special school for pupils with behavioural problems.

'I love you, Sarah,' Mum told me on the way home from hospital. 'And I always will. But I really don't like you at the moment. Why are you acting like this?'

As usual, I didn't really listen. I'd heard it all before: how I'd always been so lovely and polite but now I was like a different person, how Mum had brought me up to be better than this and how ashamed she was of my behaviour. But my brain was addled by all the drugs and alcohol and everything those men were telling me. It was like I was turning into a little robot, slowly but surely losing all sense of control over my life.

A few weeks later, Nadine turned sixteen. She told me not to tell anyone she was two-timing Amir with a white lad called Ryan. I couldn't understand why it was okay for her to sleep around with Amir's mates but not with this other guy, but I didn't ask any questions.

Nadine and Ryan saw each other a few times a week, but I still chilled with her loads. When she wasn't there, I'd hang around with Hayley, Jade and Leah, or the taxis would pick me up on the street and take me to a house party.

Soon, we were hanging around at Hayley's dad's most of the time. If I'd thought it might have been a bit like Elaine's, I was wrong. It was ten times worse.

The first time I walked through the back door the smell was so bad I actually gagged. The kitchen was foul, with rubbish piled high in every corner. It was so minging that I quickly realised some of it must have been there for months. I don't think there were any dishes or cutlery, and even if there were, it would take you forever to wade through the mess and find them.

The living room was no better. There were empty cans of lager and fag ends everywhere, and I immediately recognised the horrible smell of damp that I've come to associate with all of the houses I visited around that time. There were no sofas and the carpet was so frayed and stained it looked like it had been there for decades. None of the light bulbs worked, but in the darkness I could see around a dozen Asian men spread across the floor, laughing and talking in a mix of English and Punjabi.

'They all come to chill here because they know my dad won't mind,' Hayley explained. 'He even gives us all fags.'

It was no wonder Hayley's dad never gave her a curfew or quizzed her about who she was bringing into the house. I soon realised he was barely conscious for long enough to notice what she was up to. Hayley led us into the dining room, where he was lying face down on the only couch they appeared to own. He was wearing nothing but a tatty pair of old blue boxer shorts, and his body was covered in little tufts of grey hair. Even in the half light, I could see he'd shit himself. I still feel sick, thinking about it now.

'He's passed out again,' Hayley said. 'Typical.'

Even at twelve I could see Hayley's dad was a raging alcoholic. He was in no fit state to care for a child and he clearly needed help. But Hayley's school didn't seem to be aware of this, and if she had a social worker, he or she clearly wasn't up to the job. The only adults who knew what she was up to appeared to be the taxi drivers and takeaway workers who congregated in her living room.

Jade and Leah were used to Hayley's house and they didn't seem bothered by how disgusting it was. I thought I'd never be able to stay over there, but after a few visits I kind of got used to all the minging sights and smells. The guys that visited always made sure I was either drunk or high, so I suppose that helped.

There were a few other girls our age who sometimes popped by. Hayley never went to school much so her mates were mainly people she'd met through the older men she hung around with. Most of the guys had taxis, so sometimes they'd disappear off with one of the girls and bring them back a few hours later. One night, Hayley went off with a guy called Sajid. She came back around an hour later and, while we were having a fag in the kitchen, she told me he'd driven her to an industrial estate, where they'd had sex.

'It was right good,' she said. 'Don't tell Leah, though, as she gets dead weird about stuff like that.'

It was true. Leah was a tearaway like the rest of us, but she was the only one who realised it was wrong for men in their thirties to be having sex with twelve-year-olds.

Sajid worked in one of the local takeaways. He was a regular at the house, and a few nights later he brought a mate along who called himself Raj. I'm pretty sure that wasn't his real name but some of the men, usually the more savvy ones, were only known to us by their nicknames. Many years later, I discovered that lots of them were living a double life and had wives and children at home.

Raj was a taxi driver, and within minutes of arriving he'd taken Leah and Hayley out for a spin in his car. I barely noticed they were gone because Omar had turned up with weed and vodka. Half an hour later, they came back and Hayley called me into the dining room. As usual, her dad was lying face down on the couch in his pants, oblivious to the sordid mess unfolding around him.

'Raj wants to take you out in the car,' Hayley told me. Her voice dropped to a whisper as she added: 'He says he likes you.'

Leah elbowed Hayley and shot her a look before turning to face me. 'Don't go, Sarah. He's just asked me for sex.'

But I was already on my way out. I could hear Leah running after me, and she managed to grab hold of my arm.

'Sarah, seriously,' she said. 'He's, like, thirty-five or something. He'll try and shag you. He's a total paedo.'

'I'm not stupid, Leah,' I snapped. 'I can handle this.'

I don't know what was going through my head. Leah had called Raj a paedo and she was right, but it was like I hadn't heard her. Nadine was still taunting me about being a virgin and I thought I'd seem older and cooler if I'd had sex. Besides, it was just the done thing. All the girls at Hayley's were losing their virginity one by one, and I didn't want to be the last one left, unable to join in the conversations about who was good at shagging.

Plus, the guys might start to think I was a bit uptight, that I wasn't any fun. What if they stopped inviting me out? Then who would buy me booze and give me the drugs I loved so much? Maybe the guy who'd given us the chicken kebab in the takeaway a few weeks ago was right; perhaps we couldn't keep taking all this free stuff without doing something to earn it.

Maybe it was time to start giving these men something in return. I closed the door behind me and walked out to the taxi, which was sitting on the street with its engine running. I can't pretend I didn't know what was about to happen. Raj was going to try to sleep with me, and I was going to let him.

* * *

We didn't know it at the time, but we'd all been completely and utterly groomed – Leah was the only one who could see it. We had taken their alcohol and their drugs, and now they were going to claim their prize.

Raj was fat and ugly, with messy black hair that was thinning a bit on top, but I tried not to dwell on that. I climbed into the passenger seat and, without preamble, he asked how old I was. I told him I was fifteen.

We chatted a bit as he drove me to an industrial estate on the edge of the town, but I can't even remember what we talked about because I was pretty drunk and Omar had given me a joint. Raj parked up just outside Asda, across from the Gala Bingo. It was gone midnight and there was no one around but us.

'Get in the back,' he said, as he pulled on the handbrake.

I climbed over the gearstick and into the back seat, and soon he was sitting beside me, telling me to lie down. He pulled down my trousers, then my pants, and fiddled with a condom wrapper. He undid his jeans and they fell around his ankles.

Then he lay on top of me and took my virginity.

As soon as I walked back through Hayley's door, Leah looked gutted. She guessed what had happened before I'd even said a word. She was standing in the kitchen with a fag in her hand, but she stubbed it out as soon as she saw me. She pulled me out of earshot of everyone else and demanded that I tell her what Raj had done to me.

'I shagged him,' I said, trying to sound casual. 'It's not a big deal, Leah.'

'This is sick,' she replied, shaking her head. 'I'm going home.'

She slammed the door behind her and we didn't see her for a few days. Before I had time to dwell on her reaction, Hayley came into the kitchen and handed me a bottle of Mad Dog.

'What's up with her?' she asked.

'Oh, she's just kicking off because I shagged Raj,' I said, taking a swig. 'She needs to chill.'

'So, what's he like?' Hayley giggled. 'Does he have a big dick?'

'No, it's tiny! It wasn't even that sore,' I replied. 'It only lasted, like, two seconds.'

It makes me sick to my stomach to think of two twelve-year-olds having this conversation.

'You should do it with Sajid,' she said. 'His is massive!'

I wasn't sure if I wanted to have sex with Sajid, but later that week it was all arranged. I climbed into Raj's taxi, where Sajid was sitting in the passenger seat. He didn't acknowledge me, but I could see him studying my childish frame in the rearview mirror. Hayley was still in the house, trying to get fags from her dad, so Raj turned the engine off and leaned back to face me.

'Have you told anyone about what happened the other night?' he asked.

'No,' I replied. Of course, Hayley and Leah knew what had happened and I'd mentioned it to Nadine, but I didn't think he'd be bothered about them.

'Make sure it stays that way,' he said. 'Because everyone knows you're only twelve.'

I didn't know who had told Raj my real age. Maybe he'd just worked it out for himself. A few seconds later, Hayley jumped into the back seat, having blagged some fags from her dad, who was hammered as always. Sajid passed back a bottle of vodka and Hayley and I took turns to swig from it. I never did get used to the taste of straight vodka, but it was better than being sober.

Raj drove to another park a few miles from Ferham. When we arrived, Sajid told me to get out of the taxi, while Hayley and Raj stayed inside.

Sajid didn't say much as he led me across the grass towards a bench. It might have been night time but it still seemed really exposed, and I was worried we'd get caught. He wasn't as ugly as Raj but I still didn't fancy him, not that it mattered.

'You do know I'm only twelve, right?' I said. 'You heard what Raj said.'

'Shh, it's fine,' Sajid replied, tugging at my tracksuit bottoms. I didn't put up a fight and soon he was inside me. Hayley was right. He was really big down there, but that didn't make it good. It just hurt – it was much more painful than it had been with Raj. I grimaced a few times, but I didn't dare tell him to stop. It just didn't seem like an option. He was really rough, so I closed my eyes, hoping he'd soon finish. Eventually, he grunted a little and told me to pull up my trousers. It was only then that I realised my pants were covered in blood and it was running all down my legs. Sajid pretended not to notice.

'Let's go back to the car,' he said. His voice was toneless, devoid of any emotion. 'Don't tell anyone about this.'

We walked back across the grass and, as we got closer to Raj's car, I could see the windows were steamed up. When I climbed into the back Hayley's hair was everywhere and her top was on inside out. She was smoking one of the fags she'd got from her dad.

'You're right,' she whispered, as Raj turned the key in the ignition. 'It's tiny!'

CHAPTER SEVEN

TRAFFICKED

Once I'd had sex with Raj and Sajid, sleeping with other men more than twice my age just became normal.

A few weeks later, I went to chill with Nadine at an Asian takeaway on the other side of town. One of the men who worked there had stopped us on the street and invited us in. He claimed to know Amir. He told us to call him Baz and he looked like he was in his late thirties. As usual, we jumped at the promise of free vodka, and soon I was totally out of it. We rarely sat at the front of the shop; the men we hung around with always hid us away upstairs or in the kitchen.

On this occasion, the family who owned the takeaway had a little flat upstairs, but I don't think anyone actually lived there. There weren't any chairs, but there were religious pictures on the wall. Five of us all sat on the floor drinking in the cramped little living room: Nadine, Baz, his two friends and me. He told us to call the other guys Dee and Gus, though of course those weren't their real names. Many of the guys we hung around with had fake, English-sounding aliases.

Nadine was still sleeping with both Ryan and Amir, but that counted for nothing when she'd been plied with free booze. Soon, she was telling me she was going into the other room to have a threesome with Baz and Dee.

I barely registered what she was saying. I was so drunk I could hardly keep my eyes open, and I must have dozed off because soon I became aware of a crushing weight on my body. I opened my eyes to find Gus lying on top of me, pawing at my tracksuit bottoms. He was a big guy and I struggled for breath as he pressed down on my ribcage.

I opened my mouth to protest, but I couldn't find the words.

He smelled of sweat and the ghee from the curries, and he was at least twenty years older than me. Even in my drunken stupor, I had to fight really hard not to scream as he entered me. It was agony and the pain must have been etched all over my face, but he didn't stop. I closed my eyes and breathed in, praying he'd finish soon, but it seemed to go on forever.

Finally, he stopped, panting in sick satisfaction. It was only when he climbed off me that I opened my eyes. Nadine was standing over me, watching, but she seemed to think the whole thing was really funny.

'Hey, you've just had some donkey dick!' Gus said, in his thick Pakistani accent as he pulled his trousers up. Everyone burst out laughing. Everyone, that was, except me.

It might sound crazy, but I didn't think Gus had raped me. I'd gone to this flat willingly and I hadn't paid a penny for all the vodka he and his mates had given me. What did I expect to happen? To me, this was what sex was: rough, emotionless and something I didn't have a say in. When I gossiped with Nadine and Hayley, I sometimes pretended I enjoyed it. Inside, though, I was confused and angry, and I always wanted to lash out, especially at anyone who might have dared to suggest I was being exploited by all my older Asian 'mates'. I was drinking heavily most nights now, as well as taking loads of hard drugs. Soon, even the specially trained teachers at the behavioural school couldn't control me, and the council spent ages trying to figure out what to do with me.

I think it was at this point that I was referred to social services. I was assigned two social workers, Phil and Kate, but I thought they were horrible. They always moaned to each other about the size of their caseloads in front of us and I hated how they talked to Mum like she was stupid. Even though Mum and I argued all the time, I still didn't like other people giving her any hassle. It was quite clear the social workers saw me as a burden and they spent more time telling me off than trying to help me. I think Kate even moaned that she was scared of me. I'm sure social workers have a really hard job and I know there are some who try really hard to rescue girls like me, but that wasn't the case with Phil and Kate.

Mum suspected I was having sex – she wasn't stupid – but I don't think she had any idea of just how many men were involved at first. Still, she'd go on and on about how I could end up pregnant, or with some sort of horrible sexually transmitted infection if I wasn't careful.

'If you get pregnant I'll make sure you get put in a mother and baby hostel,' she'd tell me over and over, but her threats felt hollow. Loads of the men had condoms, especially the ones who already had a family at home. I was usually too drunk or high to be sure they'd used one, but I didn't even think about getting pregnant. I just pushed it to the back of my mind.

Not long after I got chucked out of the behavioural school, Mum insisted I take a pregnancy test, even though I hadn't missed a period. She took me to see the doctor, who told me to pee into a little tube. I told Mum she was an idiot and I claimed I was still a virgin. I didn't dare think about what I would do if it came back positive, because if it had happened to me the father could have been any one of several men. Thankfully, it was negative.

Mum was also really annoyed that my education was in limbo, but I didn't care. While the authorities worked out where to put me I had loads of freedom, and Mum couldn't keep track of me because she was usually juggling a couple of jobs. Sometimes, I'd sleep until the early afternoon, unless someone had given me phet or ecstasy, which made rest impossible. If I was on a come-down, I'd walk up to Kimberworth Comp to meet some mates and they'd wag classes to hang out with me.

That was when I first met Azim.

He was sitting outside the school gates in his car as I made my way along the road. It was a green Skoda Octavia. I remember it well because it looked like a taxi and I was squinting to see if I recognised the driver. Azim was on the phone and I didn't think he'd noticed me at first, so I kept on walking.

I'd certainly noticed him, though. He was much better looking than most of the guys I chilled with and definitely way fitter than Raj or Sajid or Gus. He was loads younger too. Gradually, I became aware of the low hum of his car crawling along beside me.

'Hey,' he said, rolling down the window with a smile, his deep brown eyes lighting up. 'Need a lift?'

Azim was a total stranger but I was so brainwashed by all the other men by this point that I thought nothing of jumping in his car.

'Are you a taxi driver?' I asked.

He laughed. 'No, I'm not. I'm a doctor. Has anyone ever told you you're really pretty?'

Azim told me he was in his early twenties and lived in Halifax, which was about an hour away in the car. I told him I was just about to turn sixteen, although I still looked about ten or eleven. I didn't know what he was doing in Rotherham but I guessed he was probably on his way home from helping at the hospital or something. He asked for my number, and when I told him I didn't have a phone he gave me an old Nokia 3210, just like that. It looks like a brick now, but I'd just turned thirteen and I thought it was the coolest thing ever.

'Now I can text you,' he grinned.

The next weekend, Azim picked me up in his Skoda and we drove to Doncaster. I told Mum I was staying at Hayley's. Doncaster was only about half an hour away and hardly the most exciting of places, but I thought I was dead grown up, sitting in the front seat of Azim's car as he sped up the M18. He'd booked a hotel room, and as we pulled up in the car park I went to get out.

'Stay here, babe,' he said. 'I'll check in and then I'll text you and tell you what room I'm in. Okay?'

'Why can't I come in with you?' I asked, confused.

'Just trust me on this one,' he said. A few minutes later, my new phone beeped and I walked through the doors of the hotel. The receptionist was tapping away on her computer, but she looked up just as I got to the double doors that led to the rooms on the ground floor.

'Excuse me,' she called after me. She had a sharp voice, a bit like a teacher's, and her hair was wound into a tight bun on top of her head. 'Are you staying here?'

'Yes,' I replied.

'Well, I haven't seen you here before,' she said. 'Has your family just checked in today?'

'I'm not here with my family,' I told her. 'I'm with my boyfriend.'

Her eyes narrowed and she pushed her glasses up to get a better look at me. I was wearing a black tracksuit and trainers and my hair was scraped back in a ponytail. I certainly didn't look like a grown woman on a romantic weekend away.

'Your *boyfriend*?' she echoed.

I nodded and she asked me my room number. When I told her, she just stared at me, bewildered. She'd obviously given Azim the key a few seconds before I'd arrived and I could see her brain working overtime. We both stared at each other in silence for a few seconds while she worked out what to do with me.

'On you go, then,' she said eventually. I thought she seemed like a snooty cow, but if she did tell anyone, they obviously decided it wasn't worth pursuing because we never heard anything more about it.

Azim was stretched out on the double bed when I got to the room, and he kissed me as I lay down beside him. The bed was quite hard and the room was clean but basic. It didn't seem like the kind of hotel you'd book if you earned loads of money working as a doctor, but I didn't really mind because it was cool enough to be out overnight with a fit older guy who told me I was his girlfriend. There was a bottle of vodka on the bedside cabinet and he poured some into two flimsy plastic cups he'd got from the bathroom, the kind you'd use to wash your mouth out after brushing your teeth.

Azim wanted sex a few times that night and, of course, I felt like I had to do it because he'd gone to all this trouble to whisk me away. It wasn't too bad, I suppose. I lay there in silence, letting him do what he had to do, just happy that he wasn't as rough as Sajid or Gus or some of the others. He used a condom and afterwards he told me he loved me.

'One day, I'll take you to meet my family,' he promised. 'Then we can get married and have children.'

The next day, he bought me a McDonald's from a motorway service station and topped up my phone with a fiver so I could keep in touch with him during the week.

I believed I was in love with Azim. I was only thirteen and I had no idea how a proper relationship worked. He only ever wanted to see me at the weekends, and never in Rotherham. He always booked us into a budget hotel, usually in Doncaster but sometimes in Sheffield or Halifax. He told me he worked all week in a hospital, and it seemed dead romantic that he was off saving lives like I'd dreamed of doing as a kid when I'd wanted to be a nurse.

I only wanted to be with him, not with any of the other guys, but it was hard because, now I had a mobile, loads of the men I'd been hanging around with had my number. I had no idea that there were several rival gangs of Asian men in Rotherham, all tussling to control and exploit vulnerable white girls like me. I just knew that whenever my phone rang, I had to go where I was told to go – it was like I owed it to them for all the drink and drugs they gave me, and it was clear what they expected in return.

My abusers had it all worked out. By now, I drank almost every night and I was taking more and more drugs just to get through the day. If they gave me a bottle of vodka or a line of cocaine, they could do anything they wanted, Azim or no Azim.

It wasn't long before they were taking me all over the country and pimping me out to their friends. Of course, I didn't see it like that at the time. It was just part of the deal, the price I had to pay to get the drink and drugs that I needed.

There was an older guy I came to know called Jamal who drove a van. He hadn't been in England long after coming from Pakistan, and his English wasn't great. He never touched me, but he took me to plenty of men who did. The first time he picked me up, Amir and Nadine came too. There were only two seats so Nadine and I had to sit in the back, where there were no seatbelts. We were sitting next to a guy called Farooq who looked roughly the same age as Nadine, and he kept asking me for a blow job. As well as underage girls, Jamal transported scrap metal, and there was barely enough room for us among all of the poles and pallets. We'd been driving for ages when he braked suddenly and Nadine was thrown forward, knocking herself out on a huge iron bar. She was fine, but I think Jamal got a bit spooked because he took us home after that.

That was the only time we were given a reprieve. At first, we didn't go too far, just to places like Sheffield and Bradford. Sometimes we went to back rooms in takeaways and other times we'd go to houses or flats. There would always be alcohol and drugs, but they would always come at a price. Quite often, the charade would be the same. We'd sit in a circle, drinking or taking whatever was on offer, before one of the men would tell me he wanted to speak to me in private. I'd go into another room with him – sometimes the bathroom, sometimes a bedroom – and we'd both know that I'd do whatever he wanted me to do. Some of the men would bring a mate in for a shot once they'd finished, but normally I was so off my face I wasn't even sure who'd done what to me. Some of them were really violent, though, and I'd wake up the next day with crippling pain down below. Still, I always prayed they'd ask for sex and not a blow job. Sex could be sore, but at least I was really out of it so I could lie there and pretend I was somewhere else, that it wasn't happening to me. With blow jobs, I had to play an active part, to pretend I was enjoying what I was doing. It always took everything in my power not to gag.

Eventually, Kimberworth Comp agreed to have me back but the teachers thought I was too disruptive, so I had to have my lessons away from everyone else, in some little huts at the bottom of the playground.

It was then that I got to know Sarah Hughes. Sarah worked for Risky Business, an outreach project run by the council that targeted young girls at risk of sexual exploitation. But Sarah wasn't like my social workers or the coppers or the teachers. She was really cool and she really listened. I'd later learn that Risky Business was the first public service to acknowledge that hundreds of girls in Rotherham were falling prey to these British Pakistani sex gangs, but that would come much later.

Sarah would take me to McDonald's for a drink and some chips, or she'd sit with me in my classes to help me when I was struggling to readjust to the school day. Sometimes, she'd even take me to Sheffield, where she let me try on dresses in TK Maxx and have my make-up done. She told me I could tell her anything, so I boasted about all my older mates and all the 'fun' we had drinking and taking drugs and having sex. She never told Mum or my social workers, but she gently tried to explain that my so-called friends were taking advantage of me. As much as I liked Sarah, it would be a long, long time before we could see eye to eye on this issue. As far as I was concerned, I was still in control. I was no victim.

Sarah knew about the parties I went to because I'd often tell her about them when she picked me up for our weekly meetings, but she didn't judge me. Sometimes, I felt like she was the only adult who didn't think I was a waste of space.

Nadine always came with me in the vans and taxis at first, but by the winter of 2004, I noticed that Jamal and the other men were picking her up less and less. I didn't understand why. She seemed to enjoy sex much more than me and she didn't take half as many drugs, either. Surely they preferred a girl who got into the swing of things and made all the right noises to one who just lay there, semi-conscious, hardly knowing what day of the week it was?

Now, it all makes perfect sense, of course. Nadine was almost seventeen by this point. She was getting too old. As the New Year rolled round, we saw less and less of each other. If I wasn't spending my nights in budget hotels with Azim, I was being whisked off in vans and taxis to all over Yorkshire and beyond.

I thought Nadine might be disappointed. She'd always gone on and on about how much she loved chilling with the Asian guys, but she didn't seem bothered that they were leaving her behind. She even seemed to be drifting apart from Amir.

By early 2005, she was virtually ignoring me, but I'd sometimes see her in the street. Then I heard that she'd left Rotherham for good – and moved to London with a friend. I hoped she really had escaped.

But while Nadine had outgrown our old life and found an escape, there seemed to be no way out for me.

There was a time when I would have been gutted to lose her as a friend, but now I was numb to any kind of emotion. The only people who mattered were the men who controlled me and gave me alcohol and drugs. As soon as my phone began ringing, I had to leave the house. I didn't have any choice. Mum would sometimes wake up in the middle of the night to find a group of Asian men waiting in a car outside our front door. She tried locking the doors and hiding the keys, but I'd climb out of a window, lured by the promise of a line of coke or a bottle of cheap cider and some fags. I'd often push her out of the way as she begged me not to go. My need to get high blocked out every other thought – drugs and alcohol had taken over my life. Most nights Laura would appear behind her, drowsy and with sleep in her eyes, having been woken by the commotion yet again.

'Just keep the fuck out of my life,' I'd tell Mum as she tried to block my exit with her petite frame. 'It's nothing to do with you where I go.'

I was so coked up to my eyeballs that I don't really remember Jamal and his mates turning up one night with a can of petrol, threatening to set it alight outside the house if I didn't come out, but Mum does. There were nearly thirty Asian men on the street, shouting and swearing. Mum was hysterical, obviously, and she hugged

Laura to her protectively as I barged past them, off into the night.

'Paki shagger!' Laura called behind me, but I didn't even care enough to tell her to shut up.

That might have been the time I woke up in a bathtub, with no idea what had happened the night before, or the night I was raped on top of a car bonnet – but I can't say for sure. The gangs were getting bolder and taking me further afield. By the summer of 2005 it wasn't unusual for them to drive me to Manchester or London. We'd go all around the Midlands and way up north too. Sometimes, they'd make Hayley and Jade come, but usually I'd be alone with them. I'd only have an idea of where I was if I was sober enough to read the signs on the motorway, which wasn't very often.

There was never a ringleader. When Mum confiscated my phone to try to keep me away from the gangs, she found the phone numbers of 177 Asian men. She wrote them all down and gave them to the coppers, but they said they couldn't do anything and palmed her off with some rubbish about the Data Protection Act.

Sometimes, if I'd taken coke or phet, I'd become feisty and put up a fight, but they'd tell me I was a slag and a white bitch and threaten to leave me stranded if I didn't do as they said. So I did just that, because how would I find my way back to Rotherham from a downtrodden house in Redcar, or Walsall, or Stoke-on-Trent? I was thirteen and I didn't have a penny to my name.

We were in Walsall the night I found myself in the house with the cobweb and the mouldy blue walls. An Asian guy, who called himself Jay, picked me up as I was walking down Ferham Road on my own. I'd never seen him in my life before, but he pulled over by the phone box and just told me he was taking me to a party near Birmingham. There was a bottle of vodka on the floor on the passenger side, and by the time we'd turned off the dual carriageway I'd drunk most of it. He stopped in a dank, forgotten street, and before we went into the house he gave me a warning.

'Just listen to what they say to you,' he said. 'And remember, do whatever they want.'

I was so unsteady on my feet that Jay had to practically hold me up as we walked to the front door. I think there were three men sitting on mismatched, threadbare chairs in the living room, four at most, and they gave me another couple of vodka shots for good measure before they took me upstairs. As each man came to me on the dirty, lumpy mattress, I hoped he'd be the last, but with every second that passed there seemed to be more voices downstairs, chattering away in Punjabi, laughing and joking as if they were playing a game of cards and not taking it in turns to rape a thirteen-year-old girl. When they were done, they left me there for two whole hours, wincing in agony as I slowly and painfully began to sober up. Eventually, Jay came upstairs and told me we could go home if I cleaned myself up. I was too sore to speak much on the long drive back to Yorkshire. When he dropped me off at home, Jay took my number and told me he'd see me around.

A few nights later, Azim picked me up near Ferham Park and we drove to a service station, where he bought me some chips from the McDonald's drive-thru. I was still in pain from my trip to Walsall but I knew he'd want sex. I consoled myself with the fact that he'd at least tell me he loved me afterwards, instead of leaving me to fester on a dirty mattress without saying a word. He'd just leaned in to kiss me when my phone – the phone he'd given me – began to ring.

Suddenly, Azim – sweet, caring Azim who called himself my boyfriend – was purple with rage.

'So it's true, then?' he said, prising the phone from my hand. Jamal's name had flashed up on the screen. 'You've been cheating on me. You little slag!'

I opened my mouth to speak, to explain, ready to deny everything, but Azim wasn't listening. He was still calling me a little slag, telling me he'd heard all the rumours about how many men I'd been shagging behind his back. I raised my voice to argue with him but it was like he didn't hear me. He was deaf to everything but the sound of his own voice, saying I was a whore – a dirty, stupid white whore.

Then he smacked me hard across the face.

CHAPTER EIGHT

A MUM'S AGONY

Most of the time when I was being raped, I didn't cry. I was too numb with drink and drugs, and it seemed pointless because it wouldn't change anything and the guys would think I was a wimp. But as soon as Azim's cold hand collided with my face, tears sprang to my eyes and I started sobbing. He'd hit me really hard and I could see in the rearview mirror that I had a big red mark on my right cheek.

'What did you do that for?' I asked him. 'I haven't done anything!'

I thought he'd soften and apologise, put his arms round me and tell me he was sorry and he'd made a mistake, but his face was like thunder as he started up the engine and tore out of the car park. As he indicated to rejoin the motorway, he had a menacing look in his eyes. I'd never seen this side of him before.

'You'd better be telling the truth,' he said. 'Or I'll kill you.'

We drove the rest of the way back to Rotherham in silence.

Thankfully, by the time I got home the red mark had faded, but Mum was really upset. I'd told her I was at Jade's and she obviously figured out that wasn't the case, so she'd reported me missing. To me, it was water off a duck's back. By now, I was going missing more often than I was at home.

A few nights later, I disappeared again. Mum had now taken to locking all of the windows as well as the doors because as soon as my phone went I had to find a way out. I thought these men were my mates, but I'd heard all sorts of horror stories about what they did to girls who disobeyed them. Loads had been beaten up. Some men even threatened to kill the girls' families if they didn't do what they were told.

The only window Mum couldn't lock was in the bathroom, on the first floor. It was my only escape route and it just had to do. I'd climb out and scale down the drainpipe, hoping I didn't fall and break my neck in the process. It was really dangerous, but because I'd usually taken so many drugs it didn't even seem that big a deal.

Jamal had a friend who we called Sav, and he'd arranged to pick me up by the phone box on Ferham

Road. Sav was annoying because he was really, really stupid, but he always had vodka and sometimes coke. I never slept with him but, like Jamal, he always took me to houses where there were lots of eager men waiting for me. As usual, Mum phoned the coppers and told them I'd vanished. She spoke to a male officer and the sigh was almost audible on the other end of the phone as she gave them my details.

'Just give us a ring when she turns up,' he told her.

Mum was dismayed. 'But it's your job to look for her!' she said. 'These horrible men keep taking her away – you have to do something.'

The copper didn't seem unduly worried about my safety but Mum was frantic. She tried to talk to the social workers, but all she got was a lecture about her parenting. Phil even suggested that Mum give me a curfew, as if it was that simple! It was like they couldn't accept that so many girls were being abused under their noses, so they buried their heads deep in the sand.

Sarah from Risky Business was the only professional who took Mum seriously, and soon she was close to her too. Sarah had gathered so much information about the sex gangs that she'd tried her best to find out where I was when I vanished, but Mum could also phone her for a chat whenever she was feeling overwhelmed and frustrated, which really helped her.

However, two days later there was still no sign of me. I was abused by so many men that it's hard to remember what happened when, but I think that was the time when Sav took me to a horrible dosshouse on the outskirts of Rotherham. Sarah says loads of underage girls got taken there, and she could always tell straight away who'd been inside the house because it had a really distinctive smell that would cling to us. I can't remember what it was like – I'd been in so many foul houses I was immune to their filthy odours – but Sarah said it was like a mix of damp, cigarette smoke and festering rubbish.

I think that was when I woke up in bed in the morning with a man who looked at least fifty. I had a vague memory of throwing up the night before, then of everything going black. Even for me, it was rare to blackout completely – and that scared me. I was still wearing the clothes I'd arrived in, but I had no idea if this man had done anything to me or what his mates had given me. He smelled and looked filthy, and he was snoring really loudly next to me, his huge, unshapely body rising and falling with every breath. I closed my eyes and pretended to be asleep too, praying he wouldn't wake up and decide he was in the mood for some 'fun'.

Thankfully, he soon got up and left me alone in the bed, but it would be another day before I'd be allowed to leave. I disappeared like this once or twice a week, but the school rarely phoned Mum to tell her I hadn't turned up. I think they were just glad I wasn't there so they didn't have to deal with me kicking off. By now, I was so trapped in my vicious cycle of drug and alcohol abuse that I was lashing out at everyone, especially anyone who tried to stop me meeting up with the only people who'd provide the substances I craved so badly. I'd drink all night, but I'd usually take phet or coke or pills too, so I could keep going for longer – but when I did want to stop, sleep was impossible without a joint or two. It fills me with shame to admit this, but I'd once been so desperate for a fix that I wrestled Mum to the ground and dragged her across the floor by her hair because she took my phone off me.

There is a paper in Sheffield called *The Star* and it had an office in Rotherham, so while I was imprisoned in the dosshouse, Mum decided to go down there, armed with a recent picture of me. No one had really heard of Facebook back then, so this was the only way she could get the word out quickly that I was missing. Of course, there was no way of her sharing a digital picture either, so she'd had to get my photo developed in the old-fashioned way and take a print of it with her.

'My daughter has been missing for two days and the coppers are doing nothing,' Mum told the receptionist, breathless with worry. 'Could you put her picture in the paper in case anyone has seen her?'

The receptionist took the photograph from Mum and said she'd speak to the news desk. One of the reporters started looking into the story, and after they'd called the police for a comment, Mum's phone rang straight away. It was the same copper she'd spoken to earlier.

'What's this all about?' he said, not bothering to ask how Mum was or if she'd had any news about me. 'What are you doing going to the paper, saying we're not doing our jobs properly?'

A few hours ago he had been indifferent, but he was now tetchy and uptight. He wasn't worried about me, of course; he was worried that the police would look bad in the paper. It took everything in Mum's power not to go mad.

'I can't find my daughter and I'm getting really, really worried,' she replied slowly. 'It's been two days. You haven't been keeping in touch with me. You're not looking for her ...'

The copper cut her off. 'Just because we've not been in touch doesn't mean we're not looking.'

But Mum wasn't giving up. 'Well, what are you doing, then?' She was fighting back tears, but she wasn't going to let the copper know that. 'She's got phone numbers for nearly 200 men, and every night they phone her up and threaten to petrol bomb my house if she doesn't go off to God knows where with them. I've got other children at home and I'm terrified. What are you going to do?'

The copper's tone was flat. 'We've circulated a photo and a description.'

He'd hung up before Mum could reply that the coppers didn't have a photo of me.

It was around this time that I met Latif. Azim picked me up one evening and Latif was sitting in the passenger seat. It was a bit weird, because Azim didn't really explain who he was or why he was coming with us. This time, we didn't go to a hotel for an overnight; instead Azim drove us to Huddersfield and gave me a joint as we sat in a car park on an industrial estate. Latif smoked one too, but he never said a single word to me. It was really weird and I felt a bit like I was invisible – he was chatting to Azim like I wasn't there. Yet as I got out of the car, I could see his eyes fixing on my body, boring into my still-developing breasts.

Azim had been a bit distant since the incident in the car, but I was almost immune to the fact that he appeared to be going off me. He was only picking me up on the odd occasion and now we rarely spent an overnight together. He still wanted sex sometimes, but it was usually just in the back of the car. He'd stopped telling me he planned to take me home and introduce me to his parents, or that he wanted marriage and babies. I think I'd even begun to doubt that he was a doctor because he always clammed up if I asked him anything about work.

But I only realised he'd decided to pass me on to Latif when I got a phone call a few days later.

'It's Latif,' he said. 'Azim gave me your number. Are you chilling?'

He was sharp and to the point, but I think in a weird way I was flattered that he'd decided to call me after ignoring me in Azim's car. Like many of my abusers, he was a taxi driver, so he picked me up in his car and drove me to his house.

He wasn't overly chatty, but he gave me a tumbler of whisky and a joint. I'd never tried whisky but he said it was his favourite drink. Latif was around Azim's age but I'd always associated whisky with old men in slippers. I took a gulp and it was foul, but after a few minutes I stopped noticing the taste and concentrated on the effect it was having on my body.

I'd only just finished my whisky when Latif pinned me down on the sofa. I'm not sure if I wanted to sleep with him, but that hardly mattered. People might wonder why I didn't resist, why I just lay there without a word of protest. But it's hard to explain just how brain-washed you can become. To me, this was normal.

Latif began to call himself my boyfriend, though all we did together was get drunk or high and have sex. He could go ages without calling me, but as soon as his number flashed up on my phone I knew I had to make myself available to him.

There was never much small talk; he'd just pour me some whisky and get down to it. Although he didn't hit me like Azim had, the sex wasn't loving or tender like you'd expect in a relationship. Latif wasn't happy unless he was holding me down, or physically overpowering me, though I hardly put up much of a fight. He had sex with me like he was angry at me, and I was always pretty sore by the time he finished.

Although Azim had always acted like we were a couple, he never officially broke up with me. I just stopped hearing from him as soon as Latif took an interest in me. One night, Latif and I had just finished having sex when his bedroom door burst open.

Azim was standing there, hand in hand with a girl called Lucy. She lived quite near Mum, so I knew who she was, but she was much older than me. In fact, she was probably the same age as Azim.

Instinctively, I pulled the duvet round me to cover my naked body, despite the fact that Azim had seen it hundreds of times before. Even though he was with another girl, I worried that he might go mad and hit me again. Although he hadn't called me for months, my mind flashed back to how angry he'd been when Jamal had called me in the car, and for a second I wondered if he thought we were still a couple. But he didn't even flinch.

'Oh, nice to see you, Sarah,' he said, without a hint of awkwardness. Then he closed the door behind him and led Lucy off, giggling, to another bedroom, as if what had happened was the most normal thing in the world.

Meanwhile, things at home were getting worse and worse. Mum was crying out for help, but her pleas were falling on deaf ears. She was really scared for the rest of the family, so she even asked Phil and Kate if I could be taken away from the house for a while so my abusers couldn't find me. It was very much a last resort. The idea of me being taken into care broke Mum's heart, but she felt it was the only way she could keep me – not to mention my siblings – safe. It was total chaos, and Phil and Kate should have done everything in their power to remove me from the situation. Instead, they told Mum in no uncertain terms that they'd have her charged with neglect if she tried to move me away from the family home.

Their indifference was truly staggering.

We'd once been so close, but I was now like a stranger to Laura. I had quite the reputation, and her friends on the estate told her lots of stories about what I'd get up to. When she was feeling brave she'd call me a slapper or a dirty Paki shagger, because that's what everyone said I was. She'd always regret it, though, because I'd fly into a fit of rage and we'd start scrapping.

One thing Phil and Kate did do was put Laura on a special register, saying she was at risk of being exploited by older men from the Pakistani community because she lived in the same house as me, but what they did to protect her, I don't know. This was all the proof Mum needed that they knew all about what was going on, but with me they just sat back and did nothing. Occasionally, the council would have meetings about cases like mine, and Sarah from Risky Business would try to fight my corner, begging the police and social services to help me. She'd tell them that beneath the threatening, violent front I put on, I was an impressionable but bright girl with the potential to really make something of my life. Phil and Kate would shout at her and tell her to wind her neck in and let them do their jobs, but that was the problem – they weren't doing their jobs.

Mum was at the end of her tether. She was so stressed she had to give up work and she never got a wink of sleep. She'd tried as hard as she could for as long as she could, but every time my phone sounded, with its familiar Nokia ringtone, she'd be on the verge of a breakdown, wondering if this would be the time I wouldn't come home at all. Sarah and her colleagues would never have said this publicly but they were convinced it was only a matter of time before one of the girls caught up in this twisted web of depravity was murdered. Mum was thinking exactly the same thing, and she was terrified that that girl would be me.

One afternoon, my phone began to ring. It was Jay, the guy who had picked me up by the phone box and taken me to Walsall. There was a party, there would be coke and vodka, he'd pick me up in ten minutes. I put on my coat, but when I got to the front door Mum was blocking my way.

'No, Sarah,' she said. 'No. You're not going.'

I glared at her and gave her a little shove before making for the bathroom so I could climb out of the window, but Mum was quicker than usual that day. She raced upstairs behind me, taking the steps two at a time, and launched herself at the bathroom door, gripping onto the handle with all her strength.

'Fucking let me out, you stupid cow!' I thundered, shaking with rage and desperation.

'No, Sarah.' Mum's voice was wavering, but there was a steely determination in her eyes. 'I said no, you can't go.'

We stood staring at each other for a minute while I tried to figure out my next move. I'd had a line of coke a few hours earlier, but the effects were beginning to wear off. I was sweaty, agitated and filled with rage. I needed another fix and Mum was the only person standing in my way.

What happened next fills me with such shame and horror that I can hardly bear to speak about it.

I tore downstairs and ran through the house, Mum never more than a few steps behind me. It took me a few minutes to decide what to do, but somehow I found myself in the kitchen, rummaging through the drawers. I caught sight of a big carving knife and, before I had time to think, it was in my hand.

Mum's hands were clasped to her face in shock. She was crying and screaming. I didn't care. All I could think about was drugs and the men who would give me them – and what might happen to me and even to my family if I left them waiting a minute longer.

I chased Mum into the living room, the huge knife clasped tightly in my hand. Laura and Robert were sitting on the sofa, and Laura began screaming too when she saw me in the doorway. I was shouting and squealing and swearing, calling them all every name under the sun and telling them I was going to kill them if they didn't let me out, but it was like someone else had taken over my body and I wasn't responsible for the venom coming from my lips.

The three of them were cowering on the sofa, all scared for their lives. It horrifies me now when I picture the scene: my mum, sister and brother, my own flesh and blood, clinging to each other and sobbing because they thought I was going to stab them. But at the time I didn't care. I was fixated on what I needed – the drugs – and I was ranting and raving, possessed by the demons I'd found in the hell that had become my life, desperate to get out of the house and to the men who now controlled me.

Laura was wailing loudly in sheer terror but her cries were driving me insane. The knife was still in my hand when I started kicking her, and she yelped in fear and pain, curling up in the foetal position. Tears were rolling down Mum's face and I was vaguely aware of her telling me to stop, to please, for God's sake, stop, but I couldn't. Eventually, somehow, Robert managed to pull me away from Laura. I think he tried to get the knife off me, but that made me even angrier because soon it was leaving my hand, flying through the air as I'd launched it at my family.

It was a minor miracle, but it landed just between Mum and Laura, plunging straight into the sofa and making a big hole. Everyone was still crying and shouting, but Mum and Robert had their phones out. Robert was calling the coppers and I was screaming that he was a grass and Mum was breaking down again as she spoke to Auntie Annette, telling her to get to the house, and fast.

Within minutes, Auntie Annette was there. I think I went for her too, before I launched my body at the living-room door, telling Mum there was no way the piggy bastards were getting anywhere near me. I must have tried to get to the knife again, because soon Auntie Annette was sitting on top of me, begging me to calm down.

I'm not sure how long it was before the sound of sirens filled the air, but a fresh wave of rage consumed me as I heard the coppers burst through the front door. Soon there were lots of them pinning me down as I screamed at anyone who would listen that I needed to get out.

I was being handcuffed when one of the coppers turned to Auntie Annette and told her to let go of me and that they had it under control. Auntie Annette's face was flushed and she was trying not to cry.

'I don't think you do,' she said. 'I really don't think you do have things under control.'

On the sofa, Mum was holding Laura, both of them rocking and sobbing, the knife still wedged in the fabric. The police were still trying to restrain me when she finally spoke.

In barely more than a whisper, she said: 'I can't take this any more.'

CHAPTER NINE

THE RAZAQ BROTHERS

After I held my family hostage with the knife, Phil and Kate had no choice but to accept it was too dangerous for me to stay at home. Mum asked if I could be locked up in some kind of juvenile detention centre, not because she wanted to punish me but because she wanted me under lock and key so I would be safe, so that none of my abusers could reach me. She also thought it would help me break the horrible cycle of alcohol and drug dependency which had become my life.

Instead, my social workers found me a place at a local children's home.

My room was basic – just a single bed, a sink and a wardrobe – but I had all the freedom I wanted. For a girl in my situation, this was lethal. The place was full of troubled children like me and some of the boys knew a dealer who gave them weed, so we'd sneak off to smoke together all the time. The staff treated us all with utter contempt and didn't bat an eyelid if my phone rang and I disappeared in the early evening and stayed out all night or even for a few days.

Often, my abusers would send me back to the home in a taxi and the staff would even pay the fare, using money from the petty-cash fund.

They hadn't made it harder for these disgusting paedophiles to reach me; they had made it much, much easier. Mum had at least done everything in her power to stop me leaving the house, but now I could come and go completely as I pleased. Of course, at the time I thought this was great, but now I'm dumbfounded by the complacency of everyone whose job it was to protect me. One of the keyworkers, Rita, was even worse than Phil and Kate. I still remember her really well. She had loads of thick, fiery red hair and she used to look at me as if I was a piece of dog shit she'd dragged in on her shoe.

'What man are you going off with tonight, Sarah?' she'd smirk as a taxi drew up outside my new home, ready to take me off into the night. 'Who are you sleeping with now?'

'What the fuck has it got to do with you?' I'd snap back. 'Don't talk to me. Don't even look at me.'

Sometimes Latif would pick me up for rough, emotionless sex in his taxi or at his house, but most nights it was anyone's guess who I'd be going off with. I still had all those phone numbers in my phone, and as soon as my ringtone sounded I knew it was time to go. Some men took me to takeaways, others parked up in laybys and industrial estates, but the end result was usually the same. The only saving grace was that I was rarely sober enough to remember anything in any great detail.

A select few, like Jamal and Sav, didn't abuse me themselves but delivered me to the men who did. I never saw any money change hands and I certainly never received any, but, given what I now know about child sexual exploitation, I suppose that they were being paid to traffic me around the country. I guess I'll never know for sure.

Throughout everything, Risky Business refused to give up on me and they still made appointments for me at least once a week. It seemed like Sarah was the only adult – apart from Mum, of course – who realised I was a kid who was being sexually abused and exploited by men who had somehow managed to convince me they were my friends. Sarah would even drive to the kids' home and try to get me to go to school, or she'd take me into Sheffield for a coffee and a chat, just to try to convince me I wasn't on my own and none of this was actually my fault. What's more, I couldn't shock her. No matter what I told her, she'd heard it all before, from scores of girls in Rotherham who were just like me.

The staff at the home hated her, though. One day, she turned up looking for me and Rita gave her the iciest of stares.

'You're looking for Sarah?' she said. 'Where are you taking her now?'

Sarah explained that she was going to take me to Sheffield for a look around the shops to get me out of Rotherham for a few hours; a chance for a little breathing space.

'So you're rewarding her for her bad behaviour again?' Rita retorted. 'This is what she gets for not going to school and getting off her face on drugs? Treats?'

Sarah didn't rise to the bait. She calmly asked again if Rita could send for me and, within seconds, I was there. I now realise that my meetings with Sarah were the only part of my week I looked forward to.

Social services had decided it was too dangerous for me to see my family in case I did anything to hurt them, but Mum couldn't bear this. We'd meet up in town in secret, so she could check up on me. I tried to pretend that everything was fine but, of course, she knew it wasn't.

I'd also sneak back up to Ferham, sometimes because my abusers told me to be there, sometimes to see my mates. We still hung around at Hayley's. One afternoon, I'd gone up to Ferham Road to meet Jade when an old green Mercedes drew up beside us. The window rolled down slowly and the driver's head popped out. I recognised him straight away, though I'd never been properly introduced to him. His name was Taz and he always hung around in Ferham Park. He had messy black hair and a little goatee beard. He was about ten years older than Jade and me, but that was nothing. Compared to some of the men I'd slept with, he almost seemed young.

'What's happening, girls?' he said. 'Are you chilling?'

Without a second thought, Jade and I climbed into his car. He asked how old we were and I said we were fifteen. By now, we were just a few months shy of our fourteenth birthdays, so it didn't seem like as big a lie as it had done before.

At the time, I didn't know Taz's real name was Razwan Razaq and that one day it would be all over the papers. To me, he was indistinguishable from all the men who took me away in their cars and did what they pleased with me. The only difference was that Taz was so brazen he'd picked us up in broad daylight.

He drove us a few miles out of Rotherham, to an industrial estate on the outskirts of Sheffield. It was a really hot day and my legs were sticking to the leather of the car seat. I thought he might offer us some vodka, or maybe a joint, but he gave us nothing. He didn't even say much, until he found a parking spot behind an abandoned factory and told me to get out.

He left Jade in the smouldering car with the windows up. He took me just out of view and, without saying a word, he pushed me up against a wall and started to kiss me. Before I knew it, he was tugging at my trousers, pawing at the small breasts hidden beneath my T-shirt.

For once, I wasn't completely off my face. I think I'd had a joint with the boys at the kids' home in the morning, but no one had given me vodka or coke or phet. I was much more lucid than usual and I felt a wave of defiance sweep over me.

'Fuck this,' I said. 'This isn't fucking happening.'

Even though Taz was quite slightly built, he was a grown man and I was still a child. It was hard to overpower him and he pulled at my clothes, trying to stick his tongue down my throat. He wasn't half as bad looking as some of the fat, ugly old men who'd abused me, but there was something about him that really turned my stomach.

'Stop it,' I said. 'Seriously, stop it.'

He tried to kiss me again but my mouth was clamped shut, so his horrible, warm tongue collided with my face and I winced. His body was still against mine, my back against the wall, and the beads of sweat on his forehead glistened in the blistering sunshine. His crotch was against my leg and I could feel that he was starting to get hard. Even then, as I squirmed at his touch and tried to wrestle him off me, I remember thinking: how can this be turning him on? I'm a child and I'm clearly hating every second of it.

I kept repeating the word 'no', over and over again. I must have been feeling bolshie because I swore at him a few more times too. I don't know what made him stop. I wasn't screaming but I was being pretty loud, and there were a few warehouses nearby so maybe he was scared someone would hear our raised voices and come to investigate. Eventually, he got bored and went off.

I waited around a minute before I took a deep breath and ran back round the corner, hoping he had gone and that he hadn't taken Jade with him to try to force her to do what I wouldn't. I was just in time to see the old green Mercedes speeding off into the distance. Jade was sitting on the pavement.

'Looks like we're walking home,' I told her, as we turned back towards Rotherham.

I'd been at the kids' home for a few months when Mum applied for a new house outside Ferham. She had never expected the home to solve any of our problems, but she'd been willing to give anything a try. But seeing that I was even more out of control than before, she reckoned it was best to have me under her watchful eye again.

The new house was in an estate called Dalton, which was around a ten-minute drive from Psalters Lane. Phil and Kate eventually agreed I could go home as a sort of trial, although my bed in the kids' home would be left open in case I needed to go back. Mum hoped against hope that this time the men who preyed on me would leave me alone.

But, of course, Dalton was too close for comfort. Most of the men who abused me drove taxis, so a three-mile car journey was nothing. Plus, I could easily walk back to Ferham myself if I had to and Mum couldn't keep tabs on me all of the time. Within days, Latif had my new address.

I think I met Keggy in the summer of 2006, but I can't be sure exactly because he always hung around in Ferham Park. His real name was Umar and one day he would be on the front pages of the newspapers too, but I only ever knew him by his nickname.

We were just friends for a while, but shortly after my fourteenth birthday Latif and I stopped 'seeing each other' for a bit. It was then that I started spending more time with Keggy.

Keggy was far from the man of my dreams. He had a chubby face and a skinhead and he always wore trousers that were far too short for him, but everyone knew who he was and he was fairly well-connected in Rotherham. I didn't find out he and Taz were brothers until much later, but I knew he had a big family and it seemed like every second Asian man in the town was some sort of cousin or uncle.

At twenty, he was six years older than me. He knew I was fourteen, they all did, but I don't think I even attempted to lie about my age to him because at the start he never made a move on me. He didn't have a job and he was really tight, so he never had any coke, but sometimes he bought me some vodka or a spliff with his benefits money.

I think he was living with his parents when I met him, but soon he got a council flat and I thought it seemed dead grown up that he had a place of his own. I went with him to pick up the keys and, even though I didn't exactly see a future with him, I felt a little surge of excitement when he asked if I wanted to move in. I think he was half joking as we hadn't even kissed, but soon I was staying most nights and I gradually brought a few clothes round.

Even though I rarely went to school, it was the summer holidays so it made it much easier to tell Mum I was just out with mates. I'd pop back every few nights and stop for a while before heading back to Keggy. He hadn't even bothered to get a proper bed, so we'd sleep on quilts on the floor, and neither of us could cook, so we always had takeaways.

It was strange. Most nights we'd lie there, side by side on our makeshift bed fashioned from old duvets, never touching or kissing. Keggy didn't take half as many drugs as I did so some nights I'd lie awake, totally wired, while he snored next to me. Usually, he'd been drinking and would go straight to sleep, but one night he rolled over to face me. In the darkness, his hands began to wander over my body – he gripped my bum and fondled my growing breasts.

For a second I just lay there, wondering what would happen if I let him have sex with me, but something stopped me. I can't really explain it; it just felt too weird.

'No, Keggy,' I said softly.

He didn't get angry; he just turned to face the wall and went to sleep.

Even though I wasn't sleeping with Keggy, everyone assumed I was, and as a result most of the other men left me alone. The whole time I was staying at his house, only one guy tried it on with me, and even then he didn't push it when I said no. I didn't have a clue why I was being left alone by all the other men. I didn't know then that I was a victim of organised crime or that my abusers were operating in huge gangs. I had no idea that, while they mainly shared girls like me around, there were times when there was an agreement between them that one man could have a victim to himself for a while.

The next day, we were sitting on Keggy's floor eating takeaway curry when he turned to me and told me that he loved me.

'What?' I said. I suddenly felt a bit awkward because I was sure I didn't love him back and I didn't know what to say.

'I love you,' he repeated. 'But you're my property because you live with me.'

I just laughed nervously and kept eating, wondering what he meant and if he was going to try it on again, but that night he just slept on the floor with his back to me as usual.

It was around this time that my school got back in touch, through Sarah from Risky Business. For a while, they hadn't been bothered whether or not I'd been there, but now GCSEs were looming and I think they figured they'd be in trouble if they didn't at least attempt to get me to sit some. I agreed to go back for some lessons, but only because Sarah said she'd come with me.

I actually coped quite well, considering I'd hardly been at school for two years. I'd come to believe that I was stupid, that there was no way I'd ever make anything of my life, because that's how my abusers made me feel. I still had to go to the huts on my own but I had a really nice tutor called Miss Iqbal.

'You're a really bright girl,' she told me. 'You need to start believing that.'

I hadn't been learning traditional things like maths and science, but I guess my brain couldn't have been completely ruined by alcohol and drugs because Sarah noticed that I'd started to pick up a bit of Punjabi. No one had ever sat down and taught me it, and I wouldn't have gone as far as to say I was fluent, but now, when men like Keggy laughed and joked in their own language, I knew what they were saying. Sometimes they'd say nasty things about girls I knew. They often called us kafirs, which I think is an insulting way to say someone isn't a Muslim. I was sure they were calling us whores and white bitches too, but if I said anything, they always claimed I'd misheard.

I'd also started writing about how I was feeling. Whenever I'd gone to English classes I'd thought they were really boring, especially when the teacher went on and on about some poet who'd died years ago. But I'd always really liked rap music, so I decided to express my feelings in a rap song:

What's happening to Rotherham town?
Underaged drinkers each time I turn around
Bouncers must be going blind just like
Every man in the nightclubs, on the dancefloor,
Always selling drugs
Men going for underage girls thinking
They're old enough because they met in
The nightclubs, taking her back to his
Pad for two pumps and a squirt
Takes her phone number, rings a taxi,
And sends her off, the dirty pervert
Fourteen-year-old girls still walking around with
Miniskirts on and chatting fully grown men up
In cars, still claiming they're sixteen to eighteen years
Why can't this dirty crime stop, wish
We could turn back the clock
Girl's parents wondering if they have to
Have to report their baby girl missing tonight
If so, they'll be waiting up all night
Wondering if she's in a gutter somewhere
Or if she's a prostitute for these people
She's hanging around with

One afternoon, I sheepishly showed it to Sarah. I assumed she'd think it was stupid, but when she'd finished reading it she looked like she had tears in her eyes.

'Sarah, this is amazing,' she said. 'I'm so proud of you.'

I couldn't find the words to tell Sarah exactly how I'd been feeling about the men who abused me. I was still telling her I was having fun and it was all just a bit of a laugh. I suppose this was my way of reaching out, of showing that perhaps I wasn't loving every second of what was happening to me.

Whether or not I got up for school always depended on how heavy a night I'd had. One morning, my alarm went off but I decided I couldn't be bothered, so I pulled my pillow over my head and turned over. Keggy had been dozing but the sound of my alarm woke him up, and before I knew it he was on top of me. I was still wearing my clothes from the night before – I'd obviously been too out of it to get undressed – and my head was pounding. I'd had lots of vodka and a few lines of coke too, so I was feeling agitated and uptight. All I wanted was a joint to help me relax and Keggy was making me feel worse.

'No, Keggy,' I said. 'I told you before.' This time he didn't listen. He pulled my trousers down, then my pants, and I could feel my heart racing. I was nauseous and sweaty and I couldn't handle having him on top of me. 'Keggy, I feel sick. I don't want to do it.'

'Shut up,' he replied. Then he said something which made me shudder: 'You're used to it.'

Of course, it was against the law for Keggy to be having sex with me under any circumstances because he was twenty and I was fourteen, and he should never have even tried. Up until that moment I had naively thought that Keggy was better than all the others, that he wouldn't do this to me. I thought he'd stop because I was putting up a fight, like he had done when I'd told him no before, but now here he was, about to force himself on me, telling me that what he was going to do was okay because I was used to it.

Because I was used to being raped.

I tried to push him off me, but there was no point. He was much stronger than I was. He pinned my arms behind my head and a stab of pain shot through my body as he entered me. All I could do was lie there and wait until it was over.

Once he'd finished, he got up off the floor and went through to the bathroom, where I heard him brushing his teeth like nothing had happened. By the time he came back through to the living room, I had pulled my trousers up and I was sitting bolt upright. I must have been feeling brave, because I called him a prick.

'I could get you done for that,' I went on. 'I didn't want to do that and you just made me. I could go to the coppers.'

Keggy was standing in his boxers, his toothbrush still in his hand. His semen was drying on my leg, I was covered in his DNA, but he was laughing.

'You, go to the coppers about *me*? You'll never go to the coppers. They'll never believe you.' He sat down next to me and his voice dropped to a whisper as he spoke into my ear. 'No one will ever believe you, because everyone knows you're a massive slag.'

CHAPTER TEN

DOES ANYONE CARE?

After Keggy raped me, I froze for a day or so. I didn't know what to do, so I wandered around in a bit of a trance and that night I fell asleep next to him on the hard floor as usual.

The next morning, he got up and left, without saying where he was going. As the day wore on, I gradually realised I couldn't stay with him. I didn't want him to touch me and there was no way he'd leave me alone if I had to lie next to him every night. I didn't have many things at the flat, but what little I did I shoved into a carrier bag and headed round to Mum's.

'You stopping?' she asked, but I just shrugged. I'd already texted Hayley to ask if I could come round for a few hours until I figured out my next move.

It didn't take Keggy long to realise I was gone and soon my phone was vibrating in my pocket every two minutes.

'You'd better answer it,' Hayley said. 'He'll go mad if you don't.'

We were sitting in her bedroom because it was the only room with a light bulb that worked, but I could hear chattering downstairs, which meant people were already starting to let themselves in. By now, word would have spread that I'd run away from Keggy, and I'd be fair game.

'Hello?' I said tentatively.

'Where the fuck are you?' Keggy's voice boomed down the line.

'Fuck you,' I replied. 'Don't even talk to me.'

I should have known that giving Keggy cheek wasn't the best idea I'd ever had. For the next few weeks my phone rang off the hook. Some calls were from people I knew and liked, others were completely anonymous. I'd get them at all times of the day and night and they'd call me everything they could think of: whore, slut, slapper, white trash.

'You're a dirty little slag,' one male voice said. 'You'd better watch it because you're going to get beaten up soon.'

I was constantly looking over my shoulder, scared someone was about to batter me or worse. Almost every time I walked down the street someone would shout abuse at me.

I didn't see Keggy himself for a few months. I was walking past Ferham Park one night and he was standing outside with a group of his mates. I think they were smoking weed and there were a couple of girls with them who looked even younger than me.

'Not speaking to me, Sarah?' he shouted across the road. 'You're a little slag.'

His mates laughed in the background as I looked at him for just long enough to see he was still wearing the jeans that were too short for him.

'You look like your cats have died, mate,' I said with as much conviction as I could muster.

'What's that?' he shouted back. 'What did you just say, you little white whore?'

But I'd already started walking away, picking up my pace a little.

After I'd run away from Keggy's, I'd sort of drifted back to Latif. We didn't officially get back together – he just called me up one night when I was at Hayley's and I agreed that he could pick me up.

By now, I was spending most of my time at Hayley's because there were always so many drugs on offer and obviously we didn't have to pay for them, as long as we had sex with whoever was providing them. Latif sometimes asked me if I was shagging anyone else but I lied and said no. He almost definitely knew this wasn't the case but he never seemed too fussed, as long as I let him do what he wanted with me while we were together. He was still really rough in bed, but he seemed like the only constant in my life. He'd started buying me loads of stuff too, and it wasn't just alcohol and drugs. He gave me clothes and shoes, and he even bought me a really expensive jacket. I was so messed up that I felt like he provided me with a bit of security.

It was in late 2006, just after I turned fifteen, that my cocaine addiction really got out of hand. I'd always had a fondness for it, but there was so much of it at Hayley's that I was soon taking lines and lines of it every day and threatening to batter anyone and everyone if I couldn't get my hands on it. In my drug-induced haze I think I slept with Raj again, and I'm sure there were a couple of times I found myself in bed with Sajid. All of these encounters just rolled into one.

Mum suspected I was at Hayley's because it was no secret that loads of Asian men congregated there. Sometimes she'd send the coppers round to try to bring me home. They'd bang on the door and the guys would tell us all to be quiet. None of the lights worked anyway so if we stayed silent for long enough it seemed plausible that no one was in.

'They'll give up eventually,' Raj whispered as we cowered in the corner, just out of view of the window.

Mostly, they did. A couple of times someone let them in by accident, but I just gave them a fake name and date of birth. It almost makes me laugh now because I told them I'd been born in 1984. This would have made me twenty-two, but I still looked about twelve. Other times, I'd be out in a taxi or in Jamal's van and they'd pull us over. I'd repeat the same ridiculous lie and the coppers rarely asked any more questions. I often saw them laughing and joking with my abusers in the rearview mirror. A couple of times, I even caught them shaking Jamal's hand before we drove off.

I went missing so much the coppers should have known who I was. At the very least, they should have questioned why I was lying about how old I was and hanging around in a total cesspit of a house with men more than double my age, or travelling round Yorkshire and beyond in taxis I clearly had no money to pay for.

But they didn't bat an eyelid.

Sometimes, when Mum phoned them and told them she couldn't find me, they'd ring me on my mobile. I was normally so coked out of my head that I thought it was funny to call them piggy bastards then pass the phone to one of the men I was with. Still, they did nothing.

I think it was at Hayley's, while the authorities were busy burying their heads in the sand, that I met Naveed. He was older than me, but nowhere near as old as Raj or Sajid or most of the others. It sounds awful, but I can't remember much about him, apart from the fact that he always had coke. I sussed this out pretty quickly and soon we were spending loads of time together. I wasn't attracted to him, but sleeping with him was a small price to pay for what he would give me in return. He never seemed to be at work and I have no idea what he did, but he must have had a bit of money because he'd book us into a hotel at least three times a week. We'd sometimes stay in Rotherham, but other times we'd go to Sheffield or Doncaster.

I usually saw Naveed when Latif was out driving his taxi. Naveed had quite a good deal, really – he'd only have to give me a few lines of coke and I'd spend all afternoon in bed with him, letting him do whatever he wanted to me. I can't remember what the sex was like, or if it hurt – all I cared about was coke; the sex was just something I had to get through so that I could get my fix.

I was still living between Mum's and the kids' home. The home always kept my bed open, and when I got really out of control Phil and Kate would tell me I had to go back into care. On the journey to the home they'd give me the usual lectures, but I never remember having any follow-up meetings with them. Of course, they might have been overworked, but every time Mum tried to reason with them they didn't want to know. I was far more at risk from paedophiles while I was in care, but it was like they couldn't and wouldn't accept this.

Loads of the men continued to pick me up in their taxis at the home. As well as seeing Latif and Naveed, I was still being transported around the country by Jamal, Sav and loads of their mates. Every time I left, Rita would look me up and down like *I* was the one in the wrong. The coke made me so aggressive I nearly went for her a few times. I'm actually surprised I didn't hit her.

I'd usually be sent back to the home in a car around seven in the morning. I'd be hungover but wired from all the coke I'd been taking, and my clothes would be dirty. I'd smell of alcohol and the horrible houses I'd had to spend the night in. These should all have been massive red flags for Rita and her colleagues, but none of them cared. As far as I know, they never even told my social workers, but then again, my social workers probably didn't ask.

Sometimes the men who'd abused me would drive me back to the home themselves, parking right outside, bold as brass. Others would be a bit more cautious and drop me round the corner, or send me back with one of their other taxi-driver mates. Just like when I'd stayed in the home the first time, some of these men would demand that I paid them a fare for their troubles, moaning that they were missing out on other hires by driving me home. I was in so deep I didn't grasp the reality of what they were telling me – that I was supposed to foot the bill for my own abuse, that I'd have to cough up for the privilege of being plied with Class A drugs and raped by more men than I cared to remember.

Of course, I didn't have any money of my own, so I'd walk into the home, where Rita would usually be sitting behind her desk, and get her to sort it out.

'You need to pay for my taxi,' I'd tell her and she'd roll her eyes.

'Oh, really?' she'd reply. 'Who have you been with now, madam? You've been busy this week.'

'Just fucking pay for it,' I'd say. 'It's £5.50.'

Rita would purse her lips and open the drawer with the petty-cash money, shaking her head at me as she counted out the change. Then she'd walk outside, open the taxi door and look straight at a man who'd most likely had sex with me the night before – the vulnerable, drugged-up fifteen-year-old girl she was supposed to be looking after.

She never scribbled down the registration number, or made a note of the licence plate or the company the car was from. She certainly didn't phone the coppers and describe the driver, or what she suspected he'd done to me.

All she'd do was ask him to give her a receipt, worried only that she'd get a bollocking if the petty cash was a few quid down.

By early December, I begged Phil and Kate to let me go home for Christmas. They eventually relented a few days before and things appeared to be going well. I still snuck out to meet Naveed, just so he could give me some coke, but everything changed on Christmas Eve when a family friend called Peter turned up.

Peter had known Mum's family for years and he was a bit like a brother to her, but he reminded me of Hayley's dad because he was a total pisshead. He'd always fall out with his missus and come crawling round to Mum's with a bag of clothes, pleading with her to let him sleep on the sofa. Mum was the only person who was soft enough to take him in. He used to get so drunk he'd piss everywhere in his sleep.

I'd just been out for a drive with Naveed, and obviously we'd been taking coke, so when I saw a black bin bag of clothes at the door, rage tore through me. I can't explain it; even though I'd caused my mum far more heartache than Peter had, I was family. I didn't want him to be a part of our Christmas.

Mum was washing up in the kitchen when I stormed through and demanded to know what was going on.

'Is Peter here?' I said. 'He'd better not be!'

'Sarah, he's got nowhere to go,' she replied. 'It's Christmas. Have a heart.'

'He's fucking taking the piss out of you, Mum,' I said.

The next thing I knew, Peter was at the door. He'd been in the pub all afternoon, and he was so drunk he could barely stand.

'You're a fat, ugly bastard,' I told him. 'I hate you.'

Then I ran into the kitchen, grabbed a pair of scissors and cut all of his clothes into tiny pieces. It sounds crazy, but it seemed like the most natural thing to do. Mum was shouting at me to stop, that I was just causing problems, but I didn't listen.

When I'd finished, all of Peter's shirts and trousers were lying in shreds at my feet. Mum wasn't crying, like she sometimes did when I played up; she was staring at me, cold and hard.

'I don't know what you've been taking,' she said slowly. 'But this isn't you, Sarah. What have they done to you?'

'You prefer him to me, don't you?' I shouted back. 'You prefer some fat, ugly pisshead to your own daughter!'

Mum just shook her head. 'Get out, Sarah. You're not ruining Christmas for your brothers and sister.'

She slammed the door behind me and I heard the key turning in the lock. She might have been bluffing, but I didn't wait to find out.

I walked back to the kids' home. I'm not sure how long it took me, because I was so off my face. I barely even noticed how cold it was.

I woke up on my own on Christmas Day, without any presents. I don't think anyone even wished me a Merry Christmas. Mum called me in tears, but I didn't give her a chance to speak. I just hung up. I didn't have to worry about being lonely for long, though, because soon my phone was ringing again and Latif's taxi was outside waiting for me.

While Mum and my siblings ate Christmas dinner and played games, I went to a Christmas party of my own with lots of Asian men. Instead of turkey and stuffing, I had loads and loads of coke and vodka. I think I took pills too – anything to block out the horrible reality that I was spending Christmas Day with these men instead of my family. I know that I had sex with Latif, but I was so out of it I can't remember a thing about it.

I was with Latif and his mates for a few days before they sent me back to the home. I think it was one of Latif's mates who drove me back in his taxi. I was still in the clothes I'd left in on Christmas Day, and I was bleary eyed, dirty, disorientated and very agitated when I went in to ask the staff to pay the fare. Rita was on a day off, so one of the other keyworkers, Jill, went out. She wasn't as nasty as Rita but she still saw that I was in a right state.

'How long have you been gone?' she asked.

'Keep out of my life,' I told her. 'It's nothing to do with you.'

She shrugged and rifled through the petty cash until she had enough change to pay my abuser's accomplice the fare he demanded for dropping me home. I stood and watched as she counted out the silver coins and handed them to him.

'Oh, make sure you give me a receipt with that,' she said. Latif's mate scribbled on a piece of paper and handed it to her before he sped off.

I'd been doing all right at school in my lessons with Miss Iqbal and Sarah from Risky Business, but as my dependence on coke worsened, so did my attendance. I just didn't see the point. All I could think about was coke and where I was going to get it from. Amazingly, I managed to pass my mock GCSEs without revising at all, but when the time came for the real exams I couldn't be bothered getting out of bed.

The morning of my first exam – it might have been English, I'm not too sure – I woke up in a hotel room with Naveed. We'd been drinking vodka and taking coke all night, and the piercing sound of my alarm was too much to bear. I already had a missed call from Sarah from Risky Business. She'd left me a voicemail, asking where I was and telling me she'd pick me up if I needed a lift to school.

I staggered out of bed, my mouth dry from all of the alcohol, and turned my phone off. Without thinking, I went into the bathroom, where Naveed had left a few bags of coke. I emptied some out onto the toilet cistern and snorted it. Within seconds, the amazing high took hold of my body and it felt like my hangover was evaporating. As I climbed back into bed Naveed rolled on top of me. My exam was the last thing on my mind.

CHAPTER ELEVEN

MARRIAGE

After I missed my first exam I didn't see the point in sitting any others, so I just continued to spend all of my time getting out of it with Naveed. Mum told me I was throwing my future away, but the only thing I was worried about was where my next line of coke was coming from.

As my sixteenth birthday edged closer, Naveed started to become a bit distant, and in the end he stopped calling completely. I wasn't too bothered, as long as I could find someone else to give me coke.

That was never usually a huge problem as my phone was still full of men who could provide me with drugs. I still saw Latif from time to time, and if I didn't fancy spending the night at the kids' home, or at Mum's, I'd call him up and he'd let me stay, as long as we could have sex, of course.

But while Latif still wanted to sleep with me, the sex

with all of the other men was slowly but surely dwindling. Don't get me wrong, there would still be nights when I'd have to sleep with a few men in a row and I'd wake up feeling sore and dirty, but there were others when I got off scot-free. Sometimes they'd give me coke and weed and I wouldn't have to do anything to earn it. I was confused, but I wasn't complaining.

Then everything fell into place.

One night, I was chilling in a house Sav had taken me to, but no one had touched me. Amir was there with some mates. I hadn't seen him for ages, but I took it for granted that I'd have to sleep with one of the guys he'd brought along. One of his mates, a guy who called himself Billy, sat down next to me and asked if I wanted to share a spliff. I'd chilled with him once before but we'd never had sex. As I took a drag I expected him to suggest going upstairs, but he said something that sent a horrible shiver down my spine.

'Got any girls?'

Suddenly, it all made sense. By 'girls' he meant underage girls, girls who were younger than me. I realised that they were going to get rid of me, just like they'd done with Nadine, because I was getting too old. I knew that the only way I could buy myself some time – and some more drugs – was by providing them with some fresh young meat.

I had to find them some other girls to abuse, just like Nadine had found me.

I can understand why people think I should have jumped at the chance to get out, but this life was all I knew. My days were punctuated by drinking and taking drugs, and if the men who gave them to me cut me off, what would I do? All of my friends were connected to my abusers, and there was no way they'd pick me over the paedophiles who had come to rule all of our lives. My education had been over before it had really begun and I had no qualifications.

All I had to show for the last five years of my life was a cocaine addiction and a shattered sense of self-worth.

'I'm a bit of a tomboy,' I said, trying to dodge his question. 'Most of my mates are boys.'

Billy looked into my eyes and took the spliff from me. 'I'm sure you can find us some girls, Sarah.'

I'm not proud of what I did next. There were two girls I kind of knew from round Ferham called Lily and Demi. They were only thirteen and they were always drinking with Asian men in Ferham Park. I heard that Demi had shagged a taxi driver on a park bench once so I didn't see them as victims. I thought they were slags, just like me, and they'd probably just be happy to get loads of free booze and maybe even some drugs. I asked around and someone gave me Demi's number.

'Want to come chilling?' I asked her. 'It'll be right good. There's a party – I can get you picked up. We've got loads of vodka.'

Demi sounded excited. 'Cool!' she replied. 'Where is it?'

'Just be outside the phone box on Ferham Road at seven,' I said. 'Bring Lily too.'

I think it was Jamal who collected the girls. He brought them to the horrible dosshouse where I'd woken up with the smelly man in his fifties. I was waiting with Billy and Amir and a few others.

Demi and Lily couldn't believe their luck. You'd have thought the Queen had turned up. Nothing was too much trouble for the men. Demi and Lily could have anything they wanted and the vodka flowed and flowed. The guys showered the girls with compliments and one even said he'd buy Lily a new phone. I sat in the corner, my stomach tightening as the scene unfolded. These girls were the same age as Laura. I felt violently sick as I imagined my baby sister in their shoes, blushing at their flattery and drinking their alcohol, falling deeper and deeper into their trap with every sip.

What the hell was I doing?

After around an hour, Demi got up. She was unsteady on her feet and Billy reached out to hold her up.

'I need the toilet,' she announced.

I sprang to my feet. 'I'll come with you,' I said. 'Lily, you come too.'

Billy shot me a look but I pretended not to notice. I took both of the girls upstairs and locked the bathroom door behind us.

'You need to be really, really careful,' I told them. 'These guys just want sex, trust me.'

Demi giggled. 'So? Some of them are well fit.'

'Yeah, but they're old,' I said. 'Really old. And once you've shagged them, they won't leave you alone. They'll pass you onto their mates and you'll have to do it with them too, even if you don't want to.'

It was the first time I'd ever said it out loud, and I'd even surprised myself. The girls just stared at me in a confused sort of silence. I didn't let them out of my sight for the rest of the night, and I think the guys got bored because, after a few hours, Jamal reappeared with his van and we were on our way home.

A few days later, Sav called me and asked if I wanted to go to Dewsbury with him. Despite the lecture I'd given Demi and Lily, I still couldn't cut the ties that bound me to my abusers. It was one thing warning younger girls off them; it was another keeping away from them completely.

Plus, they had coke. And I really, really needed some coke.

Dewsbury was about half an hour from Rotherham. It was just Sav and me in the car and I expected he'd take me to another grim flat. I was surprised when he pulled up outside a respectable-looking semi-detached house.

'I want you to meet Aisha,' he said.

I was confused. Aisha was a Pakistani name, but in all the time I'd spent with Sav and his mates, we rarely met any Asian women. They usually targeted white girls like me because they saw us as being easy. My social workers and the coppers didn't want to admit this because they were terrified of appearing racist, but it was true.

He took me into the house. There were no fag ends scattered over the coffee table and it smelled not of festering rubbish, but of cleaning fluids. It was spotless.

Aisha was sitting on the sofa when we walked in. She was wearing a black headscarf, or hijab, but her skin was paler than mine and she had blue eyes. It was obvious she wasn't Pakistani.

'Hi, Sarah,' she said, shaking my hand as she rose to greet me. 'I've heard lots about you.'

Aisha was really nice. She explained that she'd once been called Melanie but she'd converted to Islam when she'd met her husband, Adeel. They'd been married for a year.

I'm not sure if Aisha had been groomed like I had. A couple of times, she mentioned her kids, but when I asked about them she had a sad, distant look in her eyes. Eventually, she told me that they'd been adopted. I guessed that she must have had a troubled past, just like me, but now she seemed happier than ever. I was a bit jealous.

'What time does Adeel get home?' I asked.

'He doesn't always live here,' she said. 'He has two wives, so we have to share him. His other wife is from Pakistan.'

Aisha explained that, while her marriage to Adeel wasn't legally binding, it was valid in the eyes of Islam. She said Adeel had told her he could have as many as four wives. In some countries this was legal, but not in the UK. She didn't seem to mind, though.

Soon, Sav was taking me to Dewsbury a few times a week. Aisha would tell me all about Islam and I was really interested. The more I learned, the more it appealed to me.

'I'd like to convert,' I told her one day.

Aisha gave me a warm smile. 'Would you? Perhaps I should introduce you to Khalid.'

Khalid was a friend of her husband, she said. She promised I'd like him. 'Okay,' I said.

'There's just one thing,' Aisha said carefully. 'Perhaps it isn't my place to say this, but –'

'Go on,' I coaxed her.

'Sav says you like to drink and take drugs,' she said. 'You might want to keep that quiet. Khalid's pretty strict.'

I'd known that Muslims weren't supposed to drink, of course, but most of the ones I knew ignored that rule. I knew I couldn't give up drink and drugs completely, so I concentrated on getting off coke first.

I decided I'd go cold turkey, but the next week was awful. I'd wake up in cold sweats and my heart would feel like it was bursting out of my chest. The only way I could settle my nerves was by smoking loads and loads of weed, but I figured it was better than coke.

It was horrible at first, but it gradually got easier, and a few weeks later I went to Dewsbury with Sav. Adeel was staying with his other wife, so Aisha said I could stop with her for a few days. After what she'd told me about Khalid, I was surprised when she brought out a bottle of vodka and poured me a large glass.

'One won't hurt,' she winked. She pulled off her hijab and her light brown hair tumbled round her shoulders.

The next night, I finally met Khalid. I'd popped to the corner shop and there were two men standing in Aisha's living room when I came back. My heart sank straight away when Aisha introduced the more handsome of the two as Adeel. Khalid was in his late thirties and really ugly. He was quite tall and lanky, but he had a little pot belly that looked totally out of place on his skinny frame.

His face was lined and I'd soon discover he always wore the same sour expression, like he'd just caught a whiff of a really bad smell.

He was all right, though, I guess. He'd been born in Pakistan but he'd lived in Yorkshire for years and he drove a taxi, so his English was good. He told me he had a Pakistani wife too, but he was going to divorce her.

'Then I will need a new wife,' he said.

I didn't say much, but the next time we met up Khalid asked me if I'd like to marry him. It wasn't all romantic, like you see in films. He didn't get down on one knee or give me a diamond ring. He just came out with it when we were sitting on Aisha's couch, like he was asking if I'd like a cup of tea.

'Yeah, all right, then,' I said. 'But I'll need to tell my mum first.'

Khalid told me he'd drive me back to Rotherham in his taxi and I could spend a few days with my family. Then he'd pick me up and take me to Dewsbury, where we'd visit the Imam and I'd convert to Islam. Once that was done we could get married.

'You'll need to choose another name, though,' Khalid said. 'Sarah won't do.'

Khalid told me I'd have to take his surname, Mohammed, on as my own. On the journey back to Rotherham we decided on Shazia as a first name.

'Shazia Mohammed,' I said, getting used to the sound of my new identity. 'Sounds all right, doesn't it?'

Khalid agreed that it did. 'There's just one thing,' he said. 'My wife and I aren't divorced yet. We can have an Islamic ceremony, but we'll need to wait a few months to make it legal.'

'That's okay,' I replied. 'I know you can have four wives.'

'Yes,' he said. 'But once I'm divorced I'll only want to be with you.'

I don't know how I expected Mum to react when I told her about Khalid, but she went absolutely mad. She told me I was crazy and that he was using me, but I was having none of it. We screamed at each other for days.

'How can you marry a man you barely know?' she said, over and over, as she shook her head at me.

'You don't know anything,' I told her. 'I love him.'

I think even I knew that was a lie. Khalid was old and ugly but it still seemed romantic, the idea of changing my whole life for my future husband. Plus, if I married him the guys who had been abusing me wouldn't force me to find them new girls. For me, it was a way out, and I really needed to take it.

Just before Khalid's car drew up outside Mum's to take me off to my new life, I told her I wanted her and Laura to come to my wedding.

166

'It will probably be next week,' I said. 'It would mean a lot to me if you could come.'

I could see the tears glistening in Mum's eyes.

'No, Sarah,' she said. 'I can't give you my blessing. This is crazy. You need to choose between this man and your family.'

I pulled my coat around me. 'Fine, I choose him,' I replied.

Mum was shouting at me as I stormed past her, threatening never to take me back if I went ahead with the wedding.

Just as I reached the door, she grabbed hold of my arm. 'This time, I mean it, Sarah. If you do this, don't ever come back.'

I wrestled free of her grip. 'Don't worry, I won't. And my name is Shazia now.'

I felt a little silly sitting next to the Imam as he and Khalid prayed together. I didn't know what they were saying. They weren't talking in Punjabi; the prayers were in Arabic. I was wearing a hijab and my hair was hot and sticking to my face. We were in the Imam's house, which was just a few streets away from Khalid's. The Imam's wife was there too, and she was really nice, although she was sitting a little away from us, praying quietly in the background.

Eventually, they stopped and the Imam began to speak to me. He was an old man, with a big beard and a friendly smile. He was wearing traditional Islamic dress, a big white robe and hat. He was really nice and he gave me a copy of the Qu'ran, but it was in English so I could understand it.

'Now, you must tell me,' he said. 'Do you really want to convert to Islam? It's important that you have made this choice for yourself.'

'Yes,' I replied. 'I want to do this, for my own good. I think it will help me become a better person.'

The Imam nodded. 'Very well,' he said.

He and Khalid said some more prayers and then I had to recite the Shahada, the Islamic testimony of faith. Khalid had taught me the words, and I'd learned them off by heart, even though they were in Arabic.

'*La ilaha illa Allah, Muhammad rasoolu Allah,*' I said. It meant: there is no true God but Allah, and Muhammad is the prophet of Allah.

The foreign words sounded strange as they tripped off my tongue but it was over really quickly. Khalid and the Imam chatted for a bit, and they agreed that we'd be married at home two days later. Then the Imam's wife gave us a cup of tea and served up a curry.

That night, as we drove home, Khalid told me he'd like me to wear a niqab when I went out, a full Islamic dress that went right down to my feet. If I wore it, people would only be able to see my eyes. Changing my name and giving up drinking were one thing – this was quite another.

'Ha, no way!' I said. 'I'll wear a headscarf, but that's it.'

Khalid looked mildly annoyed, but he didn't push me. 'Remember, no drinking,' he said.

The wedding was planned for the Sunday, so I stayed at Aisha's on the Saturday night. In the morning a lady called Parveen came round to help me get ready. She was Khalid's cousin's wife and I'd met her a couple of times. She was nice enough, but I hardly knew her.

Parveen helped me into a red and silver sari and told me I looked beautiful. Like most girls, when I was young I'd thought about my wedding day, but I had never thought about it being anything like this. I'd imagined wearing a big, white, princess-style gown and that Laura would be standing next to me in a bridesmaid's dress as Mum looked on, dabbing her eyes and wearing a big hat. Needless to say, I hadn't dreamed that my groom would be old enough to be my dad.

I had no idea that Mum and Sarah from Risky Business had spent the last few days desperately trying to track me down in an attempt to stop me pledging to spend the rest of my life with a man I barely knew.

It felt a bit lonely, being without my family on what was supposed to be the biggest day of my life, but in a way I was glad Mum and my siblings weren't there. It was obvious they didn't approve and they'd probably just ruin it for everyone.

There were only a handful of people in Khalid's house when I arrived. He was stood in the centre of the room wearing traditional Muslim dress, just like the Imam. He still looked old and ugly, though.

The ceremony itself was over really quickly. We said some prayers and recited some vows, though I had no idea what I was promising to do. Then we had to sign the nikah, the Islamic marriage contract. It was written in Arabic, but it had an English translation at the side. I didn't really read it, though.

Afterwards, we went for a meal at an Indian restaurant in Bradford. No one drank, obviously, and we were home by early evening. It was all a bit flat.

Khalid didn't want to have sex with me until we were married. I wondered if sex would be different, now I was a bride.

Khalid led me up to the bedroom in his little terraced house and I lay on the bed, sober and apprehensive. But as he placed his lanky, oddly shaped body on top of me, I just felt weird. I stared at the ceiling until he'd finished.

* * *

A few days later, we went to the registry office. Khalid's divorce still hadn't come through, so we couldn't make our marriage legal just yet, but he wanted me to change my name to Shazia Mohammed by deed poll. The registrar gave me a funny look and told me to come back when I was eighteen.

I'm not sure if Khalid knew quite what to do with me. I think I was a bit feistier than his Pakistani wife. I couldn't cook, so he tried to teach me how to make him a curry. He expected me to do the housework too, although he did help a bit.

The days were long when he was out working. Sometimes I visited Aisha, but I didn't know anyone else in Dewsbury so it was really boring if she was with Adeel. I was too stubborn to phone Mum or Laura for a chat, so I felt really isolated.

We'd been married for about two weeks when I was looking through the cupboards for some food. Khalid had asked me to look for some ingredients so we could make a curry together. Hidden away behind some bags of rice was a bottle of whisky. I marched through to the living room, furious.

'No drinking?' I said, thumping the bottle down on the coffee table. 'So you can drink but I can't?'

He looked flustered. He'd obviously forgotten about

the whisky. I think he'd assumed I wouldn't have been brave enough to confront him if I found it.

'Okay, okay,' he said eventually. 'Pour it down the sink.'

I got rid of every last drop. A few hours later, Khalid went out on a hire and I prepared myself for another night in alone. He'd only been gone a few minutes when my phone started ringing. I didn't recognise the number but I answered it without thinking. I guess I assumed it was one of the guys from Rotherham, so I was surprised to hear a female voice on the other end.

'Who's this?' she asked. She sounded English.

'Well, you phoned me,' I replied. 'You should know. Who is this?'

She didn't answer. 'Your number is in my boyfriend's phone.'

I tried not to roll my eyes. My number was probably in a *lot* of men's phones, most of whom likely had wives and girlfriends.

'Oh, yeah?' I said. 'You don't need to worry. I'm married now. Who is your boyfriend, then?'

'Khalid. Khalid Mohammed.'

I felt my insides twist.

'Khalid is your boyfriend? How long have you been together?'

'About three weeks.'

I took a deep breath. 'Well, he's just got married to me. I'm his wife.'

She was silent for a few seconds, but I could hear her breathing. Then the line went dead.

My hands were shaking as I dialled Khalid's number and told him we needed to talk, and fast. It was only a few minutes before he came through the door, looking confused. I already had a chapati pan in my hand by the time he arrived and I launched it at his head. He ducked, and it narrowly missed him.

'You've been cheating on me!' I thundered.

'What are you on about?' he said. 'You're crazy!'

'No, I'm not,' I replied. 'Someone has just phoned me, asking me why my number is in your phone. Apparently, she's your girlfriend.'

Khalid just stood there for a second, as if he was trying to figure out whether or not to continue lying.

'Why don't I phone her now and see what she's got to say?' I suggested.

He raised his right hand, as if to give in. 'Okay, okay,' he said. 'It was one time.'

I'd given up loads to be with Khalid: my family, my home, even my identity. I'd made a huge mistake. I quietly told Khalid I wanted to leave.

'You won't leave,' he said. 'You can't. We're married. You're mine.'

He hadn't even said sorry when he walked out the door, back to his taxi, like nothing had happened. Before I could stop myself, I'd reached for my phone and dialled Latif's number.

CHAPTER TWELVE

ESCAPE

We'd barely turned off Khalid's street when Latif turned off the engine and told me to get in the back. I wasn't surprised; I'd known exactly what to expect when I phoned him. But I didn't know what else to do. I was miles from home, I had no money and I was too stubborn to tell Mum that my marriage had failed before it had even begun.

This was the price I had to pay.

Latif pulled down my trousers and pinned me down on the back seat of the taxi. I didn't protest as he forced my arms behind my head. Soon, he was inside me. He was as rough as he'd always been, but we'd done it so many times now it wasn't as sore as it once was. I just lay there in silence and thankfully it didn't last too long.

It was only when he started up the engine again that he asked me why I'd been in Dewsbury.

'I got married,' I told him. 'But it's over now.'

He looked at me like I was crazy. 'You're talking shit. Who were you up here chilling with?'

'No, really. I got married. The guy was cheating on me, though.'

Latif shook his head. 'Bullshit,' he muttered under his breath. I couldn't be bothered arguing, so I changed the subject.

I stayed at Latif's that night because I wasn't quite ready to go back and face the music at home. Of course, that meant we had to have sex again, but it seemed like a better option than seeing my family. In the end, it was a few days before I was brave enough to go back to Mum's and admit I'd made a mistake. She was still annoyed with me, though she let me move back in, no questions asked.

'I'm happy you're home,' she said eventually. 'Please don't go back to that man.'

In all the craziness of the last few months, I'd sort of lost touch with Hayley and Jade. The days were long and boring with no job and no one to hang around with, so the next week I caved in and rang Sav to ask if anyone was chilling. He was living above a shop at this point and he told me I could come round and smoke weed with him and some of the guys. By now, few of my abusers wanted to touch me. I was almost seventeen, a proper adult.

I'd decided not to touch coke as it had been such an effort to get off it and I knew what it did to me, but I still loved weed and vodka – and there was lots to go round. But as I knew all too well, nothing in this world was ever free.

'When are you going to fetch us some more girls?' Billy asked me as we sat in a circle on Sav's floor, passing a spliff round. 'Can you get Demi to come and chill with us again?'

I mumbled an excuse about having lost Demi's number after I'd gone to Dewsbury, but I knew it was only a matter of time before I'd have to come up with the goods.

'I don't have many girl mates,' I said again. 'Not new ones, anyway. I'll ask around.'

Billy took a drag of the spliff. 'Yeah,' he said, his eyes boring into me. 'You must know someone.'

I can't remember why I went downstairs to the shop, as I was stoned and a bit drunk, but I'm really glad I did. Standing in one of the aisles was an Asian man with a grey beard. He had a bit of a belly and dark circles under his eyes, which made him look ill. He looked like he was in his mid-forties, and he was carrying a basket of groceries. He held my gaze for a few seconds and I immediately felt defensive.

'What are you looking at?' I snapped, and his face broke into a little half-smile.

'Have you been upstairs?' he asked me.

I narrowed my eyes. 'What's it to you?'

'Oh, I just wondered,' he said. 'Tell me, how old are you?'

'I'm sixteen,' I said. We stood and stared at each other in silence for a few seconds longer before he asked me my name. I was well rehearsed in giving out a fake name when I felt suspicious of someone, but for some reason I told him the truth.

'Sarah, yes,' he said, with a hint of recognition, though I'd never met him before. 'Pleased to meet you.'

I said nothing but the stranger was scribbling something down. He folded the piece of paper and handed it to me.

'I'm Hamid,' he said. 'This is my phone number.' I opened my mouth to speak, but he kept talking. 'It's not what you think – I don't want anything – but I know what these men do to girls like you and it isn't right.'

I just stood there, holding the piece of paper and staring at him. Why did he care what happened to someone like me? Surely he thought I was white trash like the rest of them did, a little slapper who deserved all she got?

'You don't have to call me if you don't want to,' Hamid went on. 'But these men you hang around with are little idiots. If you want to get away, I can help.'

* * *

It took me a few days to call Hamid. I'd kept his phone number in my pocket and I'd taken it out a few times, but then I'd lose my nerve.

It was no wonder I was wary, really. Lots of men had made out like I could trust them, but so far they'd all been the same. Even the ones who'd pretended to be my mates had abused me, or at least delivered me to others who had. How could I be sure Hamid was different?

It was a gamble. But it was a gamble I was willing to take.

Hamid's writing was messy and spidery, and I wondered if I'd got the right number as I typed in the digits. It rang three times.

'Hamid, it's Sarah.' I hadn't even bothered to say hello, my heart was beating so fast.

'Sarah, hello.' His voice was warm and kind. 'Would you like to meet up for a chat?'

We met up a few times before I told Hamid anything about my past. We usually went to McDonald's, where we'd have a Coke and some chips. The first couple of times, he did most of the talking. He told me a lot about his life, even though I didn't want to give away much about mine. His parents had come to Rotherham from Pakistan just before he'd been born. He was happily married with four children and one of his daughters was around my age. He'd worked really hard to build up his own chain of corner shops and he'd made a bit of money, but recently he'd had to take a step back and let his family take care of the business. He didn't explain this last part, but I didn't feel like asking questions.

It took me a little while to work out whether or not I could trust him. I wondered if he might lure me in with free meals and promises of kindness before he pounced, claiming that I owed him something because he'd been nice to me.

But there was a really powerful voice in my head that told me he'd never touch me. Don't ask me why I thought that – it was just a gut feeling.

'Sarah, forgive me if this sounds rude,' he said. I can't remember if it was our third or fourth meeting. 'But I've heard a lot of stories about you and the guys you've been hanging around with. I know you've been through a lot. I bet they've made you feel like this is all your fault, but it isn't.'

For the first time since the abuse began, I started to cry – to really cry. My head was in my hands as I shook with every sob, tears streaming down my face. It must have gone on for a good five minutes, but Hamid just sat there patiently. The torment that had been eating me alive for five years was finally freed and I needed to let it out.

'I'm sorry,' I sniffed, wiping my eyes. 'I don't know why I'm so upset all of a sudden.'

'Sarah, I can tell you're a nice, genuine girl,' Hamid said. 'But these men have been doing this for years. Everyone knows what's going on but they're all too scared to do anything.'

'I didn't mean for it to happen,' I replied. I was still wiping the tears from my eyes. 'I don't want to feel like a slag. It just creeps up on you all of a sudden. You think they're your mates, and by the time you realise they're not it's too late.'

Then I told him everything. I started with Nadine and how she'd taken me to Amir and Rahim so they could groom me in the playground, and then I told him about all the parties at Hayley's, about Omar and his mates and all the drugs they'd given us. I trembled as I recalled sleeping with Raj in his taxi, how Sajid had abused me on the park bench and how some of them, like Azim and Keggy, had made me feel like I was their property. The worst part was probably telling him about all the places I'd been taken by Jay and Sav and Jamal, especially the horrible house in Walsall with the mouldy blue walls. By the time I got onto Khalid and my disastrous marriage, my eyes were red and blotchy.

'Sarah, you're not a slag,' Hamid said, resting his hand on mine. 'You were a child when this happened to you. It's they who are in the wrong, not you.'

'Why do you care?' I asked. 'Why do you care about me? You don't even know me.'

'This has gone on for too long,' Hamid replied. 'These men are pathetic. If I can save just one girl from them, I'll die happy.'

It was an odd thing to say.

'I don't need to be saved,' I said. Even though I'd been crying like a baby, I didn't want him to pity me or to see me as a victim. 'They don't touch me any more.'

'They don't?' Hamid raised an eyebrow, like he didn't believe me.

'No, not really. Well, apart from Latif. They want me to get younger girls involved and that makes me feel dead bad, but I don't know what to do.'

'Who's Latif?'

'He's my boyfriend. Well, kind of my boyfriend. We're always off and on.'

Hamid asked me what age Latif was and I had to admit I didn't know. 'He's about thirty. We've been seeing each other for years.'

I didn't need to tell him how much I dreaded the rough, loveless sex.

Hamid shook his head. 'He's not your boyfriend; he's taking advantage of you.'

I dabbed my eyes again, struggling to take in what he was saying. 'But it's my fault. I always lied about my age. Most of them didn't know how young I was.'

'Sarah,' Hamid said. 'I only need to look at you and I

know you're a child, so I can't imagine how young you looked when you were eleven or twelve.'

I knew he was right, but it felt weird to say it out loud, like I was admitting my whole life up until now had been one great big lie.

'Well, what can I do?' I said. 'I can't get away from them now. They might not want me any more, but they've all got my number and they want me to find them new girls. What will happen if I say no?'

Hamid rested his chin on his hands. He was peaky and tired looking. Now that I could see his face more closely, he really didn't look too good. I guessed he was maybe recovering from a bug or something.

'We need to do something about this,' he said, thinking out loud. 'If you like, I can help you change your phone number?'

'I'm not sure,' I replied, hesitant.

'I understand,' he said. 'But while you've got your old number, these people can still reach you. They'll call you when you're drunk and you know they'll get you back there.'

'I'll think about it.'

'Okay. Well, the offer is there. If you get a new number, you have to be really careful, though. Only give it to your family and your friends. Your real friends, I mean, not these pricks.'

Hamid seemed so noble and respectable that I almost let out a little giggle when he swore. But then something quite frightening dawned on me – Nadine had gone and I'd drifted away from Hayley and Jade. Leah was lovely, but she'd always kept her distance from the men who hung around at Hayley's dad's, so we'd kind of lost touch.

'I don't think I have any real friends,' I said, and I dissolved into tears again.

Eventually, I agreed that Hamid could buy me a new SIM card for my phone. I hardly gave the number to anyone, just my close family, Hamid and Sarah from Risky Business.

I'm not going to pretend I wasn't gripped by fear as I chucked the old one in the bin. I held it in my hands for a few seconds before I dropped it into the bin bag in Mum's kitchen, the numbers of nearly 200 abusers gone, just like that. Of course I was excited at the prospect of a fresh start but, dare I say it, part of me was also a little bit confused. This had been my life for so long and it hadn't all been bad. When I wasn't being forced to do things I didn't want to do, I'd actually had some fun, or at least I *thought* I'd had fun. These men were my only friends, and without them I'd have no social life. What was I going to do?

Obviously, it wasn't as simple as just throwing my old SIM card away. They might not have been able to phone me, but I could still bump into them on the street. All it would take was for one man to stop me in his car and tell me he wanted me to get him some girls and I'd be sucked right back in. This time it wouldn't be me who'd be lying on the dirty, lumpy mattresses awaiting a steady stream of sick paedophiles, it would be another innocent girl, and I'd have convinced her it was all a great laugh.

How could I live with myself if I let them violate some other young girl like they'd violated me?

Fortunately, Hamid had a plan. Because he was wealthy, he owned two houses. He lived in one with his wife and kids and he rented the other one out, but his tenants had just moved out and it was empty.

'Stay here for a while,' he said. 'They won't find you. And anyway, I'm not scared of them.'

Mum was wary at first, but the house was at the other end of Rotherham and she agreed it would be a good idea for me to get as far away from Ferham as possible. I know it was an unconventional arrangement – and perhaps my social workers would have disapproved – but I was trapped and this seemed like the only way out.

Hamid was a very good Muslim, a proper Muslim, who really cared about other people and wanted to make the world a better place. He often greeted people by saying '*as-salamu alaykum*', which means 'peace be unto you', but he could never bring himself to say it to the men he knew were grooming girls.

'They're not proper Muslims,' he said. 'They're just sick.'

Sometimes I wonder why Hamid went out of his way to help me, a white girl who some of his community would have regarded as little more than a slapper. I later discovered that lots of the men who abused me were well connected within the Asian community; some had respectable jobs and owned businesses, and others were really involved in the mosque. Hamid was really putting his neck on the line when he shunned them.

He never introduced me to his family, though. I never felt like he was ashamed of me, but I think it would have just made everything a little bit too complicated. He was completely devoted to his wife but I think she'd have found our relationship hard to understand. A couple of times, people saw me coming out of Hamid's other house and they began to talk, as if we were having an affair or something, but it was never like that. Hamid might have had different coloured skin to me, but he was like the dad I never had.

If I needed to go anywhere, I was always far too scared to call a taxi, so I'd call Mum or Hamid and I'd have to wait until one of them was free to collect me. Even now, in my mid-twenties, I don't like travelling in taxis because I'm scared of who the driver might be. I always wear a hoodie and pull it right up to my nose so they can't see my face.

I avoided the town centre like the plague, and I didn't even like going into shops on my own because I could never be sure that I wouldn't bump into someone who'd done something to me. Loads of the shops were owned by big Asian families, and while most of them had nothing to do with the paedophiles who'd stolen my childhood, I could never be sure that I wouldn't turn the corner to see one of them stacking the shelves, wearing a horrible knowing smile.

Instead, I got Mum or Hamid to drive me to the super-market and walk round with me while I shoved my groceries in the trolley as fast as I could. One day, I'd run out of milk and Hamid drove me to the petrol station.

My heart stopped for a second when I saw Latif's taxi parked up by the petrol pumps, and I had to grab Hamid's arm to steady myself. I ran into the shop as fast as I could, but just as I reached the doorway, Latif came out. His eyes travelled from Hamid to me and back again, and Hamid gave him an icy stare.

'All right, Sarah?' Latif said, but he didn't wait for an answer, he just scurried back to his car.

'He won't touch you again,' Hamid told me. 'None of them will.'

Maybe it was because Hamid had money that people in the Asian community listened to him. I don't know what he did to stop my abusers harassing me. It would have taken him days to track them all down individually and warn them off me, but whatever he did, it worked.

Finally, at long, long last, I had escaped.

It took me a while, but gradually I plucked up the courage to come out of hiding and move back to Mum's. Hamid still let me use his extra house if I needed a bit of time to myself, though. Sometimes he'd come round for a cup of tea, and I couldn't help but notice the circles round his eyes were getting darker. When I'd first met him, he'd looked quite jolly, but he didn't even have much of a belly any more. His face was gaunt and he looked almost grey.

'I won't see you next week, Sarah,' he said one evening as he dropped round some tea bags. 'I've got to go into the bloody hospital.' He started to laugh. 'Waste of time, if you ask me.'

I had a horrible feeling in the pit of my stomach.

'You're really sick, aren't you, Hamid?' I asked. 'You look sick.'

He raised his hand, as if to wave my concerns away.

'Don't you worry about me, Sarah,' he said. 'I'm fine. Just you concentrate on getting yourself sorted out.'

CHAPTER THIRTEEN

BUILDING BRIDGES

It felt good to be back with my family, out of the clutches of my abusers, but just because I'd broken free of them, it didn't mean things had suddenly become normal again.

Mum and Laura were still living in the house in Dalton but Mark and Robert had moved out. Sure, there were no longer men outside threatening to set the house on fire if I didn't come out to chill, but it was hard slotting back into family life when I'd spent the past five years in a sort of drug-induced wilderness.

Laura and I shared a room but it took a while for us to get our relationship back on track. Laura was used to having her own space, and it must have been strange for her having me back, especially as I kept dishing out lectures. After what had happened with Demi and Lily, I was terrified my abusers would target her too, and I warned her off any man who dared look at her.

'You're not allowed a boyfriend,' I'd tell her, time and time again, as if it was up to me!

Laura still thought I was a slag. She called me one often enough, but I don't really blame her. Few people saw me as a victim, and even now I think some would still maintain that what happened to me was my own fault.

Gradually, I started to make some new friends – just some people my age from round our way. Some were white and some were from Asian families. It annoys me when people ask me how I can have Asian friends after everything that happened to me, as if a few horrible paedophiles should put me off a whole race. Despite everything, I've never judged people on the colour of their skin. Plus, most of the Asian friends I have now have lived in Rotherham their whole lives and are as English as I am. Why should I treat them any differently?

But not everyone saw it that way. I got back in touch with Anwar, a guy I knew from my brief spell at high school. He was really nice and nothing to do with anyone who'd groomed or abused me, but sometimes people would see us together and jump to conclusions.

'Paki shagger!' would always be the shout as we walked through Ferham together. Sometimes I'd shout abuse back, other times I'd just ignore them.

As I started to chat to more people in Ferham, though, I heard on the grapevine that Laura had a boyfriend called Steven Smith. He was fifteen, just like she was, but that made no difference to me, especially when one of her friends let slip that she'd lost her virginity to him.

'I'll fucking kill both of them!' I said. 'She can't be having sex – she's a child.'

Laura was three years older than I'd been when I lost my virginity to Raj in the taxi, but that made no difference to me. It was too late for me to reclaim my stolen innocence, but I couldn't handle the idea of Laura having a sexual relationship. I had such a warped view of sex that to me it was just something men used to control women. I didn't want to hear about any dirty little guy with his hands all over my baby sister, no matter how old he was.

I was just walking home to give Laura an almighty lecture when I saw Steven standing at the end of our road, chatting to a mate. I know it sounds crazy, but my first instinct was to run into the house and get something to chase him down the street with. I never intended to hurt him, just to scare him.

I must have looked like I was possessed as I tore into the house, rifling through cupboards until I found my weapon. Laura was watching a film on the couch, oblivious to my rage.

'What the hell are you doing?' she asked, turning round when she heard the commotion.

'I've just heard that little prick Steven Smith has been shagging you!' I panted, breathless with rage. 'Well, he won't fucking touch you again when I've finished with him!'

Laura was on her feet now. 'Sarah!' she said. 'You're crazy. Put the crowbar down.'

'No, he's outside,' I replied. 'No one touches my little sister. I'm going to teach him a fucking lesson.'

Laura chased me as I ran onto the street. 'Sarah, you're just going to cause problems. Leave it!'

Steven's face froze in horror when he saw me coming for him and, to be fair, he must have been terrified. He might have just been a kid, but to me he was some sleazy predator who'd preyed on my little sister. Of course, they were both too young to be having sex, but I couldn't see that Steven was as naive as Laura was. To me, this was all his fault. I needed to deal with him, and fast.

'You think you can touch my sister, do you?' I hollered across the street, but he'd already started to run. Laura was still standing behind me.

'Sarah, this is mad!' she shouted. 'Like you can talk. How many guys had you shagged when you were fifteen?'

Usually, I'd have slapped her for saying this, but I was only focused on Steven. I raced up the street behind him, but he was too fast for me and soon he disappeared out of view.

Needless to say, it was a while before Laura shared any details about her love life with me. She wouldn't speak to me for days after the crowbar incident, so I texted Hamid to see if I could stop in his empty house for a day or so until everything calmed down. He replied straight away and told me he'd give me a lift to Asda so I could get some groceries.

As soon as I got into the car, I felt my stomach lurch. It had only been a week or so since I'd last seen Hamid, but his face was thinner than it had ever been. He was really jaundiced and his clothes were hanging off him, like they were about three sizes too big. He was as jolly as ever and I tried to make cheerful small talk, but by the time we parked up I couldn't hold my tongue any longer.

'Hamid, why were you in hospital the other week?' I asked.

'Oh, nothing serious,' he replied. His smile didn't fade, not even for a second. 'Just a little stomach problem.'

My eyes travelled from his yellowing skin to his bony arms and I was far from reassured.

'Are you dying?' The words had escaped my mouth before I'd had a chance to think them through. The idea hadn't even properly formed in my brain yet, but now I'd said it out loud, it seemed all too real.

Hamid just laughed. 'Oh, no, no. Don't you worry, I'm going nowhere fast.'

'Hamid, tell me the truth. You look terrible. You're really sick, aren't you?'

He looked away, but only for a fraction of a second. 'I'll be fine,' he told me. 'I'm going back into hospital tomorrow, but after that I'll be as good as new. Why don't you visit me?'

There are three hospitals in Sheffield, and Hamid told me he was in Weston Park. I didn't really know where it was, but I borrowed some money from Mum for the bus. It was a big greyish-brown building and it looked more like an office block than a hospital.

I hadn't even walked through the entrance when a horrible feeling of dread came over me. All of the signs had something to do with cancer, with arrows pointing to wards that did everything from clinical trials to radiotherapy. There was even a wing dedicated to the hospital's own cancer charity. Hamid had texted me the number of the ward he was in, so I went to the reception desk and gave his name to the nurse. I'd chosen not to come during normal visiting hours as I knew his wife and children would be with him then, and it just didn't seem right to intrude on their time together as a family.

'We don't normally allow visitors outside of visiting

hours,' the nurse said. She paused for a second. 'But I think we can make an exception.'

She led me to Hamid's room, where he was sitting up in bed. He looked even worse than he had done when we'd gone to Asda in the car. There were a few other patients dozing in beds around him.

'Why don't I let you two have some time together in private?' the nurse said. 'There's a spare room you can use.'

We spent the next hour or so in the little side room, eating the grapes and chocolate that people had given Hamid. Even though he looked terrible, he was as happy and cheerful as ever.

'How would you like a job, Sarah?' he said, popping a grape in his mouth. He explained that one of his friends owned an Indian restaurant in town and he was looking for a waitress. Of course, he made it clear that his friend wasn't connected to anyone who'd abused me.

'I'll give it a go,' I agreed. 'Sounds good.'

The idea of having a purpose in life, not to mention having money of my own to spend, appealed to me. Plus, lots of people had told me I was lucky I was neither pregnant nor in jail, and I was determined to prove to them that I could make something of my life.

'I'll tell him you can start this weekend, then,' Hamid said with a smile.

It was only when I got up to leave that I decided to ask the question that had been on my lips since I'd arrived.

'This is a cancer hospital, isn't it?' I said.

For a few seconds we were both silent as the question hung in the air between us. I'm still not sure why Hamid felt he had to protect me from the awful truth of the situation. I suppose he just thought I'd been through enough, that I was only starting to get my life back on track and I didn't need any more bad news.

Eventually, he broke the silence by dodging the question completely. 'Come back and see me on Monday. Let me know how your first shift goes. You'll be great.'

I nodded and turned to walk away, so he wouldn't see the tears in my eyes.

I liked working at the restaurant. The owner was really nice and having something to do took my mind off things. It was hard work and I often had to be there until quite late at night, but it meant I had some money so I could go and hang out with my friends.

Laura had been doing shifts in a hairdresser's salon but she'd also signed up for college, so I decided I'd give it a go too. I enrolled in a business course but I only lasted a few days. Juggling work and studying just seemed too much, plus I just wasn't used to sitting down and learning as I'd missed so much school.

Mum did her best with me, and most of the time we got on well. My shifts at the restaurant meant I didn't have as much time on my hands as I used to, but I still kicked off sometimes, mainly if I'd been mooching around the house all day. Even without coke, I could get really angry, especially when I'd been on my own for too long and I'd had time to think about everything I'd been through.

Phil and Kate had washed their hands of me now that I was an adult. I'm sure they were both over the moon that they didn't have to deal with me any more. Instead, I was supposed to pick up the shattered pieces of my life by myself. I was never offered counselling, because then the authorities would have had to acknowledge what had happened to me. I just had to get on with it.

I was still looking over my shoulder at every turn, frightened of who I might see as I walked down the street. I didn't like leaving the house alone and I still refused to go into town unless Mum was with me. Whenever I did see one of my abusers, I'd usually put my head down and shuffle past them as quickly as possible, hoping they wouldn't make a nasty comment.

One day, I was walking through Ferham when I saw Rahim across the street. He didn't look much different, except his beard was now flecked with grey. He'd sort of drifted away from Amir, and it must have been at least three years since I'd last seen him. I was on my own and I could feel my heart starting to beat a little faster. I saw a flash of recognition cross his face and I suddenly felt vulnerable and exposed, like I was eleven again and we were back in the school playground where Nadine was bullying me into giving him a blow job. But out of the corner of my eye I could see there was a woman walking next to him, her face obscured slightly by her black hijab.

I doubt he'd have tried to speak to me while he was with his wife, but I wasn't taking any chances. I pulled my hood up and walked a little faster, pretending I hadn't seen him. Still, I couldn't help but wonder: does she know? Does she have any idea what her husband has done to me, as I drag my feet down the street, weighed down by the horrible memories inside my head?

Of course she didn't know. And even if I told her, she'd never believe me in a million years. Every day, Keggy's words still rang in my head.

No one will ever believe you, because everyone knows you're a massive slag.

Despite what Mum and Sarah and Hamid said, it was still hard for me to accept that none of this was my fault, and everywhere I turned, something reminded me of my past life.

Plus, some of the guys were harder to avoid than others. I was waiting for the bus to Sheffield one afternoon, as I'd planned to visit Hamid in hospital, when I caught sight of Amir walking towards me. The sweat prickled on the back of my neck. I'd never done anything with him as he'd always been with Nadine, but he'd watched so many others groom and abuse me.

'All right, Sarah!' he said, before I could turn away. 'I haven't seen you in ages.'

He looked dirty and unshaven, like he hadn't been home in days, and when he stood next to me he smelled of old sweat and alcohol. He tried to talk to me, but I only mumbled a few one-word answers before my bus came. I was relieved, but still the unsettling thought swirled around my head: who has he got his hands on now? Surely some other young girl has fallen into his trap?

Every time I visited Hamid he looked thinner and weaker. Still, he assured me he was getting better.

'I'll be home soon,' he'd grin. 'I can't wait to get out of here!'

I pushed my doubts to the back of my mind and tried to get on with life as best as I could. Slowly but surely, Laura and I started to get closer. We'd often find ourselves giggling on the sofa together as we watched a film, or gossiping as we shared a takeaway. Plus, she had loads of mates, who soon became my mates too. Laura had stopped seeing Steven Smith and now she thought the crowbar incident was a great laugh.

'I can't believe you chased Steven Smith with a crow-bar!' she'd giggle. 'All my mates think you're mental!'

I also started going out a bit more with some of the new friends I'd made. Sometimes I went to house parties, but they weren't like the parties at Hayley's dad's or any of the other houses I'd been taken to. People would still get wasted, but nobody expected me to have sex with them. It was still hard to get my head around it all – it was so different to what I was used to.

I also went to pubs and clubs. Of course, you were supposed to be eighteen before you were allowed in, but the bouncers turned a blind eye to the fact that we were all just a few months too young. I'd always been a tomboy, in my tracksuits and trainers, but it was nice to get dressed up from time to time and put a little make-up on.

One night, I'd just finished a shift at the restaurant when Kathryn, one of the girls I'd met through Laura, texted to see if I fancied a night out. We went to one of the clubs in town and everyone was having a laugh, danc-ing away. But after an hour or so, I just wasn't feeling up to it. I couldn't explain why; it was just like something wasn't quite right. Instinctively, I reached for my phone, but my battery had died.

I was relieved when Kathryn suggested leaving before closing time, saying that her mate Taj could pick us up.

There was another Asian guy in the passenger seat, but I wasn't really in the mood to chat. As Taj drew up outside Mum's, though, he said something to his mate that made the hairs on the back of my neck stand up.

'Terrible news about Hamid, isn't it?'

I slammed the door shut without saying bye. I legged it up the path because I didn't want to hear the rest of the conversation. I convinced myself I had misheard Taj. Maybe he didn't say Hamid after all, but another name that sounded just like it. Or even if he was talking about Hamid, maybe the unthinkable hadn't happened. After all, the terrible news could be anything, couldn't it? His business could have gone bust, or his house could have burned down.

He couldn't be dead. He just couldn't.

Mum was drinking with some friends, but when I opened the door her expression changed.

'How come your phone is off, Sarah?' she said. 'Hamid's brother has been trying to get hold of you all night.'

Dread clawed at my insides. 'The battery's dead. What's wrong? What's wrong with Hamid?'

Mum bowed her head. 'I'm afraid he's passed away, Sarah. I'm sorry.'

The next few minutes were a blur. Everything seemed to happen in slow motion. I grabbed Mum's ashtray and slammed it against the wall. I was crying, but only because I was so, so angry. Hamid was only forty-three. I had seen him getting sicker and sicker, fading away before my eyes, but still it didn't seem real. Why were my abusers allowed to walk the streets and grow old with their families when the man who had saved me from them was gone?

One of Mum's friends was speaking to me. I think she was trying to calm me down, but I wanted to punch her. How could she ever understand what this felt like, what any of it felt like? I raised my hand and I could hear people gasping. My fist was clenched but I froze.

Suddenly, I could see Hamid, peaceful, caring Hamid, as if he was standing right in front of me. I imagined him shaking his head, telling me to stop.

'What are you doing, Sarah?' he'd have said. 'You're a nice girl. There's no need for this.'

Suddenly, my insides were churning, so I dropped my hand and ran upstairs. I locked myself in the bathroom and vomited, shock cascading through my veins.

When I went back downstairs, everyone was quiet.

'I'm sorry,' I said. 'I shouldn't have done that. It won't happen again.'

CHAPTER FOURTEEN

ASHTIAQ

It was early the next morning before I managed to reach Hamid's brother, Bashir. I'd been trying to call him back the previous night, but there was no answer as the family were all at the hospital. I'd never met Bashir but, as I'd suspected, Hamid had known what was going to happen for months and he'd given him my number.

'Tell me it's not true,' I said, as soon as he answered.

'I'm sorry, Sarah,' he replied. 'I'm afraid it is. Hamid had cancer.'

I couldn't stop myself from crying. Of course, I'd known that Hamid had cancer, even though he'd refused to tell me. I wondered if he had already known he was living on borrowed time when he decided to rescue me that fateful night in the shop below Sav's flat? But I suspected I wasn't the only girl he had saved.

'He asked for you shortly before he died,' Bashir went on. 'He told me to look after you.'

The funeral was a few days later, as it is an Islamic tradition to bury the dead as soon as possible. It was only then that I realised how many lives he had touched. There were far too many mourners to fit into the mosque, so the ceremony was held in one of the local fields. I had some spare money from my shifts at the restaurant, so I went to one of the Asian clothes shops in Rotherham and bought myself a new red-and-green sari. I still had my hijab from when I lived in Dewsbury with Khalid, so I wore that too.

I went along on my own and stood apart from the other mourners, my hijab covering most of my face. I couldn't really see what was going on because of the crowds – there must have been at least 500 mourners, probably more. I'd wondered if I might be the only white person there, but there were loads of others, proof that Hamid treated everyone with respect, regardless of what colour their skin was. I'd stopped practising Islam when I'd left Khalid, but I've always believed in God and the afterlife, so I tried to join in as best I could with the prayers. There were so many people it was hard to see or hear anything, though. I overheard one man saying he'd come all the way over from the States.

I'd known Hamid for just a year, but he felt like such a huge part of my life. Even now, six years later, I still think of him loads. I can't even imagine what my life might be like now if I hadn't bumped into him in the shop that night. If there is a heaven, which I'm sure there is, I know he will be there.

Over the next few months, I tried to get on with my life as best as I possibly could. Working in the restaurant gave me a focus, which was good. Mum and Laura tried to be understanding but it felt like no one missed Hamid as I did.

Bashir did try to reach out to me, like he'd promised Hamid he would. We met up a few times but it was all a bit too difficult. Bashir looked so much like Hamid it was scary, but for me he was too painful a reminder of what I'd lost. He was a good man, but he could never be Hamid. In the end, we lost touch.

I was so wrapped up in my grief that it took me a while to notice that Laura had a new boyfriend. She'd started going out more and staying out later, perhaps slicking on a coat of mascara here and there. I just assumed she was with her mates. Things had long since fizzled out with Steven Smith, but one day she was in a right strop so Mum asked her what was wrong.

'I've just had a fight with my boyfriend,' she replied.

'Your boyfriend?' Mum said. 'First we've heard of him. Who is he, then?'

'His name is Ashtiaq,' Laura said. 'Ashtiaq Asghar.'

Like I said before, I'm far from a racist, but the

mention of an Asian name did make me stop in my tracks. I hadn't heard of an Ashtiaq before, but there was every chance he could be one of *them*. My mind flashed back to Azim and all the weekends we'd spent together in cheap hotel rooms. He'd called himself my boyfriend, but really he was a paedophile.

'How old is this Ashtiaq?' I demanded, panic rising in my throat.

'He's the same age as I am,' Laura replied. 'He's fifteen. Calm down.'

Laura was a bit moody for the rest of the day, but she eventually told us she'd met Ashtiaq at a party. There was a guy who lived in Ferham called Derek and his house had always been a bit of a dosshouse. It wasn't as bad as Hayley's dad's was or anything like that, but he was always having parties. I think he would go about telling people he was some kind of war hero, but really he was just a bit of a loser who drank a lot. Still, there was always plenty of cider on offer, so lots of people would hang around there.

'We just got talking when I was round at Derek's and he asked me for my number,' she said.

Laura and Ashtiaq made up pretty soon afterwards, but it was another few weeks before I met him. Derek was having another party and Laura asked me if I wanted to go along. I had the night off, so I agreed.

When I first saw Ashtiaq his face was hidden by the cloud of smoke from his fag and he had a bottle of vodka in his hand. He was still wearing his school uniform, but the first few buttons on his shirt were open and his tie was in a really loose knot round his neck, a bit like Nadine used to do hers.

'This is Ashtiaq,' Laura said. 'And this is my sister, Sarah.'

As the cloud of smoke disintegrated, Ashtiaq's face became visible. He was smiling but I wasn't. I was still sizing him up. I properly looked him up and down for about thirty seconds before anyone spoke. I could see Laura looking at me nervously, like I was a volcano about to erupt.

'You all right?' Ashtiaq said eventually.

I didn't reply straight away. He seemed all right, I suppose, if a bit rough around the edges. I figured he probably thought he was dead cool because he was smoking and drinking. He was quite muscular for someone so young, and he looked quite strong. He had thick black eyebrows and he'd shaved a chunk out of one of them. This made him look like a bit of an idiot, but he was only fifteen, after all.

I hadn't brought my crowbar but I still wanted to give him a good talking to, to warn him not to mess my sister around. So many men had done so many horrible things to me, I couldn't bear to think of anyone hurting Laura.

'You'd better treat her right,' I said. 'If you don't, I'll kill you.'

Ashtiaq started laughing as he slid his arm around Laura. 'Relax. I will.' He turned to my sister, and with a huge grin he said: 'She's safe with me.'

Thinking of it now, I almost want to vomit.

'So, what do you think?' Laura asked as we walked home. 'He's so fit, isn't he? And he's so nice.'

'He seems all right,' I said. 'You like him, then?'

'Yeah, I do,' she replied. 'Don't give him any shit like you did with Steven Smith.'

We were both a bit tipsy, so we started giggling.

As it happened, Laura and Ashtiaq's fight was far from a one-off. Over the course of the next few months they fell out more times than I can remember, but they always made up. Maybe, looking back, the warning signs were there, but it's easy to say that now. Back then, Mum and I just thought it was a typical turbulent teenage relationship – and Laura always gave as good as she got.

They'd fight over the smallest of things and I was usually the referee. Whenever something went wrong, both of them would phone me up and I'd have to try to make each of them see sense. They always did make up, though, and Ashtiaq spent loads of time at ours.

Despite the constant fall-outs, Laura was head over heels. She'd chatter away about how they planned to get married and have lots of babies. I had to remind her how young she was. To me, she was still a baby herself, and the idea of her doing all these grown-up things seemed absurd.

'Just don't rush into anything,' I warned her. 'Plenty time for all of that.'

Of course, I kind of figured that Laura and Ashtiaq were having sex, and I didn't like it one bit when they disappeared upstairs while Mum was out. The thought of anyone with their hands all over my sister was still enough to fill me with rage. But she'd just turned sixteen by this point and I knew I had to let her live her own life. Plus, there was no way she'd listen to me if I told her to stop. I just tried not to think about it.

I was so mixed up with all my abusers at Laura's age that I don't think I experienced the all-consuming teenage love that she had with Ashtiaq. I don't think I'd ever want to get inside his head, but I do wonder if his feelings for her were ever genuine. Part of me wants to believe he did love her at the start – that he wasn't just using her all along.

Laura's feelings for Ashtiaq were so intense that she got jealous really easily. If she found out he'd been texting another girl, however innocently, she'd go mad and cry for days. Ashtiaq would always call me and ask me to speak to her.

'You need to sort your Laura out,' he'd say. 'She won't speak to me.'

'You two need your heads knocking together,' I'd sigh.

When I think of it now, I do remember that Ashtiaq sometimes boasted about fights he'd been in. He claimed he had a gun and he once told me he'd broken someone's jaw, but I just laughed because I thought he was lying. Teenage boys always want to act the hardman, especially round our way.

Just after Ashtiaq and Laura started seeing each other, Mum got a new house back in Ferham, just a few streets away from Psalters Lane. Ashtiaq was always round at ours, but Laura admitted that she hadn't even met his parents, far less been in their house – even though they lived just round the corner.

Now, it makes perfect sense, of course. Ashtiaq's parents were very devout Muslims, and they'd come to Rotherham from Pakistan before he and his siblings were born. They lived just off Ferham Road, on the corner of a street called Josephine Road, where lots of Asian families had houses. His dad drove a taxi and his mum worked at the council, but they kept themselves to themselves. While Laura was dreaming of marrying him and having his babies, they were planning to send him back to their village in the Punjab to pick a wife.

Laura would never do. She wasn't a Muslim for a start, and although she was much better behaved than I was, she still liked staying out late and having a drink at Derek's or in the park with her mates. Ashtiaq drank more than she did, but he kept this well hidden from his parents. Either that or they pretended not to notice.

I remembered my own ill-fated marriage to Khalid, and I gently tried to suggest to Laura that she might not want to pin all her hopes on a future with Ashtiaq.

'Ashtiaq's family might not want him to be with a white girl,' I told her. 'They seem very strict.'

'I don't care,' she replied. 'I love him. We'll find a way, even if his mum and dad don't want us to be together. Anyway, you married a Muslim and you're white.'

'Yeah, and do you remember how that turned out?' I said. 'Plus, that wasn't even a real wedding.'

Maybe that was part of the appeal of the whole thing with Ashtiaq. To most fifteen-year-old girls, the idea of loving someone you're not supposed to must seem dead romantic, like something out of a film, but hardly anyone stays with someone they meet as a kid. I reckoned it would fizzle out soon enough and Laura would forget all about him.

If only that had been the case.

One night, shortly before my eighteenth birthday, I came home from the restaurant to find Laura sitting at the computer in tears.

'What's wrong with you?' I asked.

'It's Ashtiaq,' she sobbed. 'He's been cheating on me.'

At first, I was sceptical. Laura was always freaking out about Ashtiaq talking to other girls. But then she showed me a Facebook message from a girl called Nicola, who claimed to have slept with him a few nights previously.

'We're going to find him,' I announced. 'We'll find them both.'

I was really angry at Ashtiaq, of course I was, but even then the alarm bells weren't ringing. I was more disappointed in him than anything, as I'd actually thought he was a nice kid, despite all his daft bravado. I was upset he'd cheated on Laura, but I thought he was just a silly teenage boy who couldn't keep it in his pants. I never dreamed he'd put Laura in any kind of danger.

I never thought he'd want to punish her for loving him so much.

But that would come later. That night, all I wanted was to find him and give him a huge telling-off. We grabbed our coats, with Laura still sniffling and sobbing behind me as we tore up Ferham Road. When we couldn't find him in Derek's, we knocked on loads of other doors, but he was nowhere to be found. He wasn't in Ferham Park, either. I think we'd been out for about two hours when we eventually gave up.

'I'll make sure I give the little prick a right talking to when I next see him,' I told Laura. 'Don't you worry.'

'I don't know why he did it,' she replied. 'I've phoned him loads of times but he won't answer.'

'Just forget about him, Laura,' I said. 'He's not worth it. You'll find someone else.'

Laura was still crying. She wiped her eyes with the sleeve of her hoodie and bit her lip.

'I can't just forget about him,' she sobbed. 'You don't understand. I love him.'

CHAPTER FIFTEEN

LOVE TRIANGLE

I thought Laura would lock herself away for weeks after she found out about Ashtiaq and Nicola; there were lots of tears for a few days, but it wasn't long before she started going out again. Most nights, she'd either be round at Derek's or out with her mates in Ferham Park.

I'm not sure if she ever properly confronted Ashtiaq about the cheating, because shortly after we tried to find him in Ferham I moved out. I was eighteen by this point, and I'd decided it was time to get a little flat of my own. The only problem was, I'd just given up my job at the restaurant. I had to go on benefits, which wasn't ideal, especially when I had all my own bills to pay.

I'd liked my job and it had given me a sense of purpose, but a few weeks before I moved into my flat, a guy called Sadiq started working there. He was a bit older than me, probably in his mid-twenties. I'd never met him before, but he gave me a really creepy feeling because he was always looking at me funny. He didn't say much, which was even weirder, but I'd always turn round to see him standing behind me, his mouth hanging open slightly.

One night, as I rushed into the kitchen with lots of dirty plates in my hand, he made me jump.

'You look beautiful today,' he said. He'd been standing behind me, but I hadn't realised.

'Don't do that!' I snapped. 'You scared me.'

I shuddered as I walked from the kitchen back into the restaurant. I recognised the look on Sadiq's face. It was the way Rahim and Azim and Latif and all the others used to look at me, except we were both adults now. I convinced myself that I could almost see the sick thoughts running through his head.

The next night, he asked me what I was doing after work.

'Want to come chilling?' he asked. 'My mate is having a party. He has weed.'

My heart felt like it was about to burst out of my chest.

'Just leave me alone,' I said. 'Don't even talk to me!'

Sadiq looked bewildered as I tore off my apron and ran in to see the owner in his office. I told him I wasn't coming back. He was confused and asked what was wrong, but I mumbled an excuse and practically ran home. I felt really bad, as the owner was Hamid's friend, but the thought of facing Sadiq at work every day made me feel sick with dread.

It sounds drastic, I know. Sadiq wasn't that much older than me and we were both adults, so I guess there was no harm in him asking me out if he fancied me. But something about him reminded me of the men who'd manipulated and abused me for so long, and I just couldn't face him. The chances are he was harmless, but it was a chance I wasn't willing to take.

It was only then I realised my abusers hadn't just stolen my childhood. They were threatening to steal my future, too.

Sarah from Risky Business still kept in touch with Mum and me, and she told me I could go to the police if I wanted, though she was never pushy. I did speak to a really nice police officer, a lady called Laila. She was a British Pakistani and she was absolutely disgusted when I told her what I'd been through. She encouraged me to take things further, but I just couldn't face it. The men who'd groomed and abused me were out of my life now, but the thought of facing them in court was just a bit too much.

'One day,' I promised Laila. 'I'm just not ready yet.'

I was so wrapped up in what was going on in my own life that it was a few weeks before I realised Laura was seeing someone else. It was plain to see that the new guy was just a rebound. She was still head over heels for Ashtiaq.

I don't think Laura could ever bring herself to ask about Nicola. It was almost like she was in denial – if she didn't say it out loud, it hadn't happened. She couldn't bear to think of him with another girl. I think she convinced herself that Nicola was lying and Ashtiaq would come running back to her, full of apologies. He didn't, of course; not then, anyway.

So Laura decided to do what thousands of teenage girls across the country do every day. She'd make her ex-boyfriend jealous, by getting with his friend.

Ishaq Hussain was four years older than me. He'd been at my primary school and everyone called him Zac. His family was huge and mega-rich, at least compared with everyone else in Ferham. He had dozens of uncles and cousins, and they owned tons of shops and houses in Rotherham, as well as loads of stuff back in Pakistan. There was even a rumour they had their own airline! Despite this, I'd always thought he was a nice guy. He'd always chatted and said hello to me, even when I was being really badly bullied.

Like lots of Muslims in Rotherham, Zac liked to drink and go to parties, but I suspect his parents didn't know much about this. They'd arranged for him to marry a girl called Mariam. She was a Muslim too, and she'd been in his class at school. I knew her a bit and I thought she was really nice, but I always wondered if they actually really liked each other or whether it was just convenient, because it was the worst-kept secret in Ferham that Zac couldn't keep it in his pants. As well as Mariam, the word on the street was that he was also seeing a white girl called Faye, who was the same age as Laura.

It was on the morning of his wedding that Zac and Laura first caught sight of each other. Zac was twenty-one and she was sixteen, so their paths hadn't crossed, but she knew who he was because he and Ashtiaq had recently started hanging around together. Lots of people said Ashtiaq idolised Zac, and even Laura admitted that he wouldn't stop talking about his cool older friend.

Zac was standing outside one of the family shops, dressed up to the nines in all his wedding gear, but he couldn't stop looking at Laura. She was looking at him too, but neither of them said anything because his dad and loads of his uncles were there.

A few weeks later, Laura was walking down Ferham Road when she bumped into him outside a chip shop.

'Hey,' Zac said. 'I recognise you. Were you outside the shop the other week?'

'Yeah,' Laura replied. 'Nice clothes, by the way.'

Zac just laughed. Neither of them said anything about the fact that he'd been on his way to his wedding at the time. I think Laura was so blinded by her desperation to get back at Ashtiaq that she decided to ignore the fact that Zac was married. By this point, Faye had announced she was pregnant and rumours were flying around that Zac was the dad. Still, he told Laura she was pretty and asked for her number.

Within days, they were sleeping together.

Of course, it didn't last long. Laura never really had proper feelings for Zac. She didn't love him like she loved Ashtiaq, so I think she got a bit bored. I think they only really met up for a few weeks, maybe a month at most.

I didn't find out they'd been sleeping together until a few weeks after they'd stopped seeing each other. Laura just casually dropped it into conversation and I went crazy.

'Zac!' I said. 'Laura, he's married!'

'I know, I know,' she replied. 'It's over. It was just a few times, I'm not seeing him any more.'

'Good,' I said. 'Because everyone is saying Faye's baby is his. You don't want to get mixed up in any of that.'

But as the Christmas of 2009 drew nearer, Laura started to feel a bit off-colour. She kept getting tummy bugs and she missed loads of college, which wasn't like her. Maybe it's because I wasn't living at home that I didn't notice the packet of sanitary towels lying untouched in the bathroom, or the fact that her boobs were bursting out of all her tops. Maybe I just didn't want to see the signs.

Just after New Year, I was walking down Ferham Road when I spotted one of Laura's friends coming towards me. Her name was Lydia and she'd always liked a gossip.

'Hey, Sarah,' she said. 'Well, who would have thought it?'

I looked at her, confused. 'What are you on about?'

'Oh, haven't you heard?' she replied. 'Your Laura's pregnant.'

'Is it true?'

I'd burst into Mum's without so much as a hello. Laura was sitting on the couch, and I could tell she had been crying because her eyes were all red. She'd told Mum she was pregnant earlier that day and the news was somehow already halfway round Ferham. She didn't answer my question, though she didn't have to ask what I was referring to.

'I've just heard from bloody Lydia that you're pregnant,' I said. 'Please tell me she's lying.'

Both she and Mum didn't say anything for ages. I just stood there, bubbling with rage.

'Yeah,' Laura whispered eventually. 'It's true.'

I just stood and shook my head in disbelief. My mind flashed back to all the pregnancy tests I'd taken, probably about fifteen in total. Even though loads of the men had used condoms, there were times when I'd been so out of it I had no way of knowing for sure, and every time my period was a day or two late I'd get a sinking feeling in the pit of my stomach. I'd been so scared that this would have been me, crying on the couch as I tried to figure out what to do with my unplanned baby. Yet it was Laura instead.

'You fucking idiot,' I said. 'I take it you'll be getting rid of it?'

Laura was still crying, but there was a steely determination in her eyes. 'No, I'm not getting rid of it. I'm keeping it.'

Looking back, I can't believe I tried so hard to persuade my sister to destroy the little life growing inside her, because without that baby I fear our family would have shattered into a thousand pieces at a time when we needed something to live for. But then, no one could have predicted the tragedy that awaited us. At that moment, to me, an abortion was the only option.

'You can't keep it!' I cried in disbelief. 'You can't have a baby – you're only a baby yourself!'

But once Laura had made her mind up, there was no telling her.

'It's *my* baby,' she said, looking me straight in the eye. 'And I'm keeping it.'

'This is a joke, right?' I replied. 'Is it Zac's?'

Laura didn't answer for a few seconds. I think part of her really, really wanted to believe the baby was Ashtiaq's, but simple maths dictated that there was no way the father was anyone but Zac.

'Yeah,' she said. 'Zac's the dad.'

'You are crazy,' I told her. I was pacing the living-room floor like a madwoman now. I wanted to grab Laura and try to shake some sense into her, but instead I stood over her, shouting, 'You can't have a baby with Zac – he's married! What's going to happen now? Are you and Faye both going to have kids by him? Don't think he'll want anything to do with it because he won't. I know how that family works.'

It was true. Money talks and Zac's family had loads of influence in the Muslim community in Rotherham. Lots of people looked up to them because they were seen as being really honourable, and that sense of honour is so important to lots of Asian people. There was no way they'd be happy about their married son having an affair with one white girl and getting her pregnant, never mind two, because it would bring so much shame on the family. I'd thought Zac was all right before I found out he'd been having an affair with Laura, but anyone with half a brain knew he'd swear blind my sister's unborn child was nothing to do with him.

'I don't care,' Laura said. 'I'll do it all myself.'

'Are you actually out of your mind?' I was shaking with rage and frustration now. 'Mum, tell her!'

Mum shook her head. 'It's Laura's decision, Sarah,' she said. 'Whatever she does I'll support her 110 per cent.'

I couldn't believe what I was hearing, so I stormed out and slammed the door behind me. It sounds bad, but I assumed Laura would change her mind about the baby. She was only eleven weeks gone and there was still loads of time to have an abortion. I thought she might even phone to apologise and tell me I'd been right all along. Of course, she didn't.

I was so upset I didn't speak to her for weeks. She'd been doing so well at college but Mum said she'd decided to give it up and go back when the new term started because she was really sick. It was a difficult pregnancy, and Mum went with her to all the scans and appointments, but it was weeks before I could even acknowledge it was happening.

While we weren't speaking, Ashtiaq got back in touch. He wanted to speak to Laura before he went off to Pakistan and he came round to visit her. He knew she was having Zac's baby, but he still wanted to make up. They were just friends, though. Mum and I were certain he'd come back with a wife, but I think his visit made Laura hope they'd get back together one day.

However, the sad truth was that if Ashtiaq had been reluctant to introduce Laura to his family before, he would be even less keen now his friend had got her pregnant.

I think it was a whole two months before I started to accept that Laura wasn't going to have an abortion after all. She was getting bigger by the day, and at her twenty-week scan she found out she was having a little girl. She and Mum went shopping for loads of girly stuff straight away, and soon there were little pink dresses all over the house.

I realised I had to swallow my pride and pick up the phone. Laura answered and I took a deep breath.

'I get that you're keeping the baby,' I said. 'So I'm here for you. We can fetch her up together.'

I could almost feel her grinning at the other end of line. 'I've decided on a name. What do you think of Alesha?'

I could almost feel a lump forming in my throat. 'It's beautiful.'

It was a stressful time too, though. Laura was still being monitored by social workers because they were scared she'd fall prey to the same men who'd groomed me. She had to have loads of assessments done and so did Mum. She got different social workers from me, but they were just as snooty. Eventually, though, they agreed that she was fit to raise her little girl.

Laura's due date was 23 June, and a few months before she gave birth, Ashtiaq came home. We were all surprised to learn he wasn't engaged after all. At least if he was, he wasn't admitting it to anyone. He told Laura his parents had encouraged him to pick a girl to marry but he hadn't found one he liked. He was supposed to be at college, but he wagged it all the time to come round to Mum's and watch DVDs with Laura. I don't think they were sleeping together again yet – Laura was way too big and uncomfortable by this point – but they were acting as if they were a couple, and Laura had that lovesick look in her eyes again.

I had liked Ashtiaq, but I was bit more guarded now I knew what had happened with Nicola.

'Be careful,' I told Laura, but it was pointless. She'd do what she wanted, like she always did when it came to Ashtiaq.

Ashtiaq was paying Laura loads of attention, but to Zac it was like she didn't exist. He hadn't bothered to get in touch to see if she needed anything, and the word in Ferham was that he was claiming the baby had nothing to do with him, just like I'd predicted.

'He's scum,' I said to Mum and Laura. 'He'll know all about it the next time I bump into him.'

As it happened, I didn't see Zac until a few days before Laura was due to give birth. I was walking down Ferham Road with some mates, eating a takeaway, and he was walking out of one of the petrol stations. I could see that he'd seen me, but he was looking at the ground. My mates knew I was desperate to give him what for, so they kept shouting his name. They must have called out about ten times before he eventually looked up and walked over.

I remember what I was eating really clearly – doner meat, chips and mayonnaise, out of one of those little white polystyrene boxes. Zac couldn't look at me. He started making small talk with one of the other girls.

Before I'd even had time to think, I'd smashed the carton in his face. The chips fell to the ground one by one, but the stringy doner meat clung to his hair and his cheeks. Stunned, Zac rifled through his pockets, searching for a hankie as big gloops of mayonnaise ran down his face. I could hear my friends giggling, but I wasn't laughing at all.

Zac's mouth was hanging open in shock. He and his family were used to people falling at their feet. I don't think he could quite believe I'd had the guts to empty my dinner over his head. We just stared at each other in silence for about thirty seconds, as if we were each daring the other to speak first. Finally, Zac cracked.

'Do you realise how much you've just disrespected me?' he said. He was speaking in barely more than a whisper, but I could tell he was really raging. I wasn't scared of him, though.

'How much *I've* disrespected *you*?' I laughed out loud. 'Yeah, well, what about my sister? Haven't you disrespected her?'

'I don't know what she's told you,' he said. 'But the baby's not mine – I haven't fucking touched her.'

'Oh, fuck off, Zac. Everyone knows the baby's yours,' I replied. 'Laura doesn't need you, don't you worry about that, but you could at least try to be there for your child.'

Zac was barely listening. He kept going on and on about how the baby wasn't his, and I was getting more and more angry. I think I reached out to slap him because he grabbed hold of my arms.

'You've disrespected me,' he said again. 'You've fucked it.'

His face was still covered in mayonnaise as he tore off back up Ferham Road, picking bits of doner meat out of his hair.

CHAPTER SIXTEEN

ALESHA

A few days after I confronted Zac, Laura went into labour. It was a gorgeous day and she'd been round at Mum's friend Donna's, playing in a big inflatable pool in the garden, when her contractions started.

Mum knew it would take a while for the baby to arrive, as first babies often take their time. But around midnight Laura was in a lot of pain, so she drove her to Rotherham District Hospital, the same place we'd all been born.

It was a difficult labour, lasting over twenty-four hours, but Mum was by Laura's side throughout. In the end the baby was in quite a lot of distress, so the midwives told Laura they'd have to use forceps to deliver her.

Alesha eventually arrived at 11 p.m. on 23 June 2010, one of very few babies born on their due dates. Laura was exhausted, but Mum says my little sister had tears of joy rolling down her face when her little girl was placed on her chest for the first time.

'She's the most beautiful baby in the world,' she said proudly, and Mum couldn't help but agree.

Auntie Annette and Donna were in the waiting room, and they soon phoned me to tell me the good news. I was over the moon, but I didn't meet my niece until the next morning. Mum drove me to the hospital first thing.

I'll never forget the moment I first laid eyes on her. She was lying in her little cot next to Laura's bed and she had piles and piles of black hair. There were some little scratches on her face from the forceps, but to me she was perfect. Laura had already dressed her in a little pink babygrow and a matching hat. I'd been so determined that Laura should have an abortion, but as I stood gazing at this beautiful little girl, tears rolling down my cheeks, I couldn't believe that such a thought had ever entered my head.

Writing this now, my mind flashes back to when we were kids, and I remember how Laura used to play with all of her prams in the back garden of our first house on Psalters Lane. She was born to be a mum and I'm so glad she got the chance to be one, if only for a short time.

It was a few minutes before I picked Alesha up. Laura was crying and we both just sat there in tears for ages! It was one of the most special moments of my life.

Eventually, I took Alesha from her cot and held her in my arms. I couldn't believe how cute she was, with her tiny fingers and toes and her little button nose. I felt the most overwhelming rush of love for her, almost as if she was my own child. Little did I know that one day I would be bringing her up as if she *was* my own child.

All I knew then was that I'd do anything to protect her. I stroked her head and I thought about how Mum must have felt the first time she held me, how her heart must have swelled with all the hopes and dreams she had for me, only for scores of horrible men to abuse me like I was piece of rubbish. It was only now, with this tiny, fragile little girl in my arms, that I had some idea of how it must have torn her apart, and that made me cry even more. I couldn't begin to imagine how I'd feel if anyone laid a finger on Alesha, but I promised myself I'd never find out because I'd never let anyone do anything to harm her.

As I cradled my new niece and held her to me, making the most of those first, precious moments, I tried not to think about her dad and how mad he had made me a few nights previously. How could Zac ever want to deny this gorgeous little girl was his? Of course, no one had called to tell him. He'd washed his hands of Laura and Alesha so he didn't deserve to hear our happy news first-hand, though it would be all round Ferham soon enough.

'We don't need Zac,' I told Laura. 'We'll fetch her up, you, me and Mum. Everything will be okay.'

'I know,' she replied. She still had tears in her eyes.

The midwife wanted to keep Laura in for a few nights for observation, as the birth had been so difficult and she needed quite a few stitches, but she must have kicked up a right fuss because a few hours after I left she rang me to say the hospital had agreed she could come home.

Laura loved being a mum, but the next few weeks were hard. She was really nervous, probably because she was so young herself. Mum had to help her lots at first, showing her how to bathe and feed Alesha. She'd decided to bottle-feed her, which made things a bit easier, as Mum or I could step in to help if she was too exhausted.

When Alesha was around three weeks old, Laura asked me to move back in. She thought an extra pair of hands would be handy, but more than anything I think she wanted the company. I agreed straight away. I was desperate to be as big a part of Alesha's life as possible and I wanted to savour all of her early moments. Plus, it would save a bit of money too.

There's no denying it was a bit of a squeeze. Now that the boys had left home and Mum had downsized we only had two bedrooms, and obviously Alesha's cot was in Laura's room so I had to share with Mum. I didn't mind, though. Mum, Laura and I became a little team, all mucking in to change nappies and make up bottles. Soon, our days revolved around Alesha, and it was impossible to imagine life without her.

Things weren't always plain sailing, though. Laura was still only sixteen, and there were times when she struggled to deal with the responsibilities that came with having a child. She loved Alesha to bits but she still wanted to go out and have fun with her mates.

One afternoon, around a month after Alesha was born, Laura was desperate to show her off so she took her to Derek's in the pram because loads of her mates were there. People were smoking and drinking and it wasn't really the place for a kid, but Laura didn't mean any harm. She was just young and naive, and because she had slight learning difficulties sometimes it took her a while to get to grips with why she wasn't supposed to do certain things.

I got word of where she was, though, and obviously I didn't think it was a great idea, so I walked down to check on her. My eyes nearly popped out of my head when I opened the door to see Zac sat on the living room floor. Alesha was sleeping in her pram, just a few yards from him.

'So, what are you doing here?' I said, before I could help myself. 'You're happy to sit in the same room as your daughter and deny that she's yours?'

'Please, Sarah, don't,' Laura said. 'Leave it – it'll just cause problems.'

'Leave it?' I couldn't believe what I was hearing. I went to the pram and picked up my beautiful, perfect niece, and I held her in my arms as I stood in front of her dad. She stirred a little, but she didn't wake up.

'Sarah, I've got something to say to you,' Zac said. 'And it begins with an "s".'

I felt rage course through my veins, just like it had the night I'd emptied my dinner over his head. If I hadn't been holding Alesha, I might have gone for him.

'Oh, what's that, then?' I asked him. 'Scrubber? Slapper?'

'No,' he replied. 'None of those.'

'Go on, tell me,' I demanded, thinking of all the names men like Zac shouted at me every time I walked down Ferham Road. 'Slut? Slag? Go on, Zac. Say it. I dare you.'

Zac looked sheepish. 'Actually, I was going to say sorry.'

I was a bit taken aback. I certainly hadn't expected him to apologise, and for a few minutes I didn't know quite what to say. But I soon steeled myself because, unless he wanted to be there for Alesha, his words were empty.

'Fair dos,' I told him. I was still holding his sleeping daughter. 'I'll accept your apology if you acknowledge that this child is yours. If you want a DNA test, fine, you pay for a DNA test.'

'Sarah,' Laura began, but I wouldn't let her finish. She'd be softer on him than I was, and he needed a good talking to.

'You either pay for a fucking DNA test or you stop denying that this beautiful little girl is yours,' I went on. 'We know who this baby's father is; we're not paying for one.'

'I'm sorry,' Zac said. 'I know she's mine. I'm sorry. Right? Is that good enough?'

But I just looked at him in disgust. There was no way he'd ever be a father to Alesha. When he looked at her, his eyes were empty and cold. He didn't even look like he wanted to pick her up.

'I'm taking Alesha home,' I told Laura. 'She shouldn't be here.'

There might have been a point when Zac and his family would have scared me, with all their money and influence and power, but those days were long gone. I think by then I was almost past caring. I'd been through so much that I wasn't bothered any more. I didn't see why Zac should be allowed to treat my sister and my niece like shit and get away with it, so I wheeled Alesha out of Derek's and took her home to Mum's.

I can't remember if I told Mum that Laura had taken Alesha to Derek's but someone did, because she went mad and gave Laura a massive lecture about how it was no place for a child. Derek was way over thirty but all the girls that went round there were Laura's age. I don't know if he ever touched any of them, but he definitely gave them all booze and I've heard that he's now banned from having kids in the house. It was all just a bit weird.

All things considered, Mum was right to have reservations about Laura going round there, especially with Alesha, but Laura couldn't see what the problem was. She went in a right strop and stormed out, taking Alesha with her. We were frantic – we had no idea where they were – and Mum ended up phoning the police. I felt really bad because it was only when I saw her crying over Laura and Alesha that I realised how much I must have put her through when I disappeared all those times.

Thankfully, it didn't take the coppers too long to find her. She'd stayed overnight with a woman called Ruby, who lived a few streets away. We were just glad both Laura and Alesha were safe.

Still, because Mum had phoned the police, social services had to get involved again. The social worker was called Anne. She wasn't as bad as Phil or Kate, but I think she scared Laura a bit because she gave her a huge row for taking Alesha to places like Derek's.

'And you can't go to Ruby's either if you're with Alesha,' she told her sternly. 'We've assessed her house before and it's not suitable for a child.'

I think Laura was a bit scared Alesha would be taken into care, because the social workers had been the ones who took me off to the kids' home, so she started to toe the line a bit after that. Soon, she didn't have much energy to go out anyway, because she'd started back at college. She found it tough, balancing the sleepless nights with studying, so sometimes Mum would do Alesha's night feeds so she could get some rest before her classes.

I thought it was important she got a break from time to time, so sometimes I'd watch Alesha for a few hours to let her go out with her mates. She was easily pleased, really. Loads of teenagers today expect the world on a plate, but Laura was never happier than when she'd saved up a couple of quid for a bottle of cherry Lambrini. We did make a big fuss of her on her seventeenth birthday, though. Mum looked after Alesha, and Auntie Annette and I made cocktails before taking her into town clubbing.

Most times, though, she'd come home early with Ashtiaq in tow, and she seemed to be at her happiest when they were snuggled up on the sofa watching a film. It didn't take a genius to work out they were sleeping together again. But while Laura was back to dreaming about their wedding day, I could see that Ashtiaq was having his cake and eating it. It was plain to see that Laura was mad about him, so he knew he could say a few nice things here and there and he'd get what he wanted from her, but she loved him so much that she wouldn't give him any shit, even if he messed her around. She wanted them to be boyfriend and girlfriend again, but Ashtiaq seemed reluctant to make things official.

He must have thought he'd won the lottery. He had all the fun of being with Laura, with none of the shame of admitting to his family that he was going out with a white, unmarried teen mum. For all that he and Laura fell out, I don't think he ever expected her to stand up to him, not properly.

He thought he could get away with using her forever, and it made me mad.

Mum and I tried our best to get her to see sense, but it was hopeless. She was only seventeen and she thought Ashtiaq was the man of her dreams.

'He's using you, love,' Mum told her one afternoon. Laura had been on the phone to Ashtiaq and she wouldn't tell us what he'd said, but she was in tears. 'There are loads more lads out there; you'll find someone else.'

'He's not using me,' Laura insisted. 'He loves me.'

Later that night, I tried to tell her the same thing. We'd got really close again and she'd started sharing all her problems with me, but I always told her straight.

'I know you want a future with Ashtiaq,' I said. 'But it's not going to happen. His mum and dad want him to marry a girl from Pakistan. They won't have it.'

Laura was wearing a black-and-gold Adidas jacket that Ashtiaq had left at Mum's a few nights before. She wouldn't take it off. I think it smelled of his aftershave.

'We'll be able to work something out,' she said. 'Even if his mum and dad don't want it. I know he loves me.'

'Laura,' I said, as gently as I could. 'It's never going to happen. I'm sorry, but it's not. Especially now you have Alesha.'

She pulled up the hood of Ashtiaq's jacket and turned away, as if she hadn't heard me.

CHAPTER SEVENTEEN

A FATAL DECISION

Wednesday 6 October 2010 was just like any other day. Mum had agreed to babysit Alesha, so Laura and I had gone to my friend Kathryn's flat. It was nice for us to get a chance to socialise together, as one of us was usually in charge of Alesha.

It wasn't a party really, as there were only five of us: Laura, Kathryn, Anwar, his friend Kaleem and me. As we sat there, having a quiet drink, I had no idea that what was about to happen would alter the course of our lives forever.

Thinking about it now, it's like it happened just yesterday.

We'd just been chatting, having a bit of a laugh, when Kaleem's phone buzzed and his expression changed. Someone had texted to tell him his little brother was drunk out of his head. He was only thirteen and Kaleem wasn't happy, so he asked me to help him find him.

We decided to go round Ferham, looking in all of the usual places. Kaleem was raging. I know it sounds hypocritical, because we all drank loads when we were thirteen, but what happened to me when I was thirteen was exactly why I felt so overprotective of all the younger people I knew.

Kaleem's brother wasn't in Ferham Park, or in any of the usual dosshouses where teenagers often went to drink. We were trying to work out where to look next when my phone rang. It was Laura.

'Sarah,' she said, breathlessly, as soon as I answered. I could tell she was trying not to cry. 'Ashtiaq's done it again.'

I didn't need to ask what had happened. I knew Ashtiaq had been with someone else, though I wasn't sure who. I told Laura to stay where she was, and Kaleem and I met her on the corner of Hartington Road, just next to the park. She was standing with Kathryn and Anwar, and she looked really upset.

'I'm going to kill him,' she said. 'He's been with Nicola again. Or so she says. She's just sent me another Facebook message.'

I can't explain what happened when Laura told me this. I think something inside me just snapped. Although I'd known Ashtiaq and Laura never had a future, he was really taking the piss now, and I couldn't stand to see my sister being messed around any more.

'That's it,' I said. 'I'm not having this. I'm going round there.'

I'm not going to lie: I'd had a *lot* of vodka, so I was feeling braver than if I'd been sober. But Ashtiaq had told me he'd look after my sister and he'd let us all down again. Someone needed to tell him he couldn't keep messing her around.

'What are you going to say?' Laura asked.

'I'm going to tell him he's a little prick and he can't treat you like this,' I said. 'It's not on.'

I expected Laura to protest, to tell me I was just causing problems. I suppose I was a bit of a loose cannon. Since the day in Derek's, I'd had a few run-ins with Zac. Predictably, he wasn't prepared to acknowledge Alesha in public, or have anything to do with her in private. He'd even warned Laura not to tell his parents that Alesha was his daughter.

It only takes about two and a half minutes to walk from Ferham Park to the corner of Holmes Lane and Josephine Road, where Ashtiaq's family lived in one of the little red terraced houses. Laura and my friends were following behind, but I was on a mission. When I got to the front door of the Asghar house, I banged as hard as I could with my fist.

It was about 9 p.m., so it was dark and quite cold. Laura, Kathryn, Anwar and Kaleem were standing a few yards away, on the corner of the street. None of them had come right to the door. I think they were waiting to see what I'd do. I don't know if anyone believed I'd be brave enough to go through with it.

But I was determined.

I kept hammering on the door, as loudly as I could. I could see the curtains twitching, so I knew someone was home, but for some reason they'd decided not to answer. I wasn't giving up, though.

'Ashtiaq?' I shouted. 'Get out here now. I know you're in there.'

Ashtiaq's mum opened the bedroom window slightly. She had a face like thunder. I didn't realise at the time, but I was making such a racket that some of the neighbours were looking out of their windows, trying to work out what was going on.

I just wanted her to fetch Ashtiaq so I could give him a right telling off, so I kept shouting at her, telling her to bring him out to me. Still, she wouldn't answer the door.

'White bitch,' she hissed through the open window. She was small and stout and her hair was pulled into a tight plait. I even remember the brown-and-red sari she was wearing. Ashtiaq sounded just like Laura and me, but his mum still had a hint of a Pakistani accent. I was surprised that she'd sworn at me but I wasn't scared of her.

'Just get him out here,' I shouted.

'No, fuck off,' she snapped back. There was a look of pure venom in her eyes. I hadn't exactly expected her to roll out the red carpet for me, but I was a bit taken aback by how raging she was. She was more than angry; it was like she'd already decided she hated me, even though I'd barely said two words to her. Ashtiaq's dad was standing behind her now, wondering what all the fuss was about. 'He's not here, you stupid white bitch.'

I was trying to keep calm, but I was beginning to lose my rag a bit.

'Tell your son to get out here now,' I said again. Ashtiaq's dad was at the window now. He was slightly built and really short. He looked even more annoyed than his wife. I wasn't bothered, though. After everything I'd been through, they couldn't scare me.

'You're a fucking white bitch,' he said in an accent just like Ashtiaq's mum's. 'We told you he's not here. Now, fuck off.'

Suddenly, I could hear Laura's voice, calling me from the corner of the street.

'Sarah!' she was shouting. 'Sarah, he's here!'

I turned round to see Ashtiaq walking up the street towards his house. He was with Zac. As soon as I saw his face I flew towards him. I tried to slap him but Zac moved him out of my way.

'Woah,' Zac said. 'Woah. Calm down, Sarah.'

I was far from calm, though. I tried to slap Ashtiaq again but he ducked out of my way just in time.

'Fuck you,' I said. 'You really are a fucking prick. I thought you were all right but I was wrong. How can you treat my sister like this?'

I'm not sure when Ashtiaq's mum and dad came out of the house, but by the time I turned round they were on the street. His mum was holding a slipper, which seemed a bit weird. Laura was trying to talk to her, but she was calling her a white bitch too.

'You don't understand,' Laura kept saying, over and over. 'I love Ashtiaq.'

Every time she said it Ashtiaq's mum got more and more wound up, and she was shouting at Laura in a mix of English and Punjabi. By now, most of the neighbours who'd been watching from behind their curtains were out in the street. Some of them were white, but loads were Asian. I think some of them were enjoying it; they probably thought it was more entertaining than what was on TV. Now, I realise how shameful such a public spectacle would have been to Ashtiaq's family, especially as lots of the neighbours were people they'd see at the mosque. I suppose it didn't help that Laura and I had been drinking. It was funny that they seemed so protective of their so-called honour when really they were all behaving in a way that didn't seem honourable at all.

'Shut up, shut up!' Ashtiaq's mum's voice was getting louder and more high-pitched. She was chasing Laura down the street with the slipper now. I turned to look at Ashtiaq, just to see what his reaction was, as part of me really wanted to believe he'd stick up for Laura, or at least tell his mum not to be so nasty to her. But he was nowhere to be seen. Like a massive coward, he'd fled the scene, unable to cope with the fact that his lies had caught up with him in a very public way. Zac was gone too.

'I love him,' Laura said again. 'I really love him.'

Ashtiaq's mum was still waving the slipper at my sister as people nudged each other and pointed. 'Dirty white bitch,' she replied, shaking her head. 'You should learn to keep your legs closed.'

I didn't think Ashtiaq's mum could go any more mental, but then Laura said something that made her really freak out. The two of them were standing next to a row of parked cars, just outside the Asghars' house. Ashtiaq's mum was still hurling abuse at her, but it was like Laura couldn't hear her.

'I want to get married to Ashtiaq,' she said. It was only then that I noticed she was wearing Ashtiaq's black Adidas jacket, as she pulled it round her body to protect herself from the biting October air. 'He's the only man I want to be with. I want to have babies with him.'

Ashtiaq's mum didn't react for a second. She just stood

there, holding the slipper in mid-air, shocked into silence as she no doubt contemplated the thought of her precious son being married to a white girl who sometimes got drunk in the park and already had a baby with his friend. She was shaking with rage as she narrowed her eyes and fixed them on Laura.

'He'll never be with you,' she said. At first, she spoke in barely more than a whisper, but her voice got stronger with every word. 'He'll *never* be with you, you dirty, stupid white bitch!'

Then she took the slipper and whacked Laura hard on the leg. Laura gave out a little yelp, and it was a second before I realised what was going on. If I thought Ashtiaq's mum might stop after the first blow, I was wrong. It was like she was possessed, screaming abuse at Laura as she tried to hit her over and over again. Most of the time she missed, but I sprinted to my sister's side.

'Stop it!' I said to Ashtiaq's mum, as peacefully as I could. I spoke in Punjabi, hoping she might calm down at the sound of her native language. It was a while since I'd used the words, but I still remembered them. 'Sister, stop it.'

But she didn't like that one bit.

'Fuck off,' she replied in English. 'White bitch.'

I grabbed Laura's arm, and without another word we ran in the opposite direction, leaving the neighbours to gasp and gossip behind us. Ashtiaq's mum was still in the middle of the street, holding her slipper and nursing her shame.

'Let's go to Zac's,' Laura said breathlessly. 'Why not? His parents deserve to know about Alesha.'

I didn't attempt to stop her; in fact, I egged her on. Why shouldn't Zac's parents know about Alesha? She was their granddaughter, after all, and she hadn't done anything wrong. She couldn't be a secret forever, could she?

Zac's family home was just a couple of hundred yards away. They owned so many houses we didn't really know which one to go to, but we decided to try the one next to their shop first.

Laura knocked on the door, but she was much more polite than I'd been when I'd gone to the Asghars'. She waited patiently and Zac's mum came to the door. She was already in her nightie. I'd seen her around before. She was a plump woman and her two front teeth stuck out a bit.

She gave Laura a strange look, like she was a piece of dirt she'd picked up on her shoe. She seemed like a right stuck-up cow, but at least she wasn't aggressive like Ashtiaq's mum had been. I could see Zac's wife, Mariam, standing meekly behind her mother-in-law. Zac's mum didn't speak great English, but she asked us what we wanted.

'I'm sorry to bother you,' Laura said. 'I've not come here to fight or argue. My name is Laura and I've got a daughter called Alesha.'

Zac's mum raised an eyebrow.

'She's three months old,' Laura went on. 'Your Zac – I mean Ishaq – is her dad. I thought you had a right to know.'

I put my hand on Laura's arm, ready to haul her out of the way because I was sure Zac's mum would go absolutely mad too. But she didn't. She just stood there, looking at us like we'd just told her we were planning to fly to the moon. Then she said something really weird.

'But Ishaq has left his family,' she replied. 'He is now with his wife.'

Looking back, I wonder if Zac's mum already knew about Alesha and she just wanted to wash her hands of the whole situation. After all, most people in Ferham knew what had happened. But it seemed absolutely ridiculous – everyone knew Zac was her son. They were all still living in the same house, for goodness' sake! As usual, I couldn't keep my mouth shut.

'But Mariam is right there!' I said. 'Mariam, wasn't it *you* who married Zac?'

I'd always liked Mariam, though I didn't know her very well. She just looked a bit scared and bowed her head, pretending she hadn't heard. I don't really blame her, though. She had always been a good girl and she was hardly going to start arguing with her mother-in-law, was she? Still, it must have been painful for her, hearing all the things her husband had been getting up to behind her back.

The four of us just stood there looking at each other for a few seconds, no one knowing quite what to say.

'Come on, Laura,' I said eventually. 'Let's go home.'

By the time we got to Mum's, Laura had sobered up a bit and she'd started crying, saying she'd ruined everything with Ashtiaq.

'Why are you bothered?' I asked her. 'He's been totally fucking you about.'

'I need to apologise,' she sniffed. 'He'll be so mad. His mum will kill him. She didn't know he was seeing me and now she'll be raging.'

'Just leave it,' I said. 'It's done now.'

But Laura wouldn't let it go. When I think of it now, I do wonder if she was scared of Ashtiaq. Had he ever taken their little play fights too far? Had he threatened her when they'd fallen out? I suppose I'll never know for sure, but Laura told me everything and she never seemed to be frightened of him. On that fateful Wednesday night it just seemed like she was more worried that they'd never properly get back together now we'd got his mum involved.

Laura had no credit on her phone, so Mum let her borrow hers. She paced the living-room floor as she dialled Ashtiaq's number, but it just went to voicemail.

'He's ignoring me,' she sniffed. 'But maybe he just doesn't recognise Mum's number.'

'He's the one in the wrong, Laura,' I told her. 'He's the one who's off shagging other girls behind your back. I don't see why you should be the one apologising.'

But, as always, there was no telling Laura. She was as headstrong as ever, and she kept dialling Ashtiaq's number from Mum's phone. She might have left him a few messages, but still there was no response.

'Maybe he's lost his phone,' she said hopefully.

I tried as best I could to get Laura to forget about Ashtiaq. On the Thursday, we even ended up giggling about what had happened.

'Ashtiaq's mum is mental,' I laughed. 'I thought she was going to batter you with that slipper!'

'I know,' Laura replied. 'I can't believe how many people were out watching. God, his mum will go mad at him.'

By the end of the day, Laura was in a much better mood. She even logged on to Facebook to tell her friends what had happened. They all thought it was funny too.

None of us had heard a peep from Ashtiaq. I didn't think too much of it. Maybe he'd lost his phone, like

Laura said, or maybe he just couldn't be bothered with us any more and he was with Nicola.

'I wonder if he got my messages,' Laura said, and I just shrugged.

He'd got them, all right. His phone was right by him the whole time, but it would be a few days before he'd get back in touch with Laura.

We didn't really realise that what we'd done had sent shockwaves through the Asian community in Ferham, and loads of the British-Pakistani families were talking about it. We just thought it would all blow over in a few days.

Ashtiaq didn't, though; he knew that what we'd said wasn't going to be forgotten in a hurry. On the Friday night, while Laura was planning a trip to Sheffield to buy a travel cot for Alesha, Ashtiaq was at home, silently simmering with the rage and shame that threatened to boil over at any second.

He reached for his phone, but he didn't dial Laura's number, or text her to say he wanted to talk things through. Instead, he typed out a text to Zac.

It read: 'I'm going to send that kafir bitch straight to hell.'

CHAPTER EIGHTEEN

WHERE'S LAURA?

On the Saturday, three days after we'd confronted Ashtiaq and Zac's families, I agreed to babysit Alesha. Mum was going out for the day with Auntie Annette and Laura wanted to go to Sheffield to have a look at travel cots for Alesha, like she'd planned.

'I probably won't buy one today,' she told me. 'I'm just going to have a look.'

Aqib, her friend from college, was going to go along with her to keep her company. She didn't fancy him or anything like that, they were just good friends. Neither of them drove, so they were going to go to Sheffield on the bus.

I remember exactly what Laura was wearing: a blue, pink and green striped vest top and dark blue jeans, with black-and-gold Adidas pump-style trainers. Her shoes matched Ashtiaq's black-and-gold Adidas jacket. Even though she hadn't heard a peep from him since we'd gone to his house, she was still wearing it everywhere.

It was late afternoon when she left. It was a cold day so she put her big Helly Hansen jacket on over the rest of her clothes. She'd left a tenner lying on the side, so she picked it up and put it in her pocket. She told me she planned to buy £5 of credit for her phone on the way home, as well as a bottle of cherry Lambrini.

'What time do you think you'll be back?' I asked her.

'Not late,' she replied. 'Maybe about nine? We could get a takeaway.'

'Yeah, let's do that,' I said. I had Alesha in my arms and she was gurgling away as I stroked her head. 'We could get a pizza and watch a film.'

Thinking about that moment now, I want to reach into my memory and pull Laura to safety.

'Cool,' Laura said. She bent down and gave Alesha a little kiss on the head. 'See you at nine. Bye, Alesha.'

Nine o'clock came and went, but there was no Laura, so I gave her a ring. The first few times I called it went to voicemail, but I eventually got hold of her.

'Where are you?' I said. 'It's nearly ten now. I'm starving.'

'Sorry, I just got held up,' she replied. 'I'll be home in five minutes.'

Half an hour passed and Laura still hadn't appeared. I wasn't worried, just annoyed and hungry. I called Mum, who then spoke to her and phoned me back.

'She says she's just down at the bottom of Ferham,' Mum said. 'You're to order the food and she'll be there soon.'

'She's really taking the piss,' I told Mum. 'She's been gone ages. I don't even know what type of pizza she wants.'

Little did we know that it was the last time any of us would hear from her.

It sounds bad, but I just assumed she'd met up with some mates after she'd gone to buy her cherry Lambrini and couldn't be bothered coming home. She was only seventeen, after all, and what teenager doesn't try to bend the rules? She knew I was looking after Alesha, and I thought she was just pushing her luck.

I'm not sure if it occurred to me that Ashtiaq could have got back in touch, but of course that was what happened. After three long days of silence, he'd finally texted Laura, asking her to meet him by the canal. Laura was so in love with him that she would have dropped everything when she got his message, not thinking for a second how strange his choice of meeting place seemed.

As midnight edged closer, I was really annoyed with her. I was still ringing her, but now she wasn't answering me at all. Eventually, Anwar came round to keep me company.

'I'll kill her,' I said. 'She promised she'd be home.'

Alesha was really difficult that night, which wasn't like her. She woke up at two in the morning and screamed for ages. Nothing would settle her, and the next morning she was still crying loads. There was no sign of Laura, so I decided to take Alesha for a little walk to calm her down. Anwar said he'd come too.

Don't ask me why, but we decided to walk down to the canal.

'She'd better be home soon,' I said to Anwar as I pushed Alesha's pram along the gravel path. 'It's not fair on Alesha for her to stay out this long.'

'I bet she's back already,' Anwar replied. 'She'll probably be really rough.'

I'd placed my phone on top of the pram, so I could play some music while we walked. When we got to a certain point at the canal, it fell to the ground. I kept trying to put it back up, but it must have fallen about another four or five times. I'd done this loads of times before and the phone had always stayed put. I kept having to stop and pick it up. It was really weird.

'Looks like that phone wants to jump in the canal,' Anwar laughed. I gave a weak smile. Normally, I would have barely noticed, but I had a strange feeling in the pit of my stomach. I couldn't explain it. It just felt like something wasn't quite right, but I couldn't put my finger on what it was.

When we got home, I called out for Laura, but there was no answer. By now, it was the early afternoon and my anger was turning into worry.

'Do you think she's okay?' I asked Anwar. 'She's never been gone this long, ever. She never stays out all night. Well, hardly ever.'

It was true. While it hadn't been unusual for me to vanish for days on end when I was younger, Laura rarely disappeared. The only time she'd been missing for more than a few hours was when she'd had the row with Mum and gone to Ruby's, but since then she'd been so scared of the social workers taking Alesha that she'd always told us where she was going.

'She'll be fine,' Anwar said, but he sounded less sure than he'd been before. I tried to push my concerns to the back of my mind, but soon my phone was buzzing with a call from Mum.

She didn't waste time on pleasantries.

'Sarah,' she said. 'Should I be worried? I've just had a call from Aqib asking if we've heard from our Laura. He's not seen her since last night.'

My stomach twisted.

'I keep calling her,' Mum went on. 'It's going to

voicemail. It's really not like her. I'm just a bit worried because Aqib said when he left her last night she was going down the canal.' Mum was silent for a second. 'Do you think I should call the coppers?'

'The canal?' I echoed, as a chill shot through me.

'Aqib said she was meeting Zac,' Mum said. 'I'm going to go round to their shop and see if they've heard anything. Maybe Zac will know something.'

'Ring the coppers, Mum,' I replied quietly. 'This isn't right.'

Mum did call the police, but she didn't wait around for them. She knew how useless they could be from her experiences with me, and she didn't feel like we had time to waste. It was now approaching teatime, and our concerns for Laura were growing with every minute that ticked by.

Poor Aqib was really upset. He'd been the last person to see Laura and I think he felt responsible, although none of this was his fault in any way. I'm not sure why he told Mum that Laura was meeting Zac and not Ashtiaq. Maybe he got confused in all the chaos, or maybe Laura had not been clear about who she was meeting.

Mum and her friend Leeanne met Aqib at one of the shops Zac's family owned, the one next to their house. The girl behind the counter didn't really speak English, so they didn't get very far, but as Mum was walking home Zac's uncle's wife shouted to her to come into their house. She lived just a few doors away from Mum at that time.

'We've got Zac here,' she explained.

The kitchen was filled with Asian men. Mum reckons there must have been around ten of them. Zac was sitting at the table, his chin resting on his hands, and he was surrounded by uncles, cousins and family friends. Mum started quizzing him, asking him if he knew where Laura was.

'I don't know,' he kept saying. 'I really don't. I haven't spoken to her for weeks.'

Mum felt a bit intimidated, but she tried not to lose her nerve.

'Please, Zac,' she said. She was trying not to cry. 'Please, if you know anything, you need to tell me. I'm so worried. This is so unlike her.'

One of Zac's relatives stepped forward.

'What about Ashtiaq?' he said. 'I think you need to speak to Ashtiaq.'

Mum didn't have time to reply because the coppers were at the door. They told Mum she had to go home so they could ask a few questions. They went round to the house with her and had a bit of a search, looking under the bed and in one of the big cupboards. They didn't seem too worried.

'Why are you looking here?' Mum asked hoarsely. 'She's not here – she's missing. You should be out looking for her. You need to look down the canal.'

The coppers fobbed her off and soon they were gone. By this point Mum and I were totally frantic, so it's hard to remember what happened when, but I remember Aqib showing up and volunteering to come and search with me down at the canal. Leeanne went round to the Asghars' to try to find Ashtiaq, but no one was in. Either that or they just weren't answering the door.

Darkness was falling by now, and Aqib and I had to use our phones as torches. We walked up and down the canal for ages, but we couldn't see much. It was strange to think that I'd been here just a few hours ago, cursing my sister for staying out late. If only she'd come home, I'd never be mad at her for staying out late again.

By the time Aqib and I finished searching, it was pitch black. We'd even looked in the bird huts, but we'd found nothing.

'She's in that canal,' I said. It was the first time I'd allowed the idea to form in my brain, but now I'd said it out loud, it was all too real. 'Isn't she, Aqib?'

Aqib looked stricken. 'No, Sarah!' he replied. 'We'll find her – we will.'

I wanted to believe him, I really did. But I couldn't.

'Where are the fucking coppers?' I said, kicking the gravel beneath my feet. 'This is their job. They should be out looking.'

There were no police cars parked by the canal. I hadn't even seen a single officer. It defied belief really, as by now Mum was telling them over and over that Laura had last been seen heading to the canal.

As we walked home a thousand thoughts were running through my head. We weren't sure why Laura had come to the canal, or even who she was meeting. Zac had denied everything and no one had heard from Ashtiaq. I wondered if she'd fallen in by accident, or maybe she'd got drunk and passed out and got hypothermia? I hadn't allowed the alternative – that Zac or Ashtiaq or someone else had deliberately hurt her – to enter my head.

It was only when Aqib put a supportive hand on my arm that I realised I was crying huge, throaty, breathless sobs. He had to steady me because I felt like I was going to collapse.

'Aqib, she's dead,' I wailed. 'Our Laura's dead; she's in that fucking canal.'

By the time I got back to Mum's, loads of people were there, including Dad. I hadn't seen him for months. He hadn't even called round to congratulate Laura when Alesha was born.

'What the fuck is he here for?' I thundered.

'Sarah, calm down,' Dad said. 'Let's go to Sheffield. Maybe she's there.'

'She's not in Sheffield,' I sobbed. 'She's in the canal.'

People were trying to comfort me, telling me about all these rumours that Laura had been taken to Sheffield and Bradford and even London, where she was being held in a house. I supposed it was a possibility. I'd been bundled into plenty of vans and taxis by strange men and driven all over England, after all. But this had never happened to Laura before. She was already seventeen, and in my experience the men who did these kinds of things tended to target younger girls. It just didn't add up.

It only takes about fifteen minutes to get to Sheffield from Rotherham, but on that cold Sunday night the journey felt like it took hours. Dad drove to the red-light district and parked up on the corner of one of the streets where the prostitutes usually stood. Neither of us knew what to do next.

'What is the point in fetching me here?' I snapped. 'She's not going to be here. Why would she be here?'

'Anything's possible,' Dad said.

'She's not here,' I said again. 'Why did you come here? You're just wasting petrol.'

'We might as well look,' Dad replied.

'She's in the canal, Dad!' I was crying again. 'Take me home. You don't even care about her anyway. When was the last time you saw her? You haven't even met Alesha!'

Dad said nothing, but he did as I said and turned back towards Rotherham. When I got home Mum looked awful, like she'd aged about ten years in an hour. Her face was all white and lined with worry.

'Anything?' I asked, hoping against hope that there had been some good news, but Mum just shook her head.

'Nothing, love,' she croaked. 'The coppers say they've searched the canal but they haven't found anything.'

I wanted to believe this, I really did, but deep down I knew they hadn't looked, not properly. The next few hours passed in a blur of tears and desperate phone calls.

'Your Laura, missing,' one of the coppers said to Mum. 'I can't believe it. Of all the girls in Rotherham, I never expected her to disappear.'

It was a bit of an insensitive thing for her to say, but we all knew it was true. It was always me who'd vanished for days, not Laura. As the hours rolled by, things were looking more and more bleak.

At one point Mum went into Laura's room to get something for Alesha, and she came out clutching my sister's purse.

'Sarah, she's left her purse,' she said. 'And it's got forty quid in it.'

Money burned a hole in Laura's pocket, mainly because we didn't always have much of it, and she normally spent it as quickly as she could. The Laura we knew would be desperate to get home and spend it. Nothing made sense.

I'm not sure when Sunday became Monday, one day just seeming to roll into the next. Mum and I simply sat on the couch, staring at our phones. We tried to tend to Alesha, but we were like zombies.

Mum must have dozed off, but she'd only been asleep for about thirty seconds when she woke up screaming. I'd seen her in some states before, mainly when I'd been playing up during the abuse, but she'd never, ever been like this. Her screams were the worst sound I'd ever heard. They were shrill and blood-curdling and they chilled me to the bone.

She was in the middle of the living room now, totally hysterical.

'It's our Laura!' she panted. 'She's in the canal! She's telling me to come and get her!'

I tried to stay calm. 'Mum, you've been dreaming,' I said.

'No, no!' she cried. 'It's our Laura. She's showing me where she is.' Without warning, Mum sank to her knees and I rushed to wrap my arms round her. She was rocking back and forth, sobbing. 'She's telling me to come and get her. She's in the canal. Oh, God, she's in that canal.'

I'm not sure what time that was because it was still dark, but there was no way I could sleep. I had to bring Laura home, dead or alive. I logged onto Facebook and I began to type out a status, to share with all of my friends. I can't really remember now what I said. I just asked everyone who could help look for Laura to meet me at the green bridge by the canal at 12.30 p.m. the next day. I hoped more people would turn up with a few hours' notice.

Before I went out, I decided to take a quick shower. It sounds mad, but even washing made me feel guilty. How could I do anything normal when Laura was gone?

As I climbed in and turned the water on, though, I almost jumped out of my skin. I was so out of my mind with worry and lack of sleep that I'm not sure what was going on in my head, but it felt like I was scrubbing myself with muddy water. I turned the shower on and off a few times, but it still looked brown and felt dirty.

Suddenly, it hit me, and my legs almost buckled beneath me. It was like I was showering in water from the canal. Everything was screaming at me to get down there.

Mum and I agreed that she would stay home with Alesha while I organised everyone. I couldn't believe how many people showed up. So many of our family and friends had come to help look, but there were loads of Laura's Asian friends too, offering to drive to all corners of the country to try to find her. It was hard not to get emotional when I saw how many people wanted my sister home safe and well.

'We'll go to Bradford, London, wherever,' one guy said. 'We'll ransack houses. We'll do anything.'

'Let's concentrate on the canal for now,' I said. I had to shout so all of the volunteers could hear me. 'If you see anything – anything at all – please call me straight away. I will give you all my mobile number. I know exactly what Laura was wearing on Saturday, so if you find any clothing or anything, you have to tell me. Just call me.' My voice was breaking but I managed to keep the tears at bay. 'Just find my sister so we can bring her home.'

I divided everyone up into groups of two or three. For the next few hours we trudged through gravel, mud and swamp together, desperate for clues, but the only thing I remember seeing was a big patch of crushed cherries on the grass. At least it looked like crushed cherries, because there were loads of seeds through them. It stuck in my head because it was really near to where Anwar and I had been walking the day before, when my phone kept falling from Alesha's pram.

I stopped absolutely everyone I saw, from bikers to dog-walkers to mums pushing buggies.

'Have you seen the police here?' I asked them. 'Have they come down with their sniffer dogs?'

But no one had seen any coppers at all. I'd love to say I was surprised, but given their track record I almost expected them not to give a shit about my sister. I glanced at my phone every two seconds, my stomach somersaulting as I waited for someone to ring me, but the call never came. No one had seen or heard anything.

Then I became aware of a voice behind me. It was Auntie Annette. She had been searching the other side of the canal, but now she was standing next to the patch of grass where I'd seen the crushed cherries. I felt my whole body turn to jelly as she came into focus, her face completely ashen.

In her hand was a black-and-gold Adidas pump, covered in streaks of red.

'Sarah,' she said slowly. 'Who owns this shoe?'

CHAPTER NINETEEN

THE WORST NEWS

I was lying on the ground, my back against the hard gravel path. I wasn't sure how I had got there, but it was as if I was paralysed and a ton of bricks had fallen on top of me. There were people all around me, a sea of faces, but I didn't know how or when they had come to me. No matter how hard I tried, I couldn't get enough air in my lungs. All I wanted to do was jump into the canal and get Laura out, but I was frozen, rooted to the spot. I couldn't even sit up.

Auntie Annette was still holding Laura's shoe in her hand, shaking violently as reality slowly began to dawn.

While I lay on the ground, hyperventilating and hysterical, all I could see was the big red patch on the grass. My insides clenched as I realised we hadn't been looking at a patch of crushed cherries with seeds through them.

It was blood, Laura's blood. And what we thought were seeds were bits of gravel from the path.

'I need to get her out!' I was shouting. 'I'm going in that canal!'

But I couldn't move, no matter how much I wanted to.

People were on their phones now, buzzing around me. I think Auntie Annette was talking to Mum because she was crying. Someone must have called the police, because soon a copper was ambling towards us, holding his notepad. I don't remember any sirens or sense of urgency. You'd have thought we'd told him someone had stolen a bike or something.

As he walked towards me, flipping the notepad open and taking a pen from his pocket, I finally managed to get up. I flew at him, my fists clenched, before Auntie Annette got hold of me. I was screaming at him.

'Why the fuck weren't you down here searching?' I screamed. 'Why did I have to find this? It's your job.'

'You need to calm down,' he said flatly.

'Calm down?' I shouted. 'Calm down? My sister is in that canal and you don't even care!'

The next thing I remember is being back in Mum's living room, surrounded by people: Mum's friends, my brothers and loads of my aunties, uncles and cousins.

We were given a family liaison officer by the police, and he turned up a bit later. His name was Alan and he was actually okay, compared to the rest of them, but I didn't pay much attention to him at first because I thought all coppers were horrible.

Alan couldn't tell us anything about the investigation because it was at such an early stage. We didn't even have Laura's body yet. Of course, I knew she was dead and I'd never see her again, but I tried to convince myself it had all been a horrible accident. Still, deep down I think we were all beginning to realise what had happened.

'Do you think someone has done this on purpose?' I asked Mum through my tears.

She looked away. I think she didn't want me to see that she was crying too. 'I hope not, Sarah.'

'I think Ashtiaq is behind this,' I replied quietly. 'Him or Zac, or maybe both of them. Do you?'

Mum bowed her head. 'I don't want to believe it, but I think you might be right.'

One thing I did know was that I'd never get over the trauma of finding Laura's bloody shoe. I'm not ashamed that I went for the copper. Who wouldn't have, in my position? What had happened to Laura was bad enough; the fact that they didn't give a shit made it ten times worse. Publicly, they would obviously never admit they were in the wrong, but a few hours after Auntie Annette found the shoe, one officer had had a private conversation with Sarah from Risky Business.

'We've fucked it,' they'd admitted. 'We hadn't even started looking for her.'

I was like a shell. I couldn't eat or sleep. I couldn't even stand to be at Mum's because everything reminded me of Laura, so I went down to the canal. It was all cordoned off now and there were a couple of coppers standing guard.

'Have you found her?' I asked.

'We can't tell you anything,' one of them replied. 'The investigation is ongoing.'

'You'd better find her,' I said. 'Find my sister, like you should have done days ago.'

She didn't say anything. I went back to Mum's and once again night rolled into morning. At one point the coppers came round and asked me some questions. They wanted me to explain how I knew exactly what part of the canal Laura was in, like I'd had something to do with it. I flew off the handle, obviously.

'She's my sister!' I cried. 'I just knew. I had to look for her because you weren't!'

Sometime on the Tuesday afternoon divers recovered Laura's body from the canal.

I was round at Auntie Annette's. It was only five minutes away from Mum's, and I'd sort of wandered round there without thinking because I was in a total trance. Auntie Annette was desperately trying to get me to eat something. I wasn't hungry or thirsty but she kept going on about how I needed to keep my strength up, so I eventually agreed she could fetch me a glass of milk and a cheese sandwich.

I'd barely taken a bite when someone started hammering at the door. I ran to the door to find Mum's friend Leeanne on the doorstep. I didn't think things could get much worse, but one look at her face told me we were about to be plunged into a whole new nightmare.

'You need to get home now, love,' she said. 'Your mum needs to speak to you.'

I ran all the way home. I think Auntie Annette was behind me, but I couldn't be sure. I burst through the front door. There were loads of people in the living room, but the only face I could see was Mum's.

I've never seen such pain in someone's eyes. Words can't describe how haunted she looked. I'd seen Mum in some right states, but the image of her that day will stay in my head forever. She looked like she was dead behind the eyes. I think part of her *had* died. She tried to speak, but no words would come out.

'She's been murdered, hasn't she?' I said hoarsely.

I felt my legs buckle beneath me, just like they had when we'd found the shoe, and soon I was falling to the ground. My knees hit the carpet and I was screaming and screaming and screaming, but it was like everything was happening in slow motion. There were people all around me, crying, trying to hug me, but my empty stomach was tightening and bile was forming in my mouth. Before I could control myself I was violently sick, all over myself and the carpet.

As I lay on Mum's floor, vomiting and crying, everything began to sink into place. Someone tried to explain to me that the death was being treated as suspicious, but we didn't know anything for sure. I wasn't interested in the finer details. Someone had wanted my sister dead and they'd got their wish. I knew in that second who was behind it. It had to be Ashtiaq – and maybe Zac too.

And the reason? They wanted revenge, because we'd brought shame on their families, of course, by revealing to the whole of Ferham just what they'd been up to while they were pretending to be good Muslim boys. How the hell could we have been so naive? Why didn't we think that there would be repercussions for what we had said and done?

In that moment the pain was so great that I thought I also might die. I almost wished whoever had done this to Laura would come and take me too, just so the agony of losing her would be over. How could I keep living and breathing when it had been me who'd opened this can of worms? I'd decided to go to Ashtiaq's door, but only because I loved my sister so much and I wanted to protect her. She had a beautiful little girl to live for, a little girl who now had to grow up without a mum. Why, oh why hadn't they taken me instead?

I found the strength to stand up. I felt dizzy with grief, but I knew what I had to do. I had to find the person who had done this to Laura and make them suffer as much as she had.

'I know who's done this!' I shouted to no one in particular. 'It's Ashtiaq! Or Zac. Or both of them. I'm going to go for them now; I'm going to fucking murder them!'

I bolted for the door but loads of people grabbed hold of me, and they had to sit on top of me to stop me getting out. I'm glad they did now because I really don't know what I would have done if I'd been let out of the house.

After about ten minutes Dad showed up. He took me into his car and tried to give me a can of lager. I pushed it back in his face.

'How is that going to help?' I snapped.

Dad shrugged. 'I thought it might calm you down.'

'You really are clueless, aren't you?' I said. 'We've just lost Laura and all you can do is give me alcohol.'

I slammed the car door and went back into the house.

Alan was in the house, and he told us a postmortem

would be carried out the next day, at a police medical centre in Sheffield.

'I know who did this,' I said through my tears. 'Ashtiaq Asghar; make sure you get him, or I will.'

Bless Alan, he sat with our Laura the whole way through the postmortem, because he didn't want her to be on her own. I suppose he wasn't bad, for a copper.

Before the police could take things any further, someone had to identify Laura's body. Mum and I knew we could have asked someone else to do it for us. But we had to see her. Dad took us in the car, and Mum's friend Donna came too, but the drive was a blur.

The mortuary was in an old building and I expected it to be really dark and morbid, but the staff had tried their best to make it look as bright as possible. Alan came to meet us. He told us the postmortem had been carried out earlier that day, but all he could say was that Laura had multiple stab wounds.

'I'm afraid we can't tell you any more than that,' he explained.

I didn't understand. 'Why not? What have they done to her?'

'I'm not allowed to give you that information,' he replied. 'I'm really sorry, but I think you might be called as witnesses if the case goes to court and this could affect your testimony.' He paused. 'Also, it's probably better that you're prepared for this. As part of the postmortem we had to shave Laura's head.'

Laura was lying on a table, covered by a sheet. All we could see was her face. Her bald head had been covered, but of course we weren't allowed to know why. Mum fell to the ground as soon as she walked into the room. Somehow, she found the strength to get back up and go to her side, where she collapsed again, with her arms around my sister's cold, lifeless body.

'My baby,' she sobbed. 'My baby!'

I just stood there for a few seconds. I didn't want to move because the closer I got to Laura's corpse, the more real it would become. Mum was hysterical, and I recognised her cries straight away. They were the same guttural, piercing sobs I'd cried the night before. I was shaking but the tears hadn't started flowing again, yet.

I was just so, so angry.

Eventually, I summoned the courage to walk across the room to my sister. I'd love to say she looked peaceful, like she was just sleeping, but she didn't. There was a big gash under her eye, and I knew instantly it was a stab wound. It broke my heart to think her lovely long hair had all been shaved off. I couldn't begin to imagine why we weren't allowed to see her head. I inhaled sharply when I saw that her beautiful button nose was all wonky, like it had been broken.

It was only then that the tears came, thick and fast. Our Laura never gave in without a fight and she'd have fought for her life with everything she had.

'Laura,' I wailed. 'What have they done to you?'

I wrapped my arms around her and Mum, and I cried for a long, long time. I'm not sure how long we were there for, but after a while Alan gently told us it was time to go. I bent down and kissed my sister's cold, soft cheek.

'I love you and I will find the scum that did this to you,' I whispered to her. 'And I will make them pay.'

Later that night, Alan told us that Ashtiaq had been arrested. We weren't surprised. The coppers had questioned him on suspicion of assault to begin with, before re-arresting him in connection with Laura's murder. A short while later, Zac was picked up and arrested on suspicion of murder too. They were both bailed, which made us mad, but we had no control over anything.

As a family, we were in limbo. The only thing that kept us going was Alesha. She still needed to be fed and clothed and cuddled, and that meant we couldn't fall apart. After the arrests, Mum was in such a state the doctor gave her some sedatives, but she only took one. They made her feel really out of it, and she decided she had to be alert so she could tend to Alesha.

I turned to weed. It had been a while since I'd touched coke or phet or pills, but in those first dark days I needed a spliff or two to get me through. I never smoke weed now I'm a mum, but back then it felt like I'd explode with anger and grief if I didn't have something to calm me down.

What was worse was that we couldn't even grieve for Laura properly; the police still had her body and we couldn't organise a funeral until it was released to us.

'When will we get her back?' Mum sobbed to Alan.

'It could take several months,' he admitted. 'It might be early next year.'

'Next year?' I repeated, incredulous.

Alan explained that one of the defence lawyers had expressed an interest in carrying out a second postmortem on Laura. Within his rights, of course, but it felt so unfair when all we wanted to do was lay her to rest.

But the delay gave Mum an idea.

'I want to see her again,' she said. 'And I want to take Alesha. She needs to say bye to her mummy.'

It was around a week later that the three of us travelled to the mortuary again. As tactfully as he could, Alan told us this would have to be our last visit. As Laura's body had undergone so many examinations, it hadn't been frozen, so it was starting to deteriorate. He didn't want us to see her decomposing before our eyes.

Alesha looked lovely. We'd dressed her in a purple coat and a pink hat, which had a little flower on it. She obviously sensed something was wrong because she was a bit unsettled. It was so hard to think that Laura would miss all of her daughter's milestones. She'd never see Alesha's first steps or hear her first words. She'd miss her first day of school and she'd never meet her first boyfriend.

How could anyone with a shred of humanity in their body put us through this pain?

One of the staff members at the mortuary had been put in charge of looking after Laura, and she was really nice.

'I think you will have to say your final goodbyes today,' she said softly as we walked in. Alesha was in my arms and Laura was laid out on the table, like before, under a sheet with her head covered. 'But don't you worry. I will make her look really pretty.'

I had to catch my breath as I caught sight of Laura's wonky nose and the wound next to her eye. Although I'd seen her before, it still made my stomach churn. Mum and I looked at each other, neither of us knowing quite what to do. Eventually, Mum took Alesha and placed her next to Laura, but she screamed the place down. She was only three months old, but it was like she just knew something terrible had happened.

Mum then passed Alesha to me, and she kissed Laura on the cheek and told her she would always love her. Then it was my turn.

I knew it was the last time I would ever see my baby sister's face, but it was so surreal, so hard to take in. I still wished they'd come for me instead and that it was me lying lifeless on that cold slab instead of Laura. In time, I'd slowly begin to realise that none of this was my fault, but as I gazed at my sister's dead body there were a thousand 'if onlys' running through my mind. If only I'd kept Laura away from Ashtiaq, if only we hadn't found out about him and Nicola, if only we hadn't got drunk and decided to tell his and Zac's families exactly what they'd been up to …

I didn't yet know the circumstances surrounding Laura's death, or who had dealt the blows that had killed her. There were lots of things the coppers were still trying to work out, and Alan said he couldn't tell us anyway because the investigation needed to be top secret so Ashtiaq and Zac could get a fair trial. It seemed ridiculous that we had to think of their rights at a time like this, but we'd have done anything to get justice. The hate inside me was eating me up, but I'd already promised Laura that I'd see her killer – or killers – punished.

But this was our final moment together and I couldn't let it be about them.

'I'll look after Alesha, I promise you,' I wept. 'I will love her like she is my own. I will make you proud of her. I won't let you down.'

Then I lowered my head and kissed my sister's freezing cheek for the last time.

A few days later, we got another visit from Alan. Ashtiaq and Zac had been in court, though none of us had the strength to face them yet. Two other men had been arrested in connection with Laura's murder too, but the charges against them had been dropped.

'It's as good an outcome as we could have hoped for,' Alan said slowly. 'Ashtiaq and Zac have both been charged with murder.'

CHAPTER TWENTY

ABUSERS IN THE DOCK

In time, we were told that Ashtiaq and Zac would be tried for Laura's murder the following April, at Sheffield Crown Court. Both Mum and I would have to take the stand as witnesses. It was a terrifying thought. How could we find the strength to be in the same room as these men, knowing they'd been accused of taking Laura from us? But we'd just have to do it. I'd promised my sister I'd make her killer pay if it was the last thing I did. We just had to get justice.

Until then, we could only wait, but life would never be normal again. Laura's death had been on the front page of the local newspapers and loads of people had laid flowers for her down at the canal. In the end, a second postmortem wasn't required, so Alan told us her body could be released to us for the funeral in early December.

Soon afterwards, he had to go off on sick leave, so we got a new family liaison officer called Karen. She was really nice and helped explain the court process to us, because obviously Mum and I didn't have a clue why we weren't allowed to know certain things about the case until after we'd taken the stand.

Karen told us that the more we knew about the circumstances surrounding Laura's death, the more likely it was that our evidence could be affected. We were only allowed to talk about what we'd seen and heard ourselves, and we couldn't speculate on anything else, like how Laura had died or what injuries she had. If the coppers told us anything, Ashtiaq and Zac's lawyers could argue that they hadn't had a fair trial, and one or both of them could get off with it, even if they were guilty.

We understood how important this was, but it was still galling. If either one of these men had killed Laura, why should we give two hoots about their rights? It tore me apart, not knowing what had happened or who had dealt the fatal blow. Sometimes I'd wake up in a cold sweat and imagine her screaming for Mum or me in her last moments. We didn't even know how badly injured she'd been or how much she'd suffered. It was sheer torture.

Then, of course, there was the funeral. It was heart-breaking, but we had to start planning. First of all, there was the cost. We wanted to give Laura the best send-off we could, but funerals are really expensive and we've never had thousands of pounds going spare. We were so touched when Mum's friends told us they were organising a big fundraiser to help us out.

Mum decided that she would put any money raised towards a carriage that would be drawn by beautiful white horses. It would carry Laura on her final journey, which she'd make in a white coffin. We asked for pink flowers, as that had been her favourite colour. We'd lay her to rest on Monday 6 December.

'I'll never see her get married,' Mum said, holding back tears. 'So I want to give her the most beautiful funeral I can.'

Ashtiaq and Zac's trial wasn't the only case that was the talk of Rotherham. I'd been so consumed in my grief that another big investigation almost passed me by. A few weeks after Laura's body was found, Mum had a copy of one of the local papers lying on the kitchen table. I was in such a daze I now can't even remember which one it was, but I began to leaf through it and my eyes nearly popped out of my head.

Some eight men, all British Pakistanis from Rotherham, were on trial at Sheffield Crown Court. They'd been accused of sexually abusing various underage girls. My heart was racing as I scanned through the list of the defendants. I didn't expect to recognise most of the names, as loads of the men who'd abused and trafficked me never used their real names.

But the reporter covering the case hadn't just used their proper names, she'd jotted down their nicknames too. I felt my throat tighten as the words swam before me on the page.

On trial is Razwan Razaq, 30, also known as Taz, and his brother Umar Razaq, 24, who goes by the nickname of Keggy …

My palms were sweaty as I clutched the newspaper in my hand. I had to sit down to read the rest. Taz and Keggy had both abused me, yet I hadn't even known their real names or that they were related. Now they were in the dock, where they belonged, but my head was spinning. How had this happened? I'd thought the coppers didn't listen to girls like me.

Taz was up for having sex with two thirteen-year-old girls in 2008, more than three years after he'd tried to abuse me. The report said he'd been cross-examined the previous day by the prosecutor, Sarah Williams, but a shiver ran down my spine when I read that he already had a previous conviction for molesting a teenager that dated back to 2002, long before I'd met him on Ferham Road. The girl was just thirteen and he'd agreed to buy her some beer. The parallels were chilling.

As a result, Miss Williams told the court, he'd been banned from having access to any girls under sixteen without the permission of their parents. He'd been told specifically not to invite underage girls into his car.

Yet no one had really checked what he was up to, and he'd been free to comb the streets of Rotherham for more victims.

I'd been thirteen too when he'd picked Jade and me up and taken us to the industrial estate, though of course none of the charges related to me because I'd never felt strong enough to tell the coppers. Plus, I hadn't trusted them and I'd assumed they'd think I was making it up.

It made me really angry when I read he'd had sex with one of the girls in an alleyway in the town centre before laughing and telling her he'd 'used and abused' her, like it was all one big hilarious joke. But in the court he was full of self-pity, acting like he was the victim.

'You say in 2002 it was very unfortunate you had a sexual encounter with a thirteen-year-old girl,' Miss Williams said. 'But then in 2008, you were duped by two girls of thirteen. Are you saying that lightning struck three times?'

'It was unfortunate for me,' Taz moaned. 'Very unfortunate. It is the worst thing that has ever happened to me. The last two years have been hell. The girls were obviously quite streetwise. I looked at the way they were acting, the things they did and the way they were dressed. They were smoking and drinking and they were out until after eleven at night. They didn't look thirteen, no way. They told me they were sixteen and I believed them. It's not my fault they lied to me.'

I was so angry I could have ripped up the newspaper there and then and thrown it out of the window. How dare he claim the last two years had been hell for him? What about us, the girls he had – in his own words – used and abused? His excuses were almost laughable. I certainly hadn't looked like an adult when he'd picked me up, and I'd have put good money on the fact that these other girls hadn't either. Plus, it wasn't eleven at night when I'd got into his car. It was the middle of the afternoon, during the school holidays.

I picked up the phone and called a few of my friends, asking what they knew about the trial.

'Oh, yeah, everyone's talking about it,' my mate Kirsty replied. 'I didn't want to mention it to you because of all the Laura stuff but I've been down the court a few times. Scumbags. I hope they go down for it. Do you know Caitlin? She's one of the victims. Taz groomed her.'

I didn't know Caitlin well as she was a few years younger than me, but I'd said hello to her on the street. I was shocked. I'd had no idea she had been mixed up in all of this too.

There were so many arrangements to be made for Laura's funeral that it was hard to keep up with the case, but I read the newspapers when I could and mates kept me updated. I thought about Sarah from Risky Business. She always told me that what had happened to me was a crime and she did her best to get me to talk to Laila about it. Still, I couldn't imagine standing in the witness box, facing Taz and Keggy and their mates, like these girls had done.

I found it even harder when I heard about all the things Keggy had been accused of. Taz might have tried to do some horrible things to me, but I'd lived in Keggy's house and slept next to him every night for weeks.

Plus, he'd forced me to have sex with him against my will, and when I'd threatened to get the coppers involved he'd uttered those awful words that still rang in my head, five years on.

No one will ever believe you, because everyone knows you're a massive slag.

He was accused of one count of rape and one count of sexual activity with a child. There were alleged to be two victims. The girl who said he'd raped her had been sixteen at the time. I genuinely thought I was going to throw up when I read that a nurse who'd examined her estimated she'd been raped around fifty times, although of course she couldn't tell if it was Keggy who was responsible.

The younger girl had been just twelve when Keggy started grooming her. He met her in an alleyway near the Primark store in the town centre. A few months later, when she was thirteen, he'd tried to force himself on her, tearing her clothes from her before she somehow managed to fight him off.

Of course, he denied everything, telling the jury he'd only ever met up with her for a 'fag and a chat' and the occasional 'kiss and cuddle'. I knew he was lying through his teeth.

The trial went on for ages, and the day it all finished I was a bit preoccupied because it was just before the fund-raiser for Laura. I hadn't even realised it was all due to finish until my mobile started buzzing with a call from Kirsty.

'Well, Sarah,' she said. 'It's been a shit time for you, but I have got some good news. Taz and Keggy are going down. They've been found guilty.'

I couldn't speak for a few seconds. I just held the phone in my hand in disbelief.

'Are you serious?' I replied eventually, not daring to believe it.

'Yep,' Kirsty said. 'At last, eh?'

Taz was found guilty of having sex with both of the thirteen-year-old girls and jailed for eleven years. Keggy was convicted of abusing the girl he'd met near Primark, but he was cleared of rape, so he only got four and a half years.

In total, five of the eight defendants went down. The remaining three were found not guilty of all the charges against them.

Taz and Keggy's cousin Zaf, real name Mohammed Zafran Ramzan, was jailed for nine years. He'd raped a sixteen-year-old girl and had sex with two thirteen-year-olds. Adil Hussain, known as Ali, got four years for having sex with a thirteen-year-old in Clifton Park. Mohsin Khan, who called himself Asif, got four years too. He was quite something: a supposedly respectable businessman who worked as a mortgage adviser and owned a cafe. He'd had sex with a thirteen-year-old girl in his car. He was just like Azim in that he'd convinced the girl they were boyfriend and girlfriend and had a future together.

'You'll never believe it,' Kirsty said. 'Some of them were actually crying when they got sentenced. They've got some cheek!'

Thankfully, all the reports in the papers said the judge, Peter Nelson QC, was having none of it. He could see these men had shown no remorse for the lives they'd ruined. They just lied and lied until they could lie no more. They weren't crying for the girls they'd abused; they were crying for themselves.

'Your weeping cuts no ice with me at all,' the judge said. 'The message must go out loud and clear that our society will not tolerate sexual predators preying on children.'

When I got off the phone I was absolutely buzzing, like someone had just handed me a hundred pounds or something. I never thought anyone would listen to girls like me, let alone the coppers. I thought they just saw us as slags, because that's what people like Keggy always told me we were. But I also knew that throwing them in jail wouldn't solve the problem completely, or stop other girls being groomed. Keggy, Taz and their mates were just the tip of the iceberg. There were loads more abusers out there who were still cocky enough to believe they were untouchable. It wasn't surprising really, because up until now they had been.

The feeling of euphoria didn't last long, though. Thinking about courtrooms and lawyers just reminded me of Laura and what we'd have to go through soon, and it wasn't long before I was in tears, yet again. Every time something good happened, the happy feeling would only ever last for a few seconds and then the memories of the last few months would all come flooding back. Laura was gone. How could any of us ever be truly happy again?

Laura's fundraiser was the next night, and I went along. Loads of people turned out and, because it was

Guy Fawkes Night, there was a big firework display. Mum's friends raised a few thousand pounds and we were really grateful, but obviously we wished they'd never had to organise anything in the first place. My mind was still all over the place, trying to process everything that had happened in the last week or so.

At that time, I didn't know any of the background to Taz and Keggy's case, or the fact that it was the start of something really big – something that would send shockwaves through the whole of Britain in just a few years' time.

The men had been brought to justice as a result of an investigation called Operation Central. I'd been targeted by men of all different ages, but Operation Central had focused mainly on men in their twenties. All of the men concerned were from Asian families, nearly all British Pakistanis, and the victims were exclusively white girls. I was still in touch with Sarah, but I hadn't realised how big a role Risky Business had played in helping the coppers identify the offenders. What was really annoying was that Sarah and her colleagues felt lots more guys like Taz and Keggy could be in jail if only everyone had worked together a bit more, but meetings were always getting cancelled and postponed, and sometimes the social workers didn't turn up at all.

Don't get me wrong, I was delighted Taz and Keggy were behind bars, and it did make me think how great it would be to get even more of my abusers locked up. I knew that I could phone Sarah and she would put me straight in touch with Laila or one of the other coppers if I wanted to make a statement. But there's only so much one person can take. There was no way I could have coped with giving evidence about my sister's murder while going through loads of gruelling interviews about years and years of grooming and abuse. I had to prioritise, and justice for Laura was at the top of my list.

We also had Alesha to think of, and none of us could fall to bits when we had her to care for. Mum had to apply to the court for a residency order, and the social workers were always round, doing assessments on us. Zac and Ashtiaq were on remand, but we were absolutely dumbfounded when we were told Zac didn't want us to get custody of her. He'd never wanted anything to do with Alesha. His name wasn't on her birth certificate and he'd even denied she was his, but now Laura was dead he was telling the social workers that we were bad people and we weren't fit to raise her. Regardless of whether or not he'd killed my sister, he had some nerve.

'I'll never let him take her,' Mum said. 'No matter what happens. Never.'

It was the last thing we needed, especially as Laura's funeral was edging closer. Although we'd said our goodbyes in the mortuary, it was gut-wrenching knowing that we couldn't hold her and kiss her one last time. But Mum still wanted her to look beautiful, even though we couldn't see her. She went to the shops and bought her a beautiful cerise cocktail dress, with a matching bag and shoes.

We rarely got the chance to dress up, and this would have made Laura feel like a princess. She'd never get married or have a prom. She'd never even get to be a bridesmaid. It was nice to think she'd look beautiful, but at the same time it was just another crushing reminder of what we'd lost.

In the end, the weather was terrible on the day of the funeral. It was absolutely freezing and snowing really heavily, but in a way it felt appropriate for our sombre mood. The service was in St Thomas' Church, the Anglican church in Kimberworth. We chose three songs to play for Laura: 'The World's Greatest' by R Kelly, 'Halo' by Beyoncé and 'Gone Too Soon' by Michael Jackson. I don't remember much about the service because I was crying so much, but the vicar said some really nice things. We took Alesha along, but she was really tetchy and she cried loads. She wasn't yet six months old, but I think she somehow sensed the sadness around her, just like she had in the mortuary.

Once the service was over, the beautiful horse-drawn carriage led Laura to her final resting place, the cemetery in the churchyard. We followed behind, not quite believing it was all real. As the white coffin was lowered into the ground I wanted to jump in too. It seemed like the only way out of the endless pain and suffering that had become my life.

But I couldn't. I'd promised Laura I'd get justice for her, and that's what I had to do.

CHAPTER TWENTY-ONE

MURDER TRIALS

Somehow we managed to get through the next few months. Alesha's first Christmas should have been a happy time, but without Laura it was pretty bleak, and the first part of 2011 was all a big blur too.

The trial began in May. On the first day Karen, our family liaison officer, came to collect us early in the morning and she drove us to Sheffield Crown Court, the same place Taz and Keggy had been tried a few months earlier. From the outside the court wasn't much to look at, but inside it was like a palace, with big sweeping staircases and loads of grand-looking rooms. It was hard not to be intimidated.

Mum and I were given a little room to wait in until we were called as witnesses. Karen explained that we weren't allowed to watch the trial until we'd taken the stand, in case our evidence was affected by anything we heard in court.

Mum's friend Donna came along to support us, and lots more of our family and friends were in the public gallery. The room had a kettle and a TV, but of course none of us felt like watching it. We did make endless cups of tea, though, and while we drank them and paced around the room Nicholas Campbell QC opened the prosecution case against Ashtiaq and Zac. He told the jury that texts showed Laura had met Ashtiaq at the canal on the night she disappeared. We'd only be told after we'd given evidence that he was the one accused of stabbing Laura to death. The case against Zac seemed less solid, but the prosecution claimed he'd provided a decoy by luring one of Laura's friends away, so she was alone when she met Ashtiaq.

They'd wanted her dead, Mr Campbell said, because we'd brought shame on their families by revealing Laura's relationships with both of them. He told them all about the texts Ashtiaq had sent Zac after we'd gone to the Hussain and Asghar family homes, including the one where Ashtiaq called Laura a kafir bitch and said he was going to send her to hell. He'd also told Zac that he wanted to make 'beans on toast'. Apparently, it was a reference to spilling blood he'd got from some film called *Four Lions*, which was set in Sheffield.

'Hussain was to tell police he was trying to keep secret the existence of his child with Laura,' Mr Campbell said.

'His attitude angered her and she threatened to "grass" to his family. It became clear that Asghar was just as keen that his parents didn't find out about his relationship with Laura. The evidence of the texts that have survived reveals how much grief Laura Wilson caused.'

It was a few days into the trial before we were called to give evidence. Karen told us Mum would be first, then me.

'Good luck,' I whispered, holding back tears as a court usher came to take Mum down the long corridor into the room where the trial was being held.

Mum later told me she was so overwhelmed that her legs went to jelly and she couldn't stand up. The judge, Lord Justice Nigel Davis, said he didn't normally allow people to sit down while giving evidence, but he made an exception because Mum was so shaky.

I don't remember how long Mum was gone; I just remember someone calling me and telling me it was my turn. I can't remember who escorted me into the court-room. I'm not even sure how my legs carried me there.

Ashtiaq and Zac were sitting in the dock, both with their heads down. It was the first time I'd seen them since the night we'd gone to each of their homes, but they'd swapped their scruffy jeans for smart suits. I didn't yet know who was supposed to have done what to Laura, but at least one of them had to be guilty, and I wanted them to look at me and see the pain written all over my face.

But as I took the oath, neither of them met my eye.

Laura had got some passport photos taken shortly before she died and I'd found some of them in Mum's house. They were small enough to fit in my purse, so I'd taken one with me to court. My palms were sweaty, but I clutched it the whole time I was being questioned. It was my way of feeling like Laura was with me.

The lawyers asked me all about Zac and Laura, and how Zac had tried to deny Alesha was his. Then they moved on to the night we'd gone to confront the Hussains and the Asghars. I actually felt quite calm when I spoke, because I knew I was telling the truth. I had nothing to hide.

I didn't break down while I was giving evidence. Karen had told me the defence lawyers would make me feel like a liar, so I was prepared for that. Even when some of the jurors started crying, I kept my nerve. Thankfully, Lord Justice Davis made me feel at ease.

I knew the hard part would come afterwards because, once I'd taken the stand, the police could finally tell me all about the case. Karen took me into another room in the court and told me as much as she could about the prosecution case, how Mr Campbell would argue that Ashtiaq had killed Laura by stabbing her but that Zac had helped plot to kill her. Then, she passed me a diagram, gently explaining how it showed where all of Laura's injuries were.

At first I just held it in my hands, staring at it blankly. I was shaking violently, but I couldn't make sense of it all. Of course, the diagram didn't show Laura's actual body, but there were loads of arrows everywhere, pointing to where she'd been hurt.

I felt exactly as I had done the day we'd found her shoe. This time I was sitting down, but I could feel my legs turning to jelly and I was pretty sure I'd never be able to stand.

As calmly as she could, Karen told me that Laura had been stabbed over forty times. Most of the wounds were to her head, explaining why they'd had to shave all her hair off for the postmortem. Then, there was the wound under her eye, the one I'd seen in the mortuary.

'She had a broken nose too, didn't she?' I asked quietly, and Karen nodded.

Laura also had loads of gashes to her hands. I couldn't get enough air in my lungs as I realised that she'd have got these injuries while trying to grab the knife from Ashtiaq. She had lots of bruises too.

She'd fought for her life with everything she had.

But Ashtiaq had been determined to finish her off. He'd also stabbed her in the chest and back. She'd still been alive when he'd thrown her in the canal, but he'd kept stabbing her, just to make sure she stayed under the water.

As a final insult, he'd slit her throat.

I couldn't take any more. I'd been frozen to the spot a minute earlier, but suddenly I found my feet and I was in the middle of the room, screaming. I'd always known that hearing about Laura's injuries would tear me apart, but her death had been so much more brutal than anyone could ever have imagined.

I'm not sure what happened next, but I was out in the street, standing in front of the court building. It was almost summer, but the fresh air chilled me to the bone and I was shivering like crazy. I hadn't said bye to Karen or told Mum where I was going, but I couldn't go back into the court, not now I knew what Ashtiaq had done. If I walked back up those steps I was sure I'd run straight to the dock and pull him out, so I could do to him what he'd done to my sister.

I think I jumped on a bus back to Rotherham, but I was in such a state I can't be sure. I ended up hiding in some woods near Mum's house. I just sat behind a tree and cried and cried and cried. I imagined how hopeful Laura would have been when her phone buzzed with a text from Ashtiaq, asking to meet up after days of silence. She loved him so much. Did she think he'd texted her because he wanted to get back together? Perhaps she'd hoped he wanted to tell her everything was okay, that it didn't matter that we'd confronted his family, because all that mattered was them.

Nothing could have been further from the truth.

My mind wandered to the attack itself. What had he said to Laura before he'd pulled out the knife? My insides clenched violently and I felt sick. Maybe I was sick, I can't be sure. It broke my heart to think of my baby sister, distraught and terrified as she fought for her life and, God, she fought hard. What must have been going through her head as her childhood sweetheart turned on her in the most vicious way possible?

I didn't want to think of her last moments, but they kept creeping into my mind. There was no point in beating around the bush. This was no painless death. She'd have suffered. I could only hope that, once Ashtiaq had tossed her in the dirty water like a piece of rubbish, it was over quickly.

I couldn't believe I'd ever trusted Ashtiaq, or thought he was all right. My mind flashed back to the last time I'd spoken to Laura, and in that second I wished I'd run down Ferham Road and dragged her home myself. But it would only have been a stay of execution. Ashtiaq had texted Zac a few hours beforehand to say he needed to 'do a mission', and he'd have carried out that mission at any cost. This was no spur-of-the-moment crime of passion; it had been days in the planning and, when Ashtiaq had washed Laura's blood from his hands, he'd calmly walked into a local snooker hall and boasted to a friend that he would soon be famous.

He wasn't sorry he'd killed my sister and left her baby girl without a mum. Instead, he wanted to go down in history for teaching her a lesson.

I thought I'd never be able to walk back into the court and look at Ashtiaq in the dock, knowing what he'd done, but somehow I managed it, although I could feel the hatred bubbling up inside me every time I looked at him. I despised Zac too. I still didn't know if he'd been involved in Laura's murder, but he'd still put us through the mill by denying Alesha was his then claiming we weren't fit to raise her. It was like we were pawns in a sick game.

The prosecution case lasted several weeks and there were lots of witnesses. One of them was a taxi driver called Shaheed who'd turned up to help look for Laura when I'd organised the search at the canal. It turned out that he was possibly the last person to see her alive, because she'd got into his car and asked to borrow his phone to call Ashtiaq.

'I can't remember what she said,' he told the jury. 'But it was about meeting up for definite, down the canal.'

After three long weeks Ashtiaq was due to begin his defence, though the evidence against him seemed so overwhelming we weren't sure what that defence would be. The prosecution closed its case just before lunchtime, and Mum and Donna were standing in the corridor when one of the lawyers defending Ashtiaq brushed past them. He was speaking to a colleague and he sounded stressed.

'You need to get the Asghar family back, now,' he said. 'Ashtiaq is changing his plea to guilty.'

It was horrible for Mum to find out about Ashtiaq's guilty plea in the way she did. Mr Campbell told us later that he thought it was really unprofessional of Ashtiaq's lawyer to speak about it openly in the corridors where anyone could listen in, no matter how frazzled he was. The plea messed the whole case up too, because the judge decided Zac couldn't get a fair trial now the jury knew Ashtiaq was guilty.

So Zac would be tried again in November, with a whole new jury, and Mum and I would have to take the stand and relive the worst hours of our lives yet again. Ashtiaq was placed on remand, but he wouldn't be sentenced until the trial against Zac was over.

It was like the nightmare would never end.

Don't get me wrong, I was glad Ashtiaq had admitted killing Laura, but he'd known he was guilty all along.

Why didn't he just hold his hands up at the start and save us weeks of trauma? We weren't stupid. We didn't think for a second that he'd suddenly been filled with remorse for his crime. It didn't take a genius to work out that his barrister had told him he'd get a more lenient sentence if he changed his plea, so that's what he did.

The hatred I felt for him was eating me alive.

For Alesha's sake we had to make things as normal as possible while we waited to go to court again. It made me really sad because the first year of her life should have been so special. Laura would have beamed with pride when she took her first steps and cut her first tooth, but they were bittersweet moments for us. We did have a first birthday party for her, with lots of family and friends and presents, but without Laura it felt a bit hollow.

We spoke to her about Laura as much as we could. We told her that her mummy loved her very much but a bad man had taken her away. We didn't want to keep anything from her. We knew she'd never be able to remember Laura, not properly, so we showed her lots of pictures and talked about her all the time.

'When she's older we'll have to tell her who her daddy is,' Mum said. 'But that can wait.'

One night, just before the start of the second trial, Alesha woke in the night, screaming. She'd only really begun to talk, but she was crying for Laura.

'I want my mummy!' she wailed, as Mum tried to soothe her. 'My mummy! Where is she?'

Mum thought her heart might break as she had to explain to Alesha that her mummy wasn't here. Like I said before, I've never believed death is the end, and I think Laura visited Alesha that night. It was comforting to know she was watching over us all, but it made me so angry that she couldn't be there for Alesha like she'd have wanted to be.

The second trial started in the middle of November, and Mum and I had to take the stand again.

I suppose giving evidence was a little less daunting now we'd done it before, and there were fewer questions as the case only related to Zac. But the fact that there was only one person in the dock instead of two didn't really change anything. Laura was still gone. The only difference was that Zac didn't change his plea at the last minute. Instead, he took the stand in his own defence.

Mr Campbell quizzed him on all the texts that he and Ashtiaq had exchanged in the days before Laura's murder, but he insisted he was not involved in any plan to kill her. Now that he was giving evidence under oath, he couldn't deny the fact that he'd slept with Laura, but still he tried to shrug off any responsibility for Alesha, telling the jury he was still not convinced he was her father.

'I heard rumours she was sleeping with Ashtiaq,' he said. 'I was actually doubting the baby was mine.'

Zac's family had hired a big-shot barrister to defend him. His name was Simon Csoka and he'd travelled all the way up from London for the case, but even he couldn't deny Zac was a total tosser.

'Mr Hussain is an unfaithful philanderer whose attitude to women totally stinks,' he told the jury. 'But although he's guilty of many things, he's not guilty of murder.'

The jury went out on 1 December. They took just a few hours to find Zac not guilty.

I burst into tears as I watched his family smile and hug when the verdict was announced. It was like we were invisible. Zac might have been acquitted, but we were Laura's family and nothing would bring her back. Zac's dad had even sent a limo to collect him from court. He was still grinning from ear to ear when he climbed into it and sped away back to Ferham.

Now that Zac had been cleared, Ashtiaq could be sentenced, and Karen took us back to Sheffield Crown Court three weeks later, on 21 December. The city was ablaze with Christmas lights and families were huddled together on the street, sipping hot drinks and enjoying the festive season. It was what Laura should have been doing with Alesha, yet we were off to see her ex-boyfriend being sentenced for her murder. It was all so hard to take in.

The court was packed. Ashtiaq's mum and dad were in the public gallery, of course. They looked about twenty years older than they had done on the fateful night we'd gone to their door and supposedly shamed their family. I didn't feel any sympathy for them as they wrung their hands and choked back tears. To think they were embarrassed by the idea of their precious son going out with a white girl. Now he'd really given them something to be ashamed of.

Zac wasn't there, but loads of his family were, which kind of pissed me off. What did this have to do with them? Zac had been found not guilty, so there was no need for them to come along. I know they didn't think much of our family, but they needed to let us grieve. Some of them were even playing on their phones when the judge came out, which I thought was really disrespectful, both to him and to Laura. But as soon as Lord Justice Davis began to speak, I was kind of glad they'd come along.

'I take the view you came under the influence of Mr Hussain who is something of a mentor to you,' he told Ashtiaq. 'He seems to have regarded girls, white girls, simply as sexual targets. He does not treat them as human beings at all. You got into that mindset yourself. You no doubt once had feelings for Laura but treated her with contempt in the latter stages.'

Ashtiaq had timed things well. As he was a few months shy of his eighteenth birthday when he killed Laura, Lord Justice Davis had no choice but to give him a more lenient sentence.

He jailed Ashtiaq for seventeen and a half years. Ashtiaq burst into tears as he was led down to the cells. But he wasn't crying for Laura; he was crying for himself.

CHAPTER TWENTY-TWO

A NEW LIFE

After Ashtiaq was sentenced, all of the national newspapers wanted to speak to us. Before the trial, none of them were really interested. After all, it's a sad fact that in this country a couple of women are murdered by a current or former partner every week. Unfortunately, in any given year hundreds of families will feel the pain that we felt when we lost Laura, and it's shocking that these deaths are so common that few of them make national headlines. But all of the local papers were covering the trial, and the big papers in London must have caught wind of it because loads of reporters turned up at court. The case was even on BBC News.

What made Laura's death unique, it seemed, was the fact that Ashtiaq had apparently killed her for bringing shame on his strict Muslim family. The press latched onto this and soon everyone was calling her murder 'Britain's first white honour killing'.

Of course, Mum and I had known for months that this was the reason why Laura had been murdered, but we didn't know loads about honour killings in general. Neither of us felt strong enough to speak about Laura's death in the days after the sentencing, especially as Christmas was just a few days away and we had to concentrate on making things as normal as possible for Alesha. But a little bit later on, Mum was asked to take part in a BBC *Panorama* programme about honour-based violence, and she agreed.

That's when we started looking into the issue a bit more. We found out that experts estimate that up to twelve honour killings occur in the UK each year. In most instances, the victims are female relatives of the killers and the crimes are generally committed after the woman is deemed to have brought shame on the family. Most honour killings in the UK occur within families of South Asian or Middle Eastern origin, and victims are targeted for a variety of reasons, such as having a supposedly unsuitable boyfriend or becoming too caught up in Western culture.

Everyone is familiar with the saying blood is thicker than water, meaning family comes before all else, but we were shocked when we spoke to a forensic psychologist called Dr Keri Nixon from Liverpool University. She'd done lots of work on honour-based violence and she told us that in some families there was another saying: honour is thicker than blood. In other words, some people think it is better to kill someone than risk the family name being dragged through the mud.

Laura's case was a bit different because she wasn't killed by a family member, but the principle was the same.

We wanted to do all we could to raise awareness of the issue, but it was really strange having journalists and TV producers phoning us up all the time. We also took part in an ITV documentary called *Britain's Darkest Taboos*. We spoke about Laura's death, while Dr Nixon and other psychologists analysed the case and gave information on honour killings. It was like our old life was gone and now we had this strange, surreal new life. We'd have given it up in a second if it meant Laura could be back with us, but we just had to get used to it.

Needless to say, things weren't all plain sailing. I still had Asian friends, but my card was marked with others in the British-Pakistani community. One night, I was having a drink with Kirsty and some of my other mates in the centre of town. We were walking from one pub to another when one of Zac's brothers, Melly – I think his real name is Ishmail – came out of a takeaway and spotted me.

'Your sister got what was coming to her!' he shouted. 'And so will you, if you don't keep your mouth shut!'

Of course, I went absolutely mad. I was carrying a pint glass at the time and I lobbed it at his head. The next few minutes were chaos, and I think Kirsty had to drag me away from him because I was kicking and screaming so much, but someone had already phoned the coppers on me. Kirsty tried to get me to run away but there was no point. Every police officer in Rotherham knew who I was.

I'd stupidly hoped the coppers might be a bit more sympathetic to me considering what had happened, but they didn't seem interested. They just bundled me into the car and took me off to the cells. I told them what Melly had said to me, but they didn't take much notice.

I was on remand for a week. I'd never been in jail before, and when I'd sobered up I was a bit scared of what it would be like but, to be completely honest, it was a walk in the park. I got three meals a day and I didn't have to worry about paying bills or doing the food shopping.

In the end, I was done for common assault and given an eight-week sentence, suspended for twelve months. Nothing happened to Melly, of course. My brief time inside made me think about Ashtiaq, though, and how easy his life must be because now I knew first-hand that being in jail isn't actually that hard. Sure, he'll be in there for a lot longer than I was, but he'll only be thirty-four when he gets out, and he'll probably get shipped off to Pakistan where no one knows what he's done and he can still get married and have a career and a nice life, things that Laura will never get to enjoy.

Laura's murder was by far the worst thing that had ever happened to me, but it didn't mean the scars from my own abuse had faded. I still didn't like going into town on my own and I wouldn't get in a taxi if you paid me. One night, I'd gone to a house party with Kirsty when I noticed Caitlin sitting on the couch. She was really nice, but it gave me a bit of a funny feeling being in the same room as her, especially when the alcohol started flowing and the conversation turned to Taz. Everyone was asking her questions and I thought she'd clam up, but she was quite open about it.

'Obviously, I lied about my age at first,' she said. 'Doesn't everyone? But then I told him the truth. He knew I was thirteen but he didn't give a shit. He still made me do it.'

I didn't know what to say. What could I say? Everyone who has been groomed has had a different experience, and I didn't want to upset her by comparing her story to mine, so I stayed silent.

'I don't think he got long enough,' she went on. 'Eleven years? I bet he's out in half of that. It's shocking.'

'I know,' I said slowly. 'It is. I've been through it too, but why don't we change the subject and have a drink? We've got better things to do than waste time talking about him.'

After all these years, it was still hard to talk to virtual strangers about what had happened. Taz and Keggy might have been in jail, but I still had a niggling feeling in the back of my mind that I wasn't a victim like Caitlin, that no one would believe me and what had happened to me was all my fault. It was easier just to talk about other things.

If it hadn't been for Sarah from Risky Business – and perhaps Hamid – I'm not sure I'd have even realised that what had happened to me was wrong. Throughout all the years of abuse, Sarah was the only professional who really had any faith in me and didn't see me as a waste of space.

That's why I was absolutely fuming when we heard Risky Business as we knew it was to be shut down. Instead, it was to be incorporated into a wider child sexual exploitation team within Rotherham Metropolitan Borough Council, meaning social workers would be meddling with everything. Anyone who has been in my position will tell you that approach will never work. Sarah and her colleagues spent years working with girls like me, many of whom didn't trust or like their social workers. Now we were all back to square one.

What was worse was that the move came after a serious case review into Laura's murder, the findings of which were published a few months after Ashtiaq was jailed. Although the review found nothing could have been done to prevent him killing Laura, it did suggest that improvements could have been made by the agencies involved with both her and Alesha. Because I'd been abused so badly, social workers had identified that she might be at risk of being groomed. They knew that sometimes Sarah or one of her colleagues had taken Laura out for a while to make sure she was okay and to check she knew the risks of getting caught up with the men who had targeted me. Apparently, there were some discrepancies in the records kept by Risky Business and the social workers and, of course, Risky Business had to take the blame.

The proof was in the pudding, though. After Operation Central, the coppers started a new investigation, called Operation Czar, in a bid to get more abusers jailed. Risky Business was critical to the success of Operation Central, because the girls trusted Sarah and her colleagues so much, but in Operation Czar social workers took the lead in working with the victims. Not one person was convicted.

I'm not saying all social workers are useless, because of course that's not the case, but loads of them are already overwhelmed with work and Risky Business provided a service that I don't think they can really replicate, no matter how good their intentions are.

Sarah had been such a big part of my life that I knew we'd never lose touch. Even when she got a new job, Mum and I still saw her loads. To this day, we still count her as a really good friend. Our relationship is more personal than professional, but I can still call her for a chat any time I need to get something off my chest. My friendship with her is one of the few positive things to have come from those years in the wilderness.

Sarah always told me I could make something of my life, but it was hard to focus on anything in those first few months after the court case had finished. I still fancied being a nurse, but the incident outside the take-away meant I now had a criminal record, which made it difficult to get any job, let alone such a responsible one. It would have been easy to go off the rails again and to find solace in alcohol or hard drugs. And if it hadn't been for Alesha, that's probably what would have happened.

When I said goodbye to Laura in the mortuary, I promised to love Alesha like she was my own. As Mum and I struggled through those first dark months after the court case, she really was our salvation. We had to be okay, because she needed us to be. Without her, I'd have probably drunk myself into oblivion every night, but because of her I had a reason to get up in the morning. I had to be there for her.

As the months rolled by, Alesha grew into an amazing little girl. Mum and I would sit for hours with her, doing jigsaws and playing her favourite game, Junior Monopoly. She was so polite and sweet, and I'd just about burst with pride every time a stranger told me what a lovely little girl she was. Thankfully, Zac didn't succeed in convincing the social workers that we weren't fit to look after her, and Mum got a permanent residency order. She decided to move shortly after Laura died because the house now had so many bad memories. I moved into my own flat, but I visited every day.

All of the happy moments were tinged with sadness because Laura wasn't there, at least not in the way she ought to be. But I still think there are lots of times she's here with us in spirit. One day, Mum and I dressed Alesha up in a chef's outfit and she looked so cute we had to take a photo. Some people might laugh, but if you look really carefully I think you can see Laura in it, sitting on one of the toyboxes, leaning forward and smiling at Alesha.

We knew things would get difficult when she started nursery, because most of the other kids lived with their mummies and daddies. She was bound to ask questions, so we continued to talk about Laura as much as we could.

'Can I call you Mummy?' she asked me one day as she sat on my lap. I think she'd just turned three.

My eyes filled with tears. Alesha was like a daughter to me and I couldn't imagine loving her any more if I'd given birth to her myself. But I had to be firm.

'No, darling,' I said. 'I love you more than anything but I'm your auntie, not your mummy. Your mummy is in heaven and she's watching over you. If you look up into the sky, she's the brightest star you'll see.'

The next summer, we scrimped and saved enough money to take Alesha to Gran Canaria on holiday. Robert had some money put aside, so he helped pay for Mum and Alesha, while I had just enough money for my own fare. As soon as she got off the coach, she squealed with delight. The night sky was really clear and there was a huge shining star beaming down on us.

'Look!' she cried. 'It's Mummy! She's followed us!'

A few weeks later, Alesha started in the reception class at school. Mum went to pick her up one day and the teacher asked to speak to her. Like most people in Rotherham, she knew all about Laura and what had happened.

'I thought you might want to know this,' she said. 'It's really quite sweet. Alesha has been telling all her class-mates about how her mummy came to visit her last night. She said her mummy gave her a kiss and told her she had to say goodbye.'

CHAPTER TWENTY-THREE

TRUTH AT LAST

August 2014 was always going to be a difficult time for us, because it marked what would have been Laura's twenty-first birthday. Had she been here, we'd have no doubt been celebrating in style with a few bottles of her beloved cherry Lambrini. Instead, we had to toast her with a glass by her graveside.

It had been a tough few months. About a year previously, I'd started seeing an old friend. I'd known him for about four years and he was from a British-Pakistani family, although needless to say he had never been involved in grooming or abusing anyone. He'd always had a bit of a thing for me, but when I first met him I was far too messed up to hold down a relationship. But somehow we started sleeping together, and from there we kind of fell into being a couple. We were never dead serious or anything – we were young and having fun and it was just one of those things.

A few weeks beforehand, I'd gone to visit my friend in hospital because she'd just had a baby. But as I was walking out of the ward I suddenly felt really lightheaded and my legs went from under me. I was taken to casualty, where they did some tests.

'You do know you're pregnant, don't you?' the nurse asked me.

I could feel the room spinning like I was about to faint again. I'd always taken precautions with my boyfriend. Surely this couldn't be right? Besides, I'd always convinced myself I maybe couldn't get pregnant because I'd never been caught out before. I thought my heart problems had somehow made me infertile.

'I'm on the injection,' I said. 'Are you sure?'

'I'm pretty certain,' she replied. 'Have you missed an appointment?'

I was supposed to get the contraceptive injection every twelve weeks. Suddenly, I realised I'd forgotten to go to the surgery a few weeks earlier, and everything fell into place.

As the news sank in I was all over the place, especially when my boyfriend told me he didn't want a kid. I wasn't sure how I felt about it either, to be honest. A baby had never really been part of the plan, as I'd been so focused on Alesha. Sadly, I didn't have much time to mull over my options, though, as I miscarried about a week later. I didn't cry or anything. I just got on with it. I think, deep down, I knew it wasn't meant to be.

But, a few weeks later, as Auntie Annette and I stood by Laura's headstone, sharing all of the funny memories we had of her, I started to feel a bit weird again. I was having a few glasses of wine at the graveside like everyone else, but I just wasn't enjoying it like I usually would and I felt a bit queasy.

'I think I might be pregnant again,' I said to Auntie Annette as we walked home. 'I haven't come on my period since the miscarriage.'

'It was only a few weeks ago,' she replied. 'Sometimes it can take a while for things to get back to normal.'

I pushed the idea to the back of my head for a few weeks, but I was still feeling a bit off-colour, so I asked one of my friends to buy me a pregnancy test. I had a really strong feeling it would be positive, but it didn't stop my heart hammering in my chest when the two blue lines appeared. I wanted to be extra sure it was right, though, so I took about fifteen more! They all showed the same result.

This time, there wasn't a shadow of doubt in my mind. I was keeping my baby. Don't ask me what had changed, I just knew in that moment I was ready to be a mum. I told my boyfriend, but he wasn't very understanding and we had a bit of a row. I wasn't really bothered if he was upset with me, though; the little life growing inside me needed me more than he did.

So, I was stressed out enough when I came home from the shops on the afternoon of Tuesday, 26 August 2014, to find several journalists camped outside my flat.

'Sarah!' one shouted. 'Can we have a word?'

'Sarah, what do you think of the Jay report?' said another. 'Was Laura one of the victims?'

'What are you on about?' I asked, bemused, as I rifled through my bag for my keys.

'The report by Professor Alexis Jay into child sexual exploitation in Rotherham,' the first journalist replied. 'It's just been published.'

Before I knew it, a man with a French accent had shoved a camera and a microphone into my face and he was trying to get me to say something about Laura. I didn't have a clue what any of them were talking about, so I slammed the door in their faces and ran upstairs to call Mum.

'What's this about some report that's out about our Laura?' I asked her. 'I've got all these reporters on my doorstep wanting me to talk to them. As if I've not got enough going on.'

'It's not about our Laura,' Mum said slowly. 'Well, they do mention her, but it's not about her. It's about all the grooming in Rotherham. I've just started reading it. Maybe you should come round and I can explain. You won't believe it, Sarah. You really won't.'

Someone had told Mum the report was coming out, so she'd been waiting for it and she'd started reading it as soon as it had been published online. When I left for hers a few hours later, I had to fight past even more reporters to get out of my front door. They were all shouting my name and thrusting business cards in my face. I was hormonal and confused, and I couldn't really be bothered with them.

'I'm not speaking to any of you,' I said.

But in a few days' time, no one would be able to shut me up.

By the time I got to Mum's, she'd just about finished reading the report, all 153 pages of it. The news was on in the background and all the footage was from Rotherham. What the hell was going on?

Mum explained that Professor Alexis Jay had been commissioned by the council to put together a report about girls being groomed and abused in Rotherham, because everyone knew it had been going on for years but no one had done anything. Professor Jay was a former senior social worker but she now worked at Strathclyde University in Glasgow. The council had brought her all the way down from Scotland because they needed someone completely independent to carry out the inquiries.

'It's really quite something,' Mum said. 'Apparently, 1,400 girls have been abused in Rotherham since 1997. Well, that's the number they've given, but they've said it could be more. Can you believe it?'

Sadly, I could.

'And do you know what?' Mum went on. 'She's said in the report that all of the guys who were doing it were Asian. But everyone was too scared to do anything because they thought it would make them look racist.'

My eyes focused on the TV screen and I started to listen to what the newsreader was saying about the story. Professor Jay had spent months in Rotherham, interviewing loads of people: coppers, social workers, councillors, council staff and young girls like me who'd been abused. Some had spoken to her anonymously because they were scared of what would happen if they were identified.

'The report outlines evidence of what it calls the appalling abuse of almost 1,400 children over a period of sixteen years, from 1997 to 2013,' the presenter said. 'It details children being raped, trafficked, beaten and sometimes doused in petrol. The inquiry says almost all of the perpetrators were of Pakistani heritage. Professor Alexis Jay, a former inspector of social work in Scotland, said there were blatant failures by both the police and the council to stop the abuse. She said clear evidence, outlined in three separate reports, had been disbelieved, suppressed or ignored.'

I had to catch my breath. Could it really be happening? Could people finally be starting to listen to girls like me and parents like Mum who'd gone through hell trying to protect us from these evil men?

The screen then flashed to Professor Jay, sitting at a table and speaking into a microphone. She was a kind-looking woman, but she had a really serious expression on her face.

'It is hard to describe the appalling nature of the abuse the child victims suffered,' she said. 'They were trafficked to other towns and cities in the north of England. They were abducted, beaten and intimidated. Girls as young as eleven were raped by huge numbers of male perpetrators. The authorities have a very great deal to answer for. Their parents are rightfully very angry. The authorities should consider very carefully what their response to these parents is.'

Councillor Roger Stone, a Labour politician who'd been the leader of Rotherham Metropolitan Borough Council for the last decade, had already stood down in disgrace. There was increasing pressure on Shaun Wright, the South Yorkshire Police and Crime

Commissioner, to do the same. He'd been a Labour councillor in Rotherham too, and he'd even been in charge of children's services at the council between 2005 and 2010. He'd received a report way back in 2007 – around the time I'd gone to Dewsbury to live with Khalid – which provided hard evidence of as many as 100 cases of child sexual exploitation in the town.

But he was swearing blind to anyone who'd listen that he didn't know about all the grooming.

I didn't feel like I had the stomach to read the whole report, but I did have a look through some of it and it made the hairs on the back of my neck stand up. I felt like almost every paragraph could have been a direct reference to me and what I'd been through, though of course Professor Jay was talking about other girls because I'd never spoken to her.

Professor Jay's investigations proved what Mum and I had suspected for a long time. For many years, a large number of officers within South Yorkshire Police saw girls like me as scum. They didn't even try to help lots of us:

There is evidence that police officers on the ground displayed attitudes which conveyed a lack of understanding of the problem of child sexual exploitation and the nature of grooming. We have already seen that children as young as

eleven were deemed to be having consensual sexual inter-
course when in fact they were being raped and abused by
adults. We were contacted by someone who worked at the
Rotherham interchange in the early 2000s. He described
how the police refused to intervene when young girls who
were thought to be victims of child sexual exploitation were
being beaten up and abused by perpetrators. According to
him, the attitude of the police at the time seemed to be that
they were all 'undesirables' and the young women were not
worthy of police protection.

The coppers had been totally clueless when it came to the
ins and outs of grooming and abuse, so they assumed
we'd made a conscious choice to be drugged up to our
eyeballs and raped by loads of men. As if! What child is
capable of making any choices when it comes to sex and
drugs?

It also said that some coppers and council staff were
scared to admit that nearly all of the men who were preying on us were from the Asian community, and that most
of them were British Pakistanis. Apparently, they didn't
want to appear racist:

The issue of race, regardless of ethnic group, should be tack-
led as an absolute priority if it is known to be a significant
factor in the criminal activity of organised abuse in local

community. There was little evidence of such action being taken in Rotherham in the earlier years ... Several councillors believed that by opening up these issues they could be 'giving oxygen' to racist perspectives.

My eyes just about popped out of my head. Girls like me were being raped by six or seven men a night and they were worried about being politically correct?

'It doesn't matter what colour their skin is!' I said to Mum in utter disbelief. 'I don't care if they're fucking purple. A paedophile is a paedophile and they should be dealt with!'

Like lots of the girls Professor Jay had written about, I'd wagged school loads and I was always going missing, often when Jamal or Sav or Jay decided to drive me all over the country so I could lie in a horrible smelly room and wait for all their grubby mates to come in and do what they liked with me. Her report also said that lots of the child victims went back to their abusers because they thought it was the only way to protect their parents and siblings.

'That's exactly what it was like with you,' Mum said. 'You used to climb out that bathroom window and slide down the drainpipe because they told you they'd petrol bomb the house if you didn't come out.'

But Professor Jay wrote that many girls like me were so brainwashed that we didn't realise we were victims of

330

abuse. That was true too. There were days when I still struggled with the idea that none of what had happened was my fault, because sometimes when I got free booze and drugs I'd enjoyed myself.

All of the girls interviewed were given code names so no one could work out who they were. One of the girls was simply called Child D, but her story chilled me to the bone because it was so similar to mine:

Child D was thirteen when she was groomed by a violent sexual predator who raped and trafficked her. Police and social care were ineffective and seemed to blame the child. An initial assessment accurately described the risks to Child D but appeared to blame her for 'placing herself at risk of sexual exploitation and danger'. Other than Risky Business, agencies showed no comprehension that she'd been groomed at thirteen, that she was terrified of the perpetrators and that her attempts to placate them were themselves a symptom of the serious emotional harm that child sexual exploitation had caused her. Risky Business worked very hard with Child D and her parents. None of the other agencies intervened effectively to protect her and she and her parents understandably had no confidence in them.

My heart went out to this poor girl. Like me, she'd been through hell, but apart from the staff at Risky Business, no one believed she'd been groomed. Worse still, the coppers and the social workers actually blamed *her* for what had happened. It was all too familiar.

In fact, Risky Business was the only agency that really came out of the report with any credibility. Professor Jay said the social workers treated Sarah and her colleagues with contempt, and some were even jealous because they'd played such a big part in getting Taz and Keggy and the rest of them jailed following Operation Central. It made my blood boil that some of these people were more interested in their careers than protecting vulnerable abuse victims.

You'd have thought they'd have learned their lesson, but most of them – like Shaun Wright – were still pathetically clinging onto their jobs.

I wasn't sure how to feel as I walked home that night. I was glad the truth was out there, but I was also emotionally drained. When I got back to my flat most of the reporters were gone, but one guy was knocking on my door just as I was getting my keys out of my bag. He said his name was Dean and he worked for the *Sun*. He actually seemed all right, and he asked me if I wanted to give an interview.

332

'Do you know what?' I said. 'I think I will. I have a lot to say about this.'

I didn't speak to Dean straight away because I wanted to talk to Mum first. I never did anything without consulting her and it was vital she was on board. Luckily, she felt just as strongly about speaking out as I did.

Dean had given me his card, so I rang him the next morning and he came round to Mum's.

But as soon as he sat down we realised that there had been a whole lot of confusion.

'So, tell me about Laura, then,' he said. 'How badly was she groomed by these men before she died?'

Mum and I exchanged confused glances.

'Laura?' I said. 'It wasn't Laura who was groomed. She was murdered, but that's a whole different story. It was me who was groomed.'

It's true that Laura had been identified as being at risk of sexual exploitation because of everything that had happened with me, and because her murder was mentioned in the report I think lots of journalists assumed she'd been a victim. It was easy to see how they'd come to that conclusion, because so many girls in Rotherham had been targeted by these gangs.

Laura told me everything and, hand on heart, to this day I believe she was only ever involved with three men:

Steven Smith, Ashtiaq and Zac, all of whom were around her own age. We could spend weeks analysing her case, but all I can say is that her experience was very different to mine and to those of the girls whose case files were used in Professor Jay's report.

I spent the next few hours pouring my heart out about everything that had happened. It was tough, but in a way it was good to get it all out, and Dean was really sympathetic.

'It never stopped,' I told him. 'I was taken in by social services lots of times and I had social workers who knew what was happening. I was too scared to open up fully about what happened, I was so young. I was being viciously groomed and locked in strange homes with dirty, filthy men. I had no voice to speak. No one listened.'

The conversation then turned to Shaun Wright, who was still holding on to his job for dear life. It was no wonder, really, because he got paid £85,000 a year for doing it, money families like mine could only dream of. The more I heard about him, the angrier I got. He'd been on Sky News, where a presenter called Anna Jones had given him a right grilling. He sounded pathetic as he continued to blame everyone but himself for the scandal. Now the Labour Party had given him an ultimatum: stand down or face suspension from the party. He was so brazen that he'd decided to keep his job by declaring himself independent.

'Do you think he should resign?' Dean asked.

'He was supposed to protect me,' I said. 'Instead, he let me down and thousands of girls and their families too. He needs to face the music and be held accountable. The way he is trying to cling on to his job is a joke. You would have to hold me back strongly to keep me from unleashing my years of torment on him.'

As it happened, I did get to unleash my years of torment on Shaun Wright. We were told he was going to be at a meeting in the town hall.

'I'm going down,' I told Mum. 'I want the chance to scream at him.'

It was really strange seeing Rotherham on the news and in the papers every day, as for years it seemed like no one could have cared less what was going on here, no matter how awful it was. There were TV cameras everywhere when we went to the town hall, and there were loads of protesters with banners. Most people were exactly like us, families who had been affected and just wanted justice, but it really annoyed me when the idiots from the English Defence League turned up. They were just jumping on the bandwagon to try to make excuses for their pathetic racism. If they got their way, they'd have us believe every British-Pakistani man was a horrible paedophile, and of course that wasn't true. Hamid was a British Pakistani, yet he'd rescued me from the men who'd abused me. None of this had been done in his name, or in the name of Islam, for that matter. As I thought about him, I hoped he'd be proud of me for speaking out.

The next few minutes were a blur. Mum and I told someone who we were and asked if we could go in, but at first we were put in a little side room. Everyone we spoke to seemed to have a similar story to mine. There was a girl around my age who'd had a baby to one of her abusers, and a man who, like Mum, had tried for years to protect his daughter from kidnap and rape.

Eventually, we were taken into the main meeting room and I felt the blood rush to my head when I saw Shaun Wright sat at the front of the room, facing everyone. He was wearing a smart black suit and he looked even more smug in real life. Loads of people wanted their say, and it was ages before the microphone was passed to me, but when I finally got my turn I really let rip.

'How can you sit there and deny everything you've done?' I spat. 'How can you do it?'

He didn't say a word. He just put his head down and refused to meet my eye. This made me even more angry.

'You can't even look me in the face!' I cried in disbelief. By now, people were clapping and I was on a bit of a roll. 'Can you? Look! Look at all the hurt you've caused to us girls. We've got to live with that and you've done nothing to support us. I've had to live with this for twelve bloody years, and what have you done? You've still got your job. You should stand down!'

'Shame on you!' one man shouted from behind me, and people started nodding and clapping in agreement once more.

But still he wouldn't look at me. Someone from the council took the microphone off me and tried to shut me up, but I was having none of it.

'I don't think you're going to get any further responses from the commissioner,' an official-looking man at the front said to me. 'Please –'

'Well, why are we doing this, then, if we're not going to get any answers?' one of the other girls shouted, to loads of applause.

I didn't care that I didn't have a microphone any more. I just decided I was going to shout, very loudly.

'There are over 1,400 children who have been abused and sexually molested for the past sixteen years and you can just sit there, still in your job?' I screamed. 'How *dare* you! You should go – you should be out. You let my sister be murdered, you let us be groomed. You left us and put us in taxis with the groomers!'

Eventually, once everyone had calmed down a bit, he responded, but his answer didn't even make sense.

'The young ladies in the public gallery, without a shadow of a doubt, have been let down and they deserve every course of support and every course of justice,' he said. 'But my record in tackling child sexual exploitation as police and crime commissioner speaks for itself.'

He was right. His record did speak for itself. Hundreds of girls had been abused with impunity under his watch and their lives had been ruined beyond belief, but he could go back to his big fancy house and shut the door and forget all about us. It was a wonder he could sleep at night.

'I'm really proud of you,' Mum told me on the way home. 'Someone needs to stick up for the victims.'

'I'm so glad we went now,' I said. 'And I didn't even swear! I didn't need to.'

Incredibly, Shaun Wright clung to his job for another five days after that. All the main political parties were publicly calling for him to resign, and there were multiple votes of no confidence in him, from the councils in both Rotherham and Sheffield and by the South Yorkshire Police and Crime Panel. Keith Vaz, the MP in charge of the Home Affairs Select Committee, even asked Parliament to pass an emergency law to get him out.

He couldn't hide forever, and when my brother Mark called to tell me he'd finally resigned, I wasn't surprised to hear that he was pretending he was doing it for the victims and not because he'd been backed into a corner. It was good news, but we'd only won one small battle in the war against child sexual exploitation in Rotherham. There were loads more fights to come if we were ever going to stamp it out completely.

CHAPTER TWENTY-FOUR

BUILDING A FUTURE

After Shaun Wright stood down, Joyce Thacker, the head of Children's Services at the council, was forced to quit too – but not before receiving a £40,000 payout. After that, the TV cameras and newspaper reporters left for a while. I think some people mistakenly thought it was all over, that the grooming had stopped just like that and no other girls were being abused. They couldn't have been more wrong.

Almost every time I walked down Ferham Road, my baby bump getting bigger by the day, I'd see young girls climbing into cars with Asian men who looked years older than them. It was the same every time I popped to Asda after dark. The same cars would be parked up in the car park, and it didn't take a genius to work out what was going on inside them. Things as serious as this don't change overnight, even when the eyes of the whole country are upon you. These men had got away with abusing girls for so long that it was no wonder they thought they could keep doing it.

I heard about Daniella through some friends. At seventeen, she was a bit older than most of the girls who were targeted by the gangs of paedophiles who'd abused girls like me, but she'd been mixed up with them for years and they were feeding her loads of hard drugs every day. If my own experience was anything to go by, I knew it wouldn't be long before they'd have her out recruiting younger girls, some fresh meat for them to use and abuse. I sensed she'd been totally brainwashed, but I was going to try my hardest to get her out of the horrible situation she'd become trapped in.

One of my mates gave me her number and I called her, asking if she wanted to come and chill with us. I knew it was going to take a while to get through to her.

She was vulnerable and defensive, and I saw a lot of myself in her. She'd just got out of jail for common assault, but she wouldn't talk much about what had happened, and God knows what she'd been taking when it did. The huge shadows under her eyes betrayed the fact that she hadn't had a good night's sleep in months, and her skin was pale and blotchy. But when I quizzed her on the people she'd been hanging around with, she swore blind it was all great fun.

'It's just a laugh,' she insisted. 'They're my mates. So what if I've slept with a few of them?'

'They're not your mates, Daniella,' I replied. 'They're using you. Trust me, I've been there.'

I also tried to talk to her about my own cocaine addiction and how I was so glad I had overcome it.

'I've done pretty much every drug you can name,' I said. 'But it's really not worth it. They fuck you up and you don't need them to have fun. You can just have a drink and a laugh instead. It's much better.'

But no matter how hard I tried, Daniella kept drifting back to her abusers. Every time her phone went she just about jumped out of her skin and ran out of the door.

'You need to get out of Rotherham,' I told her. 'Otherwise things are never going to change. Is there anywhere else you can go?'

A flash of panic crossed her face, but then I saw something else in her eyes: hope. 'I could go and stay with my uncle in Manchester,' she said.

'That's probably for the best,' I replied. 'We'll plan it all out. You can stay with me for a few days and we'll book you some tickets. Just switch your phone off and don't speak to any of them. No one will know you're here.'

Daniella successfully escaped and she stayed in Manchester for a few months, but I've heard on the grapevine that she's now come back to Rotherham. I tried texting her and telling her to call me if she needed any help, but she didn't reply. I'm pretty sure she's back in the clutches of the men who made her life hell. I hope she knows I'm still here for her if she ever wants to reach out to me again.

But besides Daniella, I knew there were countless other girls in Rotherham I could help. As my pregnancy progressed. Sarah from Risky Business mentioned that another survivor of the abuse scandal had come up with the idea of starting a support group or a charity aimed at helping victims of grooming and abuse. She suggested that I could get involved, and I agreed.

'I want at least one good thing to come out of everything I've been through,' I said.

Sarah was brilliant, as always, and she helped me get chatting to other victims who were also interested in sharing their experiences in a positive way. Things are still at a really early stage, but we're going to have a big conference later in the year to share ideas. Our aim is simple: we want to increase understanding of grooming and child sex abuse by speaking to both professionals and young people about what we've been through.

I've been to loads of meetings, and I've even met ChildLine founder Esther Rantzen, who was lovely. Reaching out to other vulnerable girls has made me even more determined to make sure this doesn't happen ever again. Most people can't begin to imagine what I've been through but I'm still here, and now I want to help others.

Of course, after my picture was all over the papers the coppers were suddenly interested in speaking to me about the abuse. I was invited to the station to give a video interview but it was all really overwhelming. I had to try my hardest to remember every tiny detail of every incident, and it wasn't easy because some of them had happened over a decade ago. The coppers I spoke to weren't too bad, but it was still really stressful. In the end, I decided I had to make my baby a priority. It wasn't good for either of us if I was under a great strain, so I put everything on hold.

Don't get me wrong, I haven't ruled out trying again. I just want to make sure the time is right and that I'm mentally strong enough to go through with taking the stand if it goes to trial. I know better than anyone how daunting giving evidence in court is.

I was glad I'd decided to concentrate on my pregnancy, because it wasn't all plain sailing. My heart problems meant I had constant check-ups and hospital visits, as doctors and midwives mulled over whether or not to let me go full term or schedule a planned Caesarean section. There was one advantage, though. I got to find out the sex of my baby really early, when I was just thirteen weeks gone.

'Congratulations,' the sonographer said. 'It's a boy.'

Mum and I hugged each other with tears in our eyes. A few days later, one of my friends suggested the name Myles and I loved it.

'Myles George Wilson,' I said to Mum. 'That's his name.'

George had been the name of my granddad, the one who'd died just after I'd had the heart surgery that saved my life. Mum had desperately wished he'd lived to see me grow up but, even though I can't remember him, I've always had this really strong feeling that he's watching over me. He's like my guardian angel and I can still feel his presence. Giving Myles his name seemed a nice way to honour him.

In the end, the hospital decided it was too risky for me to give birth naturally, as they feared labour would place a huge strain on my heart. I wasn't keen on having a Caesarean section as I knew my wound would take a while to heal, but I had to accept that the doctors knew best.

Six weeks before Myles was due to be delivered, Rotherham hit the headlines again. Louise Casey, a government official working in social welfare, had been appointed to carry out an inspection into the council in

Rotherham following the Jay report. To cut a long story short, she concluded that the council wasn't fit for purpose and the people running it cared more about its reputation than they did about protecting victims like me.

Even after everything Professor Jay had uncovered, Louise Casey still found that there was a huge culture of denial in the council. Few people would address the weaknesses that had allowed widespread child abuse to go unpunished, and nearly three-quarters of the councillors in the town disputed the results of Professor Jay's inquiry.

We didn't usually buy *The Times*, but apparently a journalist called Andrew Norfolk had been writing about the cover-ups for ages after noticing a pattern in court stories about child sex abuse in the north of England. He'd begun investigating child sexual exploitation in Rotherham shortly after Taz and Keggy's trial. At first he'd hit brick wall after brick wall, as everyone who knew anything about the abuse was too scared to speak to him, but he'd eventually managed to speak to some of the girls and then a copper opened up about one of the cases. A whole year before the Jay report was published, he'd written a story about Rotherham with the headline 'Grooming Scandal of Child Sex Town'. His work was vital in bringing the problem to national attention, but the people running the council just stuck their fingers in their ears and claimed the papers were out to get them.

Louise Casey found that instead of accepting the scale of the abuse and taking positive steps to help victims, senior council staff had tried to silence whistleblowers, and in some cases there were attempts to pay off employees to keep them quiet. Even after the Jay report, hardly anyone would address the race issue, so girls were still being picked up in taxis and driven to God knows where.

As always, Mum read every word of the report.

'Have a look at this, Sarah,' she said. 'You don't need to read it all – just look at this bit.'

'Okay,' I agreed. My bump was getting bigger by the day and I was too knackered to sit down and pore over hundreds of pages myself, but I was desperate to hear what had been said. Like Professor Jay, Louise Casey had interviewed loads of people, many of whom were council whistleblowers who couldn't bear to stand by any longer and watch their bosses do nothing but bury their heads in the sand. Only two people she approached refused to speak to her. Predictably, one was Shaun Wright. The other was Roger Stone, the former council leader. The report said:

Terrible things happened in Rotherham and on a significant scale. Children were sexually exploited by men who came largely from the Pakistani Heritage community. Not enough was done to acknowledge this, to stop it happening, to protect children, to support victims and to apprehend perpetrators. Upon arriving in Rotherham, these I thought were the uncontested facts. My job was to conduct an inspection and decide whether the council was now fit for purpose. However, this was not the situation I encountered when I reached Rotherham. Instead, I found a council in denial. They denied that there had been a problem, or if there had been, that it was as big as was said. If there was a problem they certainly were not told – it was someone else's job. They were no worse than anyone else. They had won awards. The media were out to get them.

I rolled my eyes. 'Can they really still be pretending they don't have a clue? This is pathetic.'

'Wait until you see this bit about Risky Business,' Mum went on, picking up the report again. It said:

The conclusion that I have reluctantly reached is that both today and in the past, Rotherham has at times taken more care of its reputation than it has its of its most needy. Child abuse and exploitation happens all over the country, but Rotherham is different in that it was repeatedly told by its own youth service what was happening and it chose not only to not act, but to close that service down. This is important because it points to how it has dealt with uncomfortable truths put before it.

In the end, the Government accepted that the council wasn't fit for purpose and sent its own civil servants in to manage it. The Labour councillors who had been in the cabinet didn't have much choice but to quit. I'm no expert in politics, but I've got it on good authority that this more or less never happens.

The local Labour MP, Sarah Champion, was on TV loads talking about the scandal, but she had only been elected in 2012 after the previous MP, Denis MacShane, stood down. He'd been in the Labour Party too, and he'd first been elected to serve Rotherham in 1994. While girls like me were being drugged, trafficked and raped, he was too busy fiddling his expenses to look into what was going on, and he ended up in jail for fraud. You really couldn't make it up.

Mum was still getting regular requests to speak about everything that had happened to our family, both from papers and TV programmes. I expected to see some reporters in my garden when Rotherham was back in the news, but this time none of them managed to track me down. The council had just moved me into a new house so I had more room when Myles arrived, and I guess the papers hadn't managed to get my new address. In a way, I was quite relieved. I was nearly eight months pregnant and, as passionate as I was about speaking out against the abuse that had torn my childhood apart, it was good not to have to go through the stress of another interview.

So, on 18 March 2015, the waiting was finally over. I packed my bags and Mum and I travelled to Jessop Hospital in Sheffield. Because of my heart problems, I wasn't allowed to give birth in Rotherham. Jessop Hospital had a specialist maternity wing, and they'd have all the equipment to help me if something went wrong.

I was in theatre for ages before Myles was taken from my womb at 2.58 p.m., weighing 6 pounds and 10 ounces. The minutes after his birth were really chaotic and I don't remember much about them, apart from the fact that he was absolutely screaming the place down when he came out – and that he peed all over the doctors! My heart rate plummeted after the birth and the doctors had to give me a shot of adrenaline, so the rest is bit of a blur.

I'm not sure how long I had to wait before Myles was brought to me, all fresh and clean in a towel, and placed on my chest. As I looked at his tiny face, or stroked the tiny covering of jet-black hair on his perfect little head, I was overcome by the most powerful feeling of unconditional love. I'd only experienced it once before, when I first held Alesha in the hospital in Rotherham when she was just a day old. Things with Myles's dad were still a bit up and down, but no matter what happened to my relationship I vowed I'd do everything in my power to make my son the happiest and most contented baby in the world.

I was in the intensive care unit for twenty-four hours before I was moved onto high dependency and then onto a ward. I was dying to get home, but Mum and Alesha visited loads. I had wondered how Alesha would feel about the fact that I now had another child in my life, but I needn't have stressed. She was as smitten as I was.

'He's right cute,' she giggled. 'I love him!'

'They're the best kids in the world, aren't they?' I said to Mum. 'I'd do anything for them. We're so lucky.'

Eventually, when Myles was four days old, we were allowed to come home. As I carried my precious bundle of joy across the threshold of my little house, I felt a strange sense of peace and serenity that I hadn't experienced before.

I'd never forget the horrors of my teenage years, and the pain of losing Laura in the most brutal way imaginable would stay with me until my dying day. I'd been through more trauma in my twenty-three years than most people will endure in a lifetime, but I was still here. I was a survivor.

In my darkest hours I'd been convinced I'd end up in and out of jail, caught up in a life of petty crime or, worse, with an addiction to drugs or alcohol that would eventually claim my life. But none of that had happened because, thanks to everything I'd been through, I'd found a strength deep inside me I never knew I had. Now my life had the most amazing sense of purpose: not one, but two beautiful children who needed me and depended on me.

My abusers might have taken my past, but they sure as hell weren't taking my future.

As I closed the door behind me with my baby in my arms, I finally allowed myself to believe that one long, awful chapter in my life had finally ended, and a new one, filled with hope, love and dreams, was beginning.

EPILOGUE

When the idea of writing a book about my experiences was first suggested to me, I didn't know how to feel. It was September 2014; the Jay report had just been published and I was eight weeks pregnant. Until then, I'd never seen what had happened to me as being in any way extraordinary because the most horrific abuse imaginable was a daily reality for not just me, but for hundreds of my peers. It had become so normal that in some areas of Rotherham it was almost an accepted part of growing up.

It didn't have to be that way. People were being paid – and paid very generously – to protect us, and they let us down so badly that many of us wondered if what had happened was our own fault. It is only now that most of us are slowly starting to accept that we weren't the ones in the wrong. For that reason, I knew my story had to be told.

But it wasn't that easy. I was hormonal and emotionally exhausted, and I naturally feared that the stress of delving into my memory would be too much for my fragile body and the baby growing within it. There were also some emotional conversations with Mum because, until now, even she didn't know about some of the worst episodes of the abuse. However, after months of soul-searching we decided as a family that I had to go ahead and tell the world what happened, because girls like me had been silenced for far too long.

So, all I've done on these pages is tell the truth. I don't have an election to win or a list of targets to meet. My only agenda has been to give an honest account of what happened to me.

The men who passed me around like a piece of meat purely for their own sexual gratification are truly evil. I'll never know why they did what they did, and perhaps I don't want to. But the people who stood by and let it happen are complicit in the same evil and we need to work together as a society to make sure the horrors of Rotherham are never repeated anywhere again.

I know at times my story has been uncomfortable to read, but thank you for doing so, no matter how shocked and disgusted you might have been along the way. You've already done more than the vast majority of the people who were supposed to look after me because you've listened. You've helped me find my voice, and for that I am truly grateful.

ACKNOWLEDGEMENTS

I'd like to thank everyone whose passion and commitment has helped make this book a reality: Geraldine McKelvie, who helped me to put down my story on paper; Kate Latham, my editor at HarperCollins; Clare Hulton, my literary agent; and Jack Falber of Medavia, who first suggested that I should share my story with the world. I'm also grateful to Helen O'Brien for giving up so much of her time to read the drafts of my manuscript.

On a personal level, I'd like to thank Sarah Hughes. Despite everything that has happened to me, she has always believed in me and never given up on me. I'd also like to thank my dear friend Hamid for changing my life. I will never forget his kindness to me.

However, the biggest thank you of all must go to my mum, Maggie. She has been through so much because of what I suffered, but she never turned her back on me, and I love her with all my heart.

Moving Memoirs

Stories of hope, courage and the power of love…

If you loved this book, then you will love our
Moving Memoirs eNewsletter

Sign up to…

- Be the first to hear about new books

- Get sneak previews from your favourite authors

- Read exclusive interviews

- Be entered into our monthly prize draw to win one
  of our latest releases before it's even hit the shops!

Sign up at

www.moving-memoirs.com

Harper True.
Time to be inspired

Write for us

Do you have a true life story of your own?

Whether you think it will inspire us, move us, make us laugh or make us cry, we want to hear from you.

To find out more, visit

www.harpertrue.com or send your ideas to harpertrue@harpercollins.co.uk and soon you could be a published author.